S Y B E X

OFFICIAL
strategies & secrets™

AGE
of
MYTHOLOGY

FOREWORD BY
BRUCE SHELLEY

SYBEX®

DOUG RADCLIFFE
WITH CHRIS "SWINGER" RUPP

Associate Publisher:	Dan Brodnitz
Contracts and Licensing Manager:	Monica Baum
Acquisitions and Developmental Editor:	Willem Knibbe
Editor:	Michael Johnson
Production Editor:	Kelly Winquist
Proofreader:	Laura Ryan
Book Design:	Diana Van Winkle, Van Winkle Design
Book Production:	Diana Van Winkle, Van Winkle Design
Cover Design:	Victor Arre
Poster Design:	David Cherry

ISBN: 0-7821-4166-8
Manufactured in the United States of America
10 9 8 7 6 5 4 3 2 1

To Lee Morgan and Rick Rosenbaum—
two rabid Age fans! Hope this guide helps you command
those armies with vigor, invoke those god powers without mercy,
and annihilate the competition with a vengeance.

Acknowledgments

huge thanks to Sybex for their continued support and complete professionalism. It's truly a pleasure to work with everyone there. To Willem Knibbe for his incredible juggling act. You always have the time to bounce ideas, fulfill requests, listen to gripes, and just chat. The book wouldn't be the same without your efforts. To Kelly Winquist for maintaining the schedule and keeping everything on track. Thanks to Michael Johnson for his copyediting expertise and Diana Van Winkle for another beautiful design.

The acknowledgements to Ensemble Studios and Microsoft begin with the great Bruce Shelley, for his insight and for advancing the real-time strategy genre in a magnificent way. Thanks to Greg "DeathShrimp" Street for his thorough review of the technical aspects of this guide and for his speedy answers to tricky questions. A round of thanks to Lance Hoke for providing gorgeous artwork, David Cherry for the beautiful poster, Matthew Hemby for technical help, and build after build, and to David Rippy and Rich Mehler for their timely assistance.

My thanks would not be complete without showering the Ensemble Studios playtest team with praise. I'm extremely grateful to Jerry "Gx_Iron" Terry, Nate "Redline" Jacques, Matt "Maimin_matty" Scadding, Kevin "The_Sheriff_" Holme, and Justin "GX_Bear" Rouse for their invaluable contributions to this strategy guide. And finally, a very special thanks to Chris "Swinger" Rupp, also part of the Ensemble Studios playtest team and an important contributor to this book. Thanks for your advanced strategies, expert analysis, late-night chats, and generosity.

Contents

CHAPTER SIX

CHAPTER SEVEN

CHAPTER EIGHT

CHAPTER NINE

Missions 25-32 Walkthrough 167

CHAPTER TEN

Advanced Economy 189

CHAPTER ELEVEN

Advanced Military Strategies 201

CHAPTER TWELVE

Advanced Greek Strategies 211

CHAPTER THIRTEEN

Advanced Egyptian Strategies 219

CHAPTER FOURTEEN

Advanced Norse Strategies 231

APPENDIX

Appendix 241

Foreword

Ensemble Studios began working on what would become *Age of Mythology* back in 1997 when we finished the original *Age of Empires*. At that time we established a technology team to begin building from scratch a 3D engine that would run our third major game, not knowing then what that might be. The technology team continued to work on the engine while most of us concentrated on *Age of Empires II: The Age of Kings* and the *Rise of Rome Expansion*. As we neared the completion of *The Age of Kings* in 1999, we held a series of company meetings to help decide what would be the topic of our third major release. After considering everything from redoing the original *Age of Empires* to fantasy, science fiction, and modern combat, we chose mythology as our topic.

That decision was heavily influenced by several factors. First, we did not want to stray too far from what had been successful for us already. Second, we wanted to make a new RTS that remained based on the human experience, if not necessarily history. Third, we wanted the gameplay to stay reasonably familiar. Fourth, we wanted to take advantage of the capabilities of 3D technology. (Flying units? Underwater units? Special effects? Dynamic terrain?) And, very importantly, we wanted to do something relatively new and fresh for our own sakes. (We had been making the same type of game for five straight years, and the natives were getting restless.)

Mythology as a topic met all of our requirements and, in hindsight, we are hard-pressed to see what would have been better. *Age of Mythology* has been a blast to make, and we are extremely happy with the final result. At the game vision level, the topic and look and feel are clearly different from what we have done before and what our competitors have been doing. At the gameplay level, *Age of Mythology* includes a lot of innovation, inspired both within our team and by our fans around the world. Players will find it familiar to what they have played before, but at the same time there is a lot that is fresh and new.

Ensemble Studios collaborated with Sybex several years ago to produce a strategy guide for *Age of Empires II: The Age of Kings,* and we also collaborated on *The Conquerors Expansion* strategy guide. We welcomed the opportunity to work together again on a book about *Age of Mythology*. While we worked hard to provide within the game a useful tutorial, a clear and very functional interface, and easy access to in-game (often rollover) help, there is a lot to discover and learn about *Age of Mythology*. This makes it very appropriate to provide a comprehensive strategy guide for those wanting more detailed and more easily accessible information about the game.

We were very fortunate that veteran writer Doug Radcliffe was available and willing to take on the bulk of the writing as *Age of Mythology* neared completion. He has done a great job providing an overall introduction to the game, descriptions of its parts and how to play, and walkthroughs of the single-player campaign scenarios. We think one strength of the game is its flexibility—the many different ways it can be played and adjusted so individuals within a wide audience can find a style of game that particularly suits them. Doug concisely presents everything you need to know to find the style of game that suits you and start having fun.

In support of Doug, we enlisted some of the world's best *Age of Mythology* players—the balance test team from inside Ensemble Studios— to provide advanced tactics and tips that can help average players raise the level of their playing skill. Chris "Swinger" Rupp did most of the writing of the advanced material, but this part of the book draws also on the shared experience and opinions of Kevin "The_Sheriff_" Holme, Jerry "Gx_Iron" Terry (USA Champion of *The Conquerors* tournament), Matt "Maimin_matty" Scadding (world *Rise of*

Rome Champion), Justin "GX_Bear" Rouse, and Nate "Redline" Jacques. Scattered throughout the book you will find additional short tips from these Ensemble Studios balance test team experts. Our goal was to enhance Doug's fundamental work and help create a superior strategy guide that would be useful for players of all skill levels.

Part of our philosophy at Ensemble Studios is to strive for a high standard of quality in everything we do. That includes the stuff inside a game, like graphics, artificial intelligence, game balance, music, sound effects, map types, random map generation, user interface, and overall gameplay. The extra effort put into this book by our expert testers, plus the abilities of author Doug and the rest of the Sybex team, are another example of our shared commitment. We believe this strategy guide will greatly enhance your enjoyment of *Age of Mythology*.

— *Bruce C. Shelley*
Ensemble Studios/Microsoft

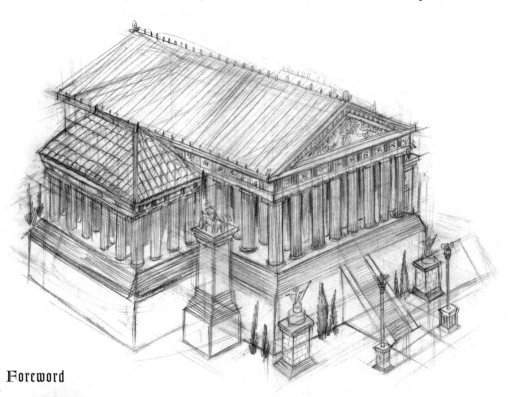

How to Use This Book

Ensemble Studios and Microsoft have created a landmark title with their third real-time strategy game, *Age of Mythology*. Expanding and refining the classic game elements of *Age of Empires* and *The Age of Kings*, *Age of Mythology* offers unparalleled variation and depth with the introduction of unique cultures, Gods, and devastating god powers. This official guide was written with the full support of the Ensemble Studios and Microsoft design teams, and assistance from the Ensemble Studios playtest team. It provides all the information and data a beginning, intermediate, or advanced player needs to understand *Age of Mythology* gameplay, units, Gods, cultures, and strategies.

Chapter 1: Managing Your Economy covers all five *Age of Mythology* resources: food, wood, gold, favor, and population. You'll discover important tips on gathering and balancing each resource to suit your current economic needs. The chapter also includes techniques for running an efficient economy, using the Market, and planning a strategic economy.

Chapter 2: Commanding Your Military provides insight on putting your resources to good use by training a powerful and effective army. The chapter presents *Age of Mythology*'s concepts of combined arms and counter units. Chapter 2 also discusses ways to improve your military, including line improvements, Armory improvements, and unique mythological improvements. You'll also find coverage of naval warfare; tips on organization, unit selection, using god powers, and unit stances; and examples of offensive and defensive techniques.

Chapter 3: The Greeks covers *Age of Mythology*'s Greek culture and how it differs from the other cultures. The chapter suggests god paths based on style of play, and offers comprehensive coverage of the Greek Major and Minor Gods, god powers, mythological units, unique improvements, and Greek military units.

Chapter 4: The Egyptians mirrors the preceding chapter, with exhaustive coverage of the Egyptian culture and its differences from the others. The chapter describes, and suggests strategies based on Egypt's god paths, Major and Minor Gods, god powers, mythological units, unique improvements, and military units.

Chapter 5: The Norse again provides exhaustive insight on the unique differences and god paths of the Norse, and suggests why your strategy also might be unique. The chapter also features extensive descriptions of, and tips regarding, Norse Major and Minor Gods, god powers, mythological units, unique improvements, and military units.

Chapters 6-9 cover "The Fall of the Trident," *Age of Mythology*'s single-player campaign. Each chapter provides comprehensive walkthroughs for eight missions. You'll get specific guidance at every turn, so you can meet every goal in the game. Map highlights presented with each of the 32 mission walkthroughs give you quick hints regarding each mission's battleground. *Age of Mythology* is so deep that all single-player missions can be completed in thousands of different ways. The walkthroughs presented in these chapters offer proven, but not the only, solutions.

Chapter 10: Advanced Economy begins our advanced tactics chapters. Written by expert *Age of Kings* and *Age of Mythology* player Chris "Swinger" Rupp, Chapter 10 provides vital instructions on running an impeccable economy, and includes the use of hot keys, the importance of villager flow, and an advanced look at resources.

Chapter 11: Advanced Military offers Chris "Swinger" Rupp's insight on advanced military techniques. It explains the advantages and disadvantages of three primary approaches to playing *Age of Mythology;* further discusses the concept of combined arms; talks about micromanaging battles; and covers the use of control groups (with unit grouping examples).

Chapter 12: Advanced Greek Strategy includes Chris "Swinger" Rupp's advanced tips and tactics for *Age of Mythology*'s Greek culture. You'll find ways to use the Greek culture's unique characteristics and Major God benefits to your gameplay advantage. Two sample Greek strategies—The Poseidon Cavalry Raid and The Hades Archer Rush—are included, to give your Greek culture a kick-start!

Chapter 13: Advanced Egyptian Strategy includes Chris "Swinger" Rupp's advanced tips and tactics for *Age of Mythology*'s Egyptian culture. Similar to the Advanced Greek and Norse chapters, "Advanced Egyptian Strategy" provides techniques for using the Egyptian culture's unique differences and Major God benefits to your advantage. Two sample Egyptian strategies—The Ra Sphinx Attack and The Isis Turtle—are included as guidance to help your Egyptian play.

Chapter 14: Advanced Norse Strategy polishes your techniques for using *Age of Mythology*'s most unusual culture. Chris "Swinger" Rupp's advanced tips-and-tactics discussion covers the unique differences of the Norse from the other two civilizations, and Norse Major God benefits. This chapter also offers two sample Norse strategies—the Loki Myth Unit, Hersir Rush, and the Thor Throwing Axeman, Dwarf Attack.

The Appendix provides comprehensive statistics for all of the three civilizations' military units, mythological units, and improvements. The section also contains a complete list of military and economic improvements, counter units, and Relics and their benefits.

Managing Your Economy

aging war, commanding groups of mythological creatures, invoking devastating god powers, researching powerful new technologies — it's all part of the incredible Age of Mythology experience. But none of these things would be possible without the resources required to fund them. In Age of Mythology, economy is the backbone of your civilization.

This section covers Age of Mythology's basic economic concepts. It includes a profile of all five resources and the effects of improvements on them. We show how strategy should dictate your economic focus, how to run an efficient economy, and how to use your Market and trade to balance resources and create an additional income. For advanced economic strategies, check out Chapter 10, written by expert player and Ensemble Studios tester Chris Rupp.

Resources

Without resources, it's impossible to train a military, advance to the next Age, or even erect a viable defense. There are five resources to collect or gain in *Age of Mythology*, and each plays a vital role—some more than others, depending on your game situation.

TIP

For detailed statistics for all general and culture-specific resource improvements, check the Appendix in the back of this book.

This section covers *Age of Mythology*'s five resources: food, wood, gold, favor, and population. Some resources are available in different types, such as food, and some civilizations collect certain resources differently, such as favor. Each culture also has a different place to deposit resources. You'll find info on the resources here, as well as charts explaining all the economic improvements that can be made to each resource.

Table 1.1 shows where each culture deposits its collected food, wood, and gold, and where it gains favor.

CULTURE	FOOD	WOOD	GOLD	FAVOR
Egyptian	Granary, Town Center, Dock	Lumber Camp, Town Center	Mining Camp, Town Center	Monuments
Greek	Granary, Town Center, Dock	Storehouse, Town Center	Storehouse, Town Center	Temple
Norse	Ox Cart, Town Center, Dock	Ox Cart, Town Center	Ox Cart, Town Center	Combat (especially with Hersirs)

Table 1.1 *Resource Deposit Sites per Culture*

Food

Food is the most important resource in *Age of Mythology* because it funds villagers, or resource gatherers, who in turn generate more food and other resources, which in turn are used to build structures, train military units, or advance to the next Age. It's a domino effect where everything can be traced back to food.

ES TIP

Egyptian laborers gather resources slower than other cultures. The only way the Egyptians can ever achieve Greek rates is with Book of Thoth improvement.
— Greg "DeathShrimp" Street

It's nearly impossible to develop an effective strategy that ignores food. While it's possible to concentrate on other resources and perform effectively, food will be your primary resource, particularly in the first Age and even into the second (see Figure 1.1). As the game progresses (when you have plenty of villagers), food becomes less important and other resources assume center stage.

There are five ways to harvest food—herding, hunting, foraging, farming, and fishing—and all of them produce at different rates. Some methods even require other resources! Generally, you should collect food starting with the fastest available method, then move on to slower methods when your first sources have been exhausted. That means you'll usually start with hunting, then go to foraging, then herding (after the animals have had time to fatten), and then farming. The map layout also plays a key role. For instance, fishing can be substituted for farming, on a water map. If there are no wild animals near your start position, begin foraging until you can hunt effectively. Let's look at the five methods in detail.

Figure 1.1 *Food is your primary concern at the beginning of the game. You need more food to fund more villagers!*

Herding

The "herdables" are domesticated animals that can be controlled instead of hunted. (Chickens are the exception: They can't be controlled, but they also don't run away, or attack villagers.) Herdables are positioned randomly on the map and begin unaligned but waiting to be captured. To capture a herdable, move one of your units within the animal's line of sight. Once captured, the herdable can be moved to any location, though most likely toward a Town Center, Granary, or Ox Cart to prepare for processing.

It's possible for an enemy player to capture one of your herdables if one of your units isn't close by. Protect these food sources well by keeping a unit close as you escort the herdables back to base.

In *Age of Mythology*, the herdable units—goats, pigs, and cows—actually fatten, or increase their food potential, over time. (Each herdable has a maximum value, however.) So, while it's important to seek out as many herdables as possible (even stealing your enemy's animals), it's unwise to process them early in a game. Instead, use two of the other food-gathering methods—hunting or foraging—before processing the herdables.

Like all animals in *Age of Mythology*, herdables slowly decay after being killed. As the animal decays, the amount of food you're able to collect decreases. Therefore, it's important to retrieve as much food as possible before the animal decays completely or stops providing food.

"Task" three to four villagers around the herdable, positioned on the side of the animal closest to the food-deposit site. Villagers on the far side of the animal might take too long to reach the deposit site, or bump into the other villagers, slowing down the gathering process. Also, only process one herdable at a time, to minimize food loss. If you task too many villagers on a herdable, the extras will simply stand around and watch—definitely bad news for an economy!

Table 1.2 shows the herdables, their initial food value (at the time they're found), and their maximum food potential if left to fatten. Research the Husbandry technology (improvement) to increase the rate of fattening on herdables, and the gathering rate of your villagers on those herdables.

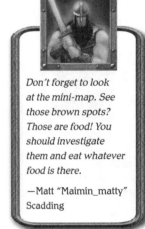

ES TIP

Don't forget to look at the mini-map. See those brown spots? Those are food! You should investigate them and eat whatever food is there.

—Matt "Maimin_matty" Scadding

ANIMAL	INITIAL FOOD	MAXIMUM FATTENING
Goat	50	300
Pig	50	300
Cow	75	400

Table 1.2 *Herd Animals Initial and Maximum Food*

ES TIP

Chickens aren't herd animals or hunted animals. They don't fatten, don't convert, and techs don't apply to them. They are really in a group by themselves with berries. Chickens start with 75 food a piece.

—Greg "Deathshrimp" Street

Hunting

Villagers gather food fastest by hunting wild animals (listed at the end of this section). However, accomplishing the task isn't always the easiest, or *safest*, method of collecting food. You can't control wild animals—instead, you must attack them. Though villagers are the primary hunters, in *Age of Mythology*, military units can join in the hunt. Some wild animals, such as walruses, boars, crocodiles, lions, and elephants, fight back, while others, such as deer, elk, zebra, and giraffe, simply try to escape. Odin is the only Major God who provides an immediate "bonus to hunting": Odin's gatherers hunt 10% faster than those of other cultures.

Even the aggressive animals, however, might run away instead of attacking, so it's difficult in *Age of Mythology* to lure wild animals to a Town Center, Granary, or Ox Cart. Often, time must be spent building a Granary or moving an Ox Cart to the wild animals' location, in order to gather the food as quickly as possible.

Use at least five or six villagers to hunt an aggressive animal. Losing villagers to animal attacks in the Archaic Age will set you back economically. After military units have been produced, use them to assist the villagers in hunting. Just as with herdables, the meat of dead huntables slowly rots, so use five or six villagers to gather as much food as possible from the slain animal.

Table 1.3 displays wild animals and their food value.

ES TIP

Get the Hunting Dogs improvement as soon as possible if you plan on hunting in the first Age.

—Nate "Redline" Jacques

ANIMAL	FOOD	ANIMAL	FOOD
Baboon	100	Crocodile	200
Crowned Crane	100	Polar Bear	200
Hyena	100	Zebra	200
Lion	100	Boar	300
Monkey	100	Giraffe	300
Wolf	100	Aurochs	400
Caribou	150	Hippopotamus	400
Deer	150	Walrus	400
Elk	150	Water Buffalo	400
Gazelle	150	Rhinoceros	500
Bear	200	Elephant	750

Table 1.3 *Wild Animals Food*

Foraging

Villagers forage from berry bushes or chickens, typically located near the Town Center in random map or multiplayer games. Foraging is one of the slower methods of gathering food. (It's not as slow as farming or fishing—at least until improvements are researched—but it's much slower than hunting or herding.) Each berry bush contains "100 food," and is far enough from the Town Center that a Granary or Ox Cart should be built or moved near the berries to hasten gathering. The farther a villager has to walk to deliver food, the more time is wasted not collecting resources!

Even though collecting from berries is slow, it's wise to use the bushes as your first food source while waiting for herdables to fatten and searching for a pack of wild animals.

Unlike animals, which decay after death, berry bushes retain their food until collected by villagers. Therefore, it's not important to place all your villagers on a single bush to minimize loss—there won't be any! Spread out your villagers to minimize bumping. Position them close to the nearest deposit site to minimize walking distance.

Farming

Farming is slow but dependable, and it's generally one of the safest methods of gathering food. Its downside is that each farm requires other resources (either wood or gold, depending on the culture), and villager "build time" to create. Once built, however, each farm provides an infinite amount of food, and never has to be replaced unless destroyed by enemy units or god powers (see Figure 1.2).

Farms become much more productive after researching the general improvements called Plow, Irrigation, and Flood Control. Research these at your culture's food-deposit site (Granary or Ox Cart) to increase farm yield by 10–15%.

Shift to farming only when other food-gathering methods have been exhausted. Multiple farms require resources, and it's typically more important in the early game to use those resources for construction, or for military units and improvements. Plus, since it's slower than hunting, herding, or foraging, farming will often become your final food source. You likely will need to switch to farms after exhausting your other sources during the late Classical Age or early Heroic Age. (Your mileage may vary, depending on your early game strategy.) Farms are extremely weak and should be protected by Towers and military units, or by placing them around a Town Center.

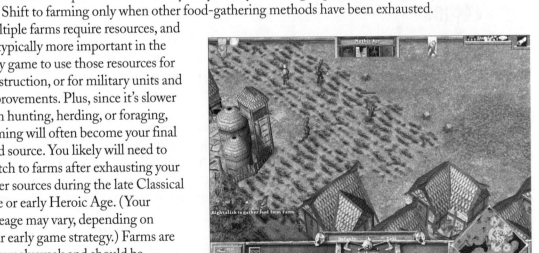

Figure 1.2 *Farming produces a slow, but steady, supply of food.*

Fishing

Fishing could be thought of as the water map equivalent to farming: It's slower than herding, hunting, or foraging, but provides a constant rate of food (and schools of fish provide an infinite amount of food). But like farming, fishing requires additional resources and build time. Fishing ships first need a Dock, which requires resources and time to construct. Then, each fishing ship requires a population slot, as well as resources and build time.

If you plan to fish, researching the Dock improvements is mandatory! The Classical Age improvement, Purse Seine, boosts fishing's gathering rate by 50%. The Heroic Age improvement, Salt Amphora, doubles the carrying capacity of fishing ships, and boosts gathering by another 25%.

Fishing can be a slow and expensive process, particularly in its early stages. It requires a lot of wood. But the longer the fishing boats operate, the more profitable the operation becomes. An important note: A school of fish can support just one boat, so you must scout out a new school for each fishing boat you build. Fishing is also more vulnerable to enemy attacks than farms.

Fishing can generate a powerful economy, particularly with its Classical and Heroic Age improvements (Purse Seine and Salt Amphora). If you can control the seas, your fishing operation becomes a second revenue stream while your opponent will only be able to use villagers on land. The heavy wood investment will pay off in the long run, with large amounts of food filling your reserves. But beware: Scout the enemy's naval power frequently to ensure your investment's safety. Since you can't construct Towers or walls in the sea, fishing ships are extremely vulnerable to enemy attack. Protect them with naval vessels or your entire investment could be sunk! You can garrison fishing boats in your Dock to protect them. The Dock does not fire back, like a Town Center, however.

Wood

Villagers gather wood from a single source: trees. You will often find single trees, sometimes called "stragglers," around your initial Town Center, and a forest of trees not far from there. While the trees around your Town Center are typically close enough to avoid needing an extra deposit site, forests are far enough away that they require one, to hasten collection and minimize a villager's walking distance.

Depending on your strategy and culture, wood may be a nearly ignored resource or one you'll focus on primarily. For instance, the Egyptian culture requires very little wood, particularly in the early Ages—none of their buildings, including farms and Towers, need wood! However, the Egyptian Heroic Age and Mythic Age Tower upgrades, siege weapons, and Archer units do require the resource. In fact, any strategy reliant on lots of Archers requires a substantial wood income.

Gold

Villagers collect gold from mines scattered across each map (or created with Thor's Dwarven Mine god power). Gold mines can differ in size; each size offers a different amount of gold. Gold isn't extremely important in the Archaic Age (though some strategies may dictate a gold economy that begins that early), but it certainly becomes vital as an *Age of Mythology* game progresses. All Age-advances after the Classical Age require gold, as do improvements, military units, and many mythological units (see Figure 1.3).

Table 1.4 reveals all gold-mine sizes, and their respective values. Thor's Dwarven Mine god power lets you place a gold mine anywhere on passable terrain. The amount of gold provided by the Dwarven Mine depends on the Age in which it's used.

Collecting gold follows the same principles as gathering food and wood. You need a deposit site close to the mine to minimize villager walking distance: The faster the gold reaches your coffers, the better, and the less time villagers spend walking (and not collecting resources), the better! Avoid placing too many villagers on gold, or time will be wasted when the villagers bump into each other trying to deliver their deposits. Five or six collectors per mine, all on the side closest to the deposit site, is optimal.

Figure 1.3 *'Twas ever thus: Funding armies takes large amounts of gold.*

The Norse can use a special gold-miner known as the Dwarf. Norse Dwarves gather gold faster than the other Norse gatherers, but gather food and wood more slowly. If you choose to worship Thor, however, Dwarven miners are cheaper, and collect food and wood on a par with other Norse gatherers.

SIZE	GOLD AVAILABLE
Archaic Age Dwarven Mine	250
Classical Age Dwarven Mine	1000
Medium Pit and Heroic Age Dwarven Mine	3000
Large Pit and Mythic Age Dwarven Mine	6000

Table 1.4 *Gold Quantity per Mine Size*

Favor

Favor, *Age of Mythology*'s fourth resource, is used to fund unique mythological units, and the improvements offered by the Gods. These powerful units and improvements give *Age of Mythology* a wealth of options, and a diverse style, unmatched in the real-time strategy genre.

The Greeks, Egyptians, and Norse gain favor from their Gods in different manners. This section details how each culture gains favor, and provides insight on how best to balance the gaining of favor against other economic needs.

Greek Favor

The Greeks gain favor by worshipping at the Greek Temple. You must manually task Greek villagers onto the Temple to begin worshipping. The Greeks are the only culture with direct control of the rate at which they gain favor. Each added villager doesn't double the rate of favor-gain, though: To balance the Greeks' direct control of gain, each subsequent villager provides less favor than the one before.

Egyptian Favor

Egyptians gain favor from their Gods by erecting Monuments. There are five Monuments in all; they must be built in the proper order; and each one adds more to favor-gain than the preceding one. Valuable food and gold resources—and the laborers' resource-gathering time—must be used to erect the Monuments. Although the Egyptians don't have the ability to increase or decrease the rate at which they gain favor, the Monuments allow for a consistent gain, which can be planned for accordingly (see Figure 1.4).

Figure 1.4 *Egypt! Increase the rate at which you gain the Gods' favor by building another Monument.*

Norse Favor

Norse warriors gain favor by fighting. Any combat will suffice, including hunting and gathering food from animals! The Gods bestow the most favor to the Norse Hero unit, the Hersir, which gains double favor from combat and even gains small amounts of favor for just being on the map. But Norse mythological units never generate Favor. As the Norse commander, it's difficult to plan for favor, since you must fight to gain some, and it can be nearly impossible to fill your favor coffers if you're faring poorly in battles.

Population

Age of Mythology's fifth resource isn't collected but instead built. Population governs the maximum number of units (military, mythological, economic, naval) you can have under your control at a particular time. Certain units occupy more population slots than others. For instance, a villager only uses one population slot while some of the larger mythology units occupy four or even five.

You can increase population by building Houses, or (after you have reached the Heroic Age) by acquiring settlements— specified areas on the map on which you can erect new Town Centers. Houses provide an additional "10 population," and each settlement provides 15 (see Figure 1.5).

You can build a maximum of 10 houses. This increases your "population cap" by only 100, but it's possible to increase population even further. To do so, acquire settlements after advancing to the Heroic Age. With settlements, there's no fixed population cap; the possible total depends on the number of settlements you acquire, the particular improvements you research, and even which Major God you choose to follow.

Figure 1.5 *Build Houses to increase your population cap, which permits the production of more units.*

Important Economy Concepts

Now that you're well versed on *Age of Mythology*'s five resources, it's time to learn how to maximize their potential. This section offers tips on directing your economy according to your strategy, managing an efficient economy, using your Market to trade resources and gain extra gold. We also offer a sample strategy to get your economy off to a profitable start.

Strategy Dictates Economy

In *Age of Mythology*, the ways in which players choose to run their economies will differ. Economies aren't the same across the board. One player may choose to emphasize wood gathering while another may put priority on favor and gold. Above all, players' military strategies determine how best to manage their economies.

Before beginning a random map or multiplayer game, consider what you're trying to accomplish in the game. Are you planning to use a strategy heavy in mythological units? Would you rather attempt an early cavalry assault? Or perhaps you're planning to play defensively, and create a massively productive economy to fund Mythic Age warfare?

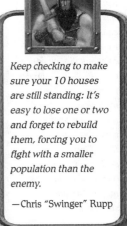

ES TIP

Keep checking to make sure your 10 houses are still standing: It's easy to lose one or two and forget to rebuild them, forcing you to fight with a smaller population than the enemy.

—Chris "Swinger" Rupp

After considering your strategic options, determine what will be required to fund that strategy. Archer-heavy strategies require a priority on wood. Big-economy strategies require a large population of villagers. Mythological-unit strategies require a consistent stream of favor. Adjust your economy accordingly, and keep in mind that you may need to adjust even further, if battles aren't going your way. Head over to Chapter 11 for more advanced tips on using the economy to fund a strategy, including the three "standard" approaches: rush, turtle, and boom.

TIP

For specific examples on developing an economy, head over to Chapters 12, 13, and 14 in our Advanced Multiplayer section. These advanced chapters on each culture offer specific strategies and include villager "build orders" and "task orders" to get you started on the right foot.

Running an Efficient Economy

Running an efficient economy doesn't mean just tasking countless villagers onto a particular resource until your coffers are overflowing. While that may fill your bank with resources to spend on units, structures, and upgrades, your opponent will likely still have more resources available—because your opponent is running a more efficient economy than you are!

Here are some tips on running an efficient economy.

ES TIP

Each random map can provide different resources. For example, Watering Hole has no berries or chickens, but overflows with huntable animals. Even within the same map, you might find less gold than you expected, but more food. Finding relics, or seeing what gods your opponent is choosing might also alter your strategy.

—Greg "Deathshrimp" Street

⊕ It's very important to minimize villager "walk time." The farther you task villagers from their deposit site, the more time that villager spends not working. Place deposit sites close to your villagers, or task them on resources close to the deposit site!

⊕ Don't task too many villagers on a particular food, wood, or gold resource. If you use too many, the villagers bump each other and increase their time spent not working. Move some off and task them on a different resource.

⊕ Carefully monitor the proportions and amounts of your resources. If you find that you're accumulating too much of one resource and it's just sitting unused, shift villagers off that resource and send them to collect another.

⊕ Check for idle villagers often (a banner appears in the upper right corner of the screen), to ensure that none of your villagers are standing around doing nothing.

⊕ When training new villagers at a Town Center, set the structure's gather point to the resource you want them to begin collecting (see Figure 1.6). Upon being trained, the villagers will automatically start collecting that resource (rather than just standing next to your Town Center, waiting for you to tell them what to do).

- Use the gathering guidelines in this chapter to determine how best to accumulate resources quickly. Don't begin farming before seeking out herds of wild animals!

- Research economic improvements as soon as you have extra resources in your coffers. Careful scouting of the enemy will determine if those resources should be spent on defense, military units, or economic improvements.

Figure 1.6 *Send villagers directly to a resource by adjusting the Town Center's gather point.*

- Treat Fishing Ships, and later Caravans, as Villagers. You may not need as many farms or gold miners if you are getting resources in other ways.

- Villagers occupy population slots too. In the late game, you may find that you have too many villagers and can't support a large army. Don't be afraid to delete villagers—you can always train more later.

Using the Market and Trade

You can build a Market upon reaching the Heroic Age (and you might as well; the structure is required in all cultures to advance to the Mythic Age). The Market is used to trade resources. For instance, if you're low on wood, you can use the Market to trade gold for more wood. If you're low on gold, you can trade food or wood for gold. The Market can't be used to trade food for wood directly.

Using the Market haphazardly isn't advisable because you incur a transaction fee with each use. It's not an even trade. In all but the rarest of instances, you'll sell off more resources than you'll receive. Considering that it took valuable villager time to gather those resources, you're automatically setting your economy back a little, particularly if your opponent has maintained an economic balance.

The Market is best used when you need just a bit more of a particular resource to fund a significant addition to your military or base. For instance, you wish to erect a Fortress, Midgol Stronghold, or Hill Fort quickly, and need just a smidgen more gold. Consider using the Market to build the structure sooner, but be cognizant of the resource penalty.

Trade Caravans are a function of your Market, and provide an extra revenue stream (of gold). Caravans travel between the Market and allied settlements, delivering extra gold into your reserves. The longer the Caravan's route, the more gold the Caravan delivers.

Commanding Your Military

Now that you have an understanding of Age of Mythology's economic system, it's time to put those resources to use, and create an army. The beauty of Age of Mythology is that you can't just mass one unit type and hope to succeed. Age of Mythology's counterbalancing military system demands planning, strategy, and careful unit selection.

This section covers Age of Mythology's basic military concepts, including how to implement combined arms, use counter units, and improve your army. You'll also find techniques for commanding your army, including tips on organization, unit stances and formations, god powers, and naval warfare.

We also offer valuable tips on battling effectively. For advanced military tactics, written by Ensemble Studios tester Chris Rupp, check out Chapter 11.

Creating an Army

This section offers guidelines on creation of your military, including how to best implement the concept of combined arms; *Age of Mythology*'s counter system and its importance in battle; and the improvements that boost the power of your soldiers.

Unit Selection

Strategic army creation requires more than just clicking military-training buttons. Strive to complement your culture and your Gods' strengths by training units with inherent benefits. For instance, Poseidon, a Major God of the Greeks, provides cheap stables and cavalry units. Although it's certainly possible to eschew cavalry under Poseidon, it's wiser to exploit these benefits to your advantage.

Likewise, consider your opponent's culture and Gods when deciding how to form your army and what improvements to research. An opponent choosing to worship Hades will likely exploit Hades' improvements to archers. Prepare to counter Hades' Archers with cavalry units, and research pierce-armor improvements to help defend your units against archer attacks.

Combined Arms and Counter Units

Age of Mythology's concept of counter units encourages—and, some could argue, forces—military commanders to train a mixture of military units, if they want to succeed. Military units follow a "rock, paper, scissors" formula. In general, infantry are most effective against cavalry, cavalry are most effective against archers, and archers are most effective against infantry. *Age of Mythology*'s military units don't *always* follow this basic rule. For instance, Norse Huskarl are infantry units that counter archers, and Greek Cataphracts are cavalry units that counter infantry.

ES TIP

Try to avoid fighting your unit's counter, because you will lose badly. If you see enemy Heroes or Priests attacking your mytho-logical units, run!

—Kevin "The_Sheriff_" Holme

Despite some variation, each *Age of Mythology* military unit is specifically built to be most effective against another type. Note that Hero units have no real counter (although Heroes don't perform as well against human units as they do against mythological units).

Training an army made up of just one type of unit is extremely unwise—the enemy could simply train units that counter your army, and win in a total landslide. Thus, in order to protect your army from a devastating counterblow, train complementing mixtures of units. For example, protect Greek Hippikon with Greek Hypaspists. The Hypaspists counter the Hoplites, Spearmen, or Ulfsarks that can counter the Hippikon.

Combining arms is only the first step in succeeding. You must actively apply strategies during the battle. A mixed army left to fight their counter units won't succeed any more than a one-unit army would, battling an army designed to counter it. In the above example, for instance, make sure the Hippikon stay away from enemy counter units and, instead, attack archers, if they are present.

An effective combined-arms force would be trained to counter anything the enemy uses. Add siege weaponry to your group to topple Towers, walls, and buildings; train mythological units for your army to battle other myth units and the enemy's human soldiers; and include Heroes in your army to counter mythological units.

Each military and naval unit in *Age of Mythology* can counter another, and often, several others. Additionally, certain units have even more bonus damage against particular units or structures. Use the stat Appendix in the back of this book as a guide when considering your army and what to use against an enemy's units. Scouting plays an integral role in deciding what units to train. Monitor the enemy's army and train your army accordingly. See the Appendix for a table that shows all *Age of Mythology* human and naval military units, their respective cultures, what the unit counters, and what unit to counter with.

Military Improvements

You've studied combined arms and counter units, but that's just the beginning: You can always improve your army. *Age of Mythology* features several ways to increase the abilities of military units. This section covers such improvements. You'll see the need to advance through the Ages, and you'll study line improvements (researched at the centers or structures where the units were produced), and Armory improvements (researched at the Armory).

TIP

For unit descriptions, head over to Chapters 3, 4, and 5 and find the unit in its respective culture. For full stats for all units, buildings, and improvements, check out the Appendix at the back of this strategy guide.

Age-Advancement

In order to develop military units to their full potential, you must advance to higher Ages. Usually, you'll begin in the Archaic Age, with nothing more than resource gatherers, a scout, and—depending on your culture—a Pharaoh, Priest, or Ulfsark. In order to train stronger military units, you must advance an Age. In order to research technologies to improve the attack, armor, and other abilities of your units, you must advance even further.

Table 2.1 shows the requirements for advancement to each Age. Note that worshipping the Egyptian Major God Isis reduces the food and gold requirements by 10%.

AGE	FOOD	GOLD	STRUCTURE
Archaic to Classical	400	0	Temple
Classical to Heroic	800	500	Armory
Heroic to Mythic	1000	1000	Market

Table 2.1 *Age Advancement Requirements*

ES TIP

Spend your resources as you get them, especially on units, until hitting your population cap. Those resources don't do you any good sitting in the bank!

—Nate "Redline" Jacques

Line Improvements

Line improvements to military units are researched at the centers where they were respectively produced. For instance, Greek Hoplites' line improvements are researched at the Military Academy. Line improvements researched here increase units' hit points, attack damage, and line-of-sight.

Each line improvement provides more "bang for the buck" because it upgrades three stats for the same cost in resources. Each Armory improvement upgrades only one statistic. In general, you should research line improvements at the units' production center before spending resources on Armory improvements.

Line improvements don't upgrade armor, though. Eventually, you should research the Armory improvements that boost armor. Make your selection based on what units your opponent has been training. If your opponent is training infantry (including Throwing Axemen), cavalry or mythological units that inflict hack damage (close-range attacks), research the "Mail" Armory improvements that upgrade hack armor; if your opponent is training archers or mythological units that inflict pierce damage (long-range attacks), research the "Shield" Armory improvements that upgrade pierce armor. See the Appendix for a table with all possible line improvements by culture, with resource requirements and benefits for each.

Armory Improvements

Each culture can research improvements at its Armory to upgrade the attack, hack armor, and pierce armor of human units, Heroes, and ships.

Table 2.2 lists all Armor improvements, with resource requirements and benefits for each.

IMPROVEMENT	AGE	FOOD	WOOD	GOLD	BENEFITS
Copper Weapons	Classical	200	-	200	+10% to all human and ship attacks
Copper Mail	Classical	150	-	150	+10% to human and ship hack armor; +15% to Hero hack armor
Copper Shields	Classical	-	150	150	+10% to human and ship pierce armor; +15% to Hero pierce armor
Bronze Weapons	Heroic	300	-	300	+10% to all human and ship attacks
Bronze Mail	Heroic	300	-	200	+10% to human and ship hack armor; +15% to Hero hack armor
Bronze Shields	Heroic	-	300	200	+10% to human and ship pierce armor; +15% to Hero pierce armor
Iron Weapons	Mythic	600	-	600	+10% to all human and ship attacks
Iron Mail	Mythic	500	-	500	+10% to human and ship hack armor; +15% to Hero hack armor
Iron Shields	Mythic	-	500	400	+10% to human and ship pierce armor; +15% to Hero pierce armor
Burning Pitch	Mythic	-	500	500	+3 to Archer and archer ship damage to buildings; +50% to Archer damage to ships; +20% to Ballista crush damage; +15% to archer ship pierce damage.

Table 2.2 *Armory Improvement Requirements and Benefits*

Note: Thor's Armory improvement requirements differ from these.

The Norse God Thor offers a special Dwarven Armory, which can be built as early as the Archaic Age. Followers of Thor can research the first Armory improvements in the Archaic Age and receive an additional set of improvements upon reaching the Mythic Age. Table 2.3 lists Thor's additional Mythic Age Dwarven Armory improvements, with resource requirements and benefits for each.

IMPROVEMENT	AGE	FOOD	WOOD	GOLD	BENEFITS
Hammer of the Gods	Mythic	500	-	500	+10% to Norse human attack.
Meteoric Iron Mail	Mythic	500	-	500	+10% to Norse human hack armor.
Dragonscale Shields	Mythic	-	500	500	+10% to Norse human pierce armor.

Table 2.3 *Thor's Dwarven Armory Mythic Age Improvement Requirements and Benefits*

Mythological Improvements

The Gods, major and minor, bestow mythological improvements. You won't be able to research all of these in a particular game, because you can only worship a total of four Gods. These improvements apply to the offensive or defensive capabilities of a particular type of unit, whether military, Hero, villager, or mythological. Research them at Temples or unit production centers. Check out Chapter 1, Managing your Economy, for mythological economic improvements.

Spending resources, particularly favor, wisely can easily determine the outcome of a game. An astute spender has a distinct advantage over a haphazard clicker. Because of their expense, it's important to choose your mythological improvements wisely. For example, don't research an improvement to a mythological unit, such as Feet of the Jackal, if you don't plan on implementing Anubites in your army. If your enemy isn't training infantry, don't bother researching Scalloped Axe, which improves Egyptian Axemen's attack.

Use mythological improvements to exploit your culture's benefits and advantages, and to counter the benefits and military composition of your opponent's culture. Refer to the Appendix for a table that lists all mythological improvements, with the God, resource requirements, and benefits for each.

Commanding the Army

Training an effective mixture of units sets you up for success. If you can't efficiently command the army, however, your training expertise will be wasted on the battlefield. This section provides tips and techniques for controlling your military, including organizing the units into banner groupings, using unit stances and formations, assisting your military with god powers, and tips on naval warfare and battling effectively.

ES TIP

If you like watching battles as much as I do, try assigning a control group to some of your buildings. For example, select all your Barracks by double-clicking them. Now hit Ctrl +5. Now when you are in a battle, press 5 and you will see that you can train units from those buildings without ever leaving the battle.

—Matt "Maimin_matty" Scadding

Organization

It's possible to spend your resources wisely, train combined arms that counter your enemy's forces, and still lose battles! You can't haphazardly send troops into battle. Organization is key. Although a disorganized army may succeed on occasion (against an opponent doing the same, for instance), it's much more sensible to organize your units for maximum effectiveness.

Organize units by using "Control" or banner groups. Select any number of units and hold the Ctrl key plus a number key. For instance, selecting your Hoplite group and pressing Ctrl and 1 assigns the Hoplites to banner group 1. You can select the Hoplites at any time by either pressing 1 or by clicking the mouse on the banner at the top left of the screen (pressing the number is much faster).

Organize your army into specific counter groups. For example, assign ranged units to their own group to keep them out of the middle of battles. The ranged units can strike from long range against their counter, typically infantry. Another example: Assign a single cavalry unit to a group so you can steer the unit easily and quickly around the battle to intercept an enemy siege weapon. There's no right way to organize your army, only better ways. For more on control groups and organization, see Chapter 11.

Unit Stances and Formations

Any *Age of Mythology* unit can be assigned its own unit stance and formation, though these functions are best assigned to organized groups of units. To use stances and formations, select a unit or unit grouping and click on the unit commands button on the unit interface. From there, toggle which stance and formation to assign to the unit or group.

Here are the three possible unit stances and suggestions on when to assign them.

◈ **Aggressive Stance.** Units will approach, chase, and engage any enemy units within their line of sight. Select aggressive stance for cavalry and infantry units (and non-ranged mythological units) when you're about to engage in battle.

◈ **Defensive Stance.** Units will remain stationary until attacked, then will approach, chase, and engage the attacker(s). Select defensive stance during non-combat situations so you aren't lured away by a scout or non-military unit into an ambush.

◈ **Passive Stance.** Units will remain stationary and attack within their range. Select passive stance to keep archers stationary and away from the close-range skirmishes. Make sure your archers stay within range of the enemy units, however—they need to assist in the battle!

While military units are automatically placed in logical formations (cavalry and infantry in front, ranged and siege in the rear), it's still possible to adjust the shape and depth of the military formation. Dense formations enable units to reach the battle quicker. The sooner you begin attacking enemy units, the better. However, if the enemy employs area effect weapons, such as a Ballista, switch to a more spread formation to avoid heavy damage when approaching the battle.

Units in formation move at the speed of the slowest unit in the formation. Protecting siege weaponry in formation is easier because your defenders remain close to the slow siege weaponry. Being closer means you can react to threats faster. But slow units approaching a line of archers can prove disastrous! The enemy archers have a longer time to inflict damage against your approaching units. In this situation, break up the formation and attack the archers with cavalry or other counters.

Divine Intervention

Invoking a god power at precisely the right moment will have a significant effect on a battle's outcome. You receive one god power for each God, major or minor, that you worship, so you can have a total of four god powers upon advancing to the Mythic Age. God powers offer both economic and military bonuses. This section focuses on the military bonuses, particularly those that can enhance your efforts in battle.

Here are some examples of offensive god powers and when to use them. For more information on all god powers, check out the Greek, Egyptian, and Norse chapters in this strategy guide.

◈ **Bolt.** Zeus' lightning kills a single unit. Use it on the enemy's most powerful unit (such as an expensive mythological unit) as you engage in battle. Or take out a villager or scout early in the game to set the enemy back.

◈ **Bronze.** Dionysus' Bronze affects both units and ships (including allies) within its area of effect, making them nearly invulnerable to attacks for a short time. Invoke it as you engage the enemy. Prepare a flank, in case the enemy considers retreating a better option than battling your Bronzed units.

◈ **Curse.** Aphrodite's Curse turns a portion of the enemy's units (based on hit points and number of present enemies) into pigs. Use on a group of villagers to set the enemy's economy back or invoke it during a battle to remove some of the enemy's military from the fight. Don't forget to claim your pigs and use them for food!

◈ **Lightning Storm.** Save Hera's Lightning Storm for large skirmishes with the enemy. Flank the enemy in an attempt to prevent the enemy's escape from the storm.

◈ **Eclipse.** Use Bast's Eclipse to increase the attack and speed of your mythological units. Save the god power until you are using mythological units, and invoke it as the battle begins.

◈ **Plague of Serpents.** The serpents will help defend an area against enemy attackers (and will keep doing so until killed) but won't follow if the enemy retreats.

◈ **Ancestors.** Nephthys' Ancestors is similar to Anubis' Plague of Serpents. Invoke the god power to help defend or attack an area. Unlike the serpents, the invoked minions will follow retreating enemies and are under your control, but automatically will die after a short time.

◈ **Son of Osiris.** Invoke this Egyptian god power to transform your Pharaoh into a more powerful warrior, with a chain-lightning attack. Especially useful against mythological units.

◈ **Undermine.** Use Heimdall's Undermine to crumble enemy walls and Towers so you can quickly and safely send in an invasion force. Follow up with another Norse offensive god power to handle the enemy's human or mythological unit defenders.

ES TIP

Get used to fighting in the second Age. Going straight up to the third Age with no army is almost never a winning strategy.

—Jerry "Gx_Iron" Terry

- **Walking Woods.** Invoke Walking Woods on forests adjacent to enemy buildings. Especially useful during a battle. The Walking Woods will pummel the enemy's buildings while his defenders are occupied in battle. Do not use Walking Woods against enemy units! It's okay against enemy units, just better vs. buildings.

- **Frost.** Use Skadi's god power to freeze enemy units in a block of ice. Although it's possible to damage the units in ice, it's very difficult. Instead, concentrate on hacking up the enemy's resource gatherers or town while the military units thaw out.

- **Flaming Weapons.** Increases the attack of all weapons (including projectiles, as from ships, siege ships, and siege weaponry) but does not affect allies. Flaming Weapons is an all-purpose offensive and defensive god power.

Naval Warfare

Age of Mythology's naval units mirror land forces: Each naval unit counters another, and can itself be countered by still another vessel. It's a "rock, paper, scissors" relationship that, once again, requires you to create combined arms to succeed. The primary naval vessels are separated into three categories: archer ships, hammer ships, and siege ships. Each culture includes one of each. There are other unique mythological naval vessels available through the worship of particular Gods. For more information on these, check out Chapters 3, 4, and 5.

Here's a list of the primary naval vessels for each culture, and the counter vessels.

- **Archer Ships**, including the Greek Trireme, Egyptian Kebenit, and Norse Longboat, are most effective against hammer ships, and are countered by siege ships.

- **Hammer Ships**, including the Greek Pentekonter, Egyptian Ramming Galley, and Norse Drakkar, are most effective against siege ships. They are countered by archer ships. They are also the best bet against naval mythological units.

- **Siege Ships** comprise Greek Juggernauts, Egyptian War Barges, and Norse Dragon Ships. Siege ships are most effective against archer ships and buildings, and they are countered by hammer ships.

Naval improvements are researched at each culture's Dock. Table 2.4 lists all naval improvements, with their resource requirements, and the benefits of each. These improvements are the same for all three cultures.

IMPROVEMENT	SHIP	AGE	FOOD	WOOD	GOLD	BENEFITS
Archer Ship Cladding	Archer Ships	Heroic	-	200	200	+10% to pierce damage; +20% to hit points; +4 to range
Reinforced Ram	Hammer Ships	Mythic	-	300	200	+10% to hack damage; +10% to hit points
Naval Oxybeles	Siege Ships	Mythic	-	500	200	+10% to hit points; +2 to bonus damage vs. buildings; +9 to range
Conscript Sailors	All	Mythic	500	-	-	Naval vessels train 20% faster

Table 2.4 *Naval Improvements and Benefits*

Here are some naval tactics for gaining the upper hand on water maps.

- Adjust your economy to meet the heavy wood requirements of naval warfare. Shift most villagers onto wood and gold to fund ships and improvements. Research wood- and gold-gathering improvements.

- Research all naval improvements to archer, hammer, and siege ships offered at the Dock. Use your food resources to research Conscript Sailors, to decrease training time. Don't forget that Armory improvements (including Burning Pitch) affect ships as well.

- Follow god paths that offer unique naval improvements and unique naval mythological units. Research the improvements and train the naval mythological units to support your ships. Learn their abilities!

- Ship construction is slow; construct multiple Docks to increase output.

- Ships do worse foundation damage than land units. It is still possible to build a Dock even if you are under attack.

- Focus your attacks. For instance, make sure all your archer ships engage one specific enemy naval vessel. Attack any damaged enemy vessels first. A naval battle is a numbers game: More often than not, the fleet with the more vessels will win the skirmish.

- Use combined arms. Attempt to avoid fighting counter ships, but attempt to counter the enemy's ships with your own.

- Maintain pressure near the enemy's Docks. Set your own Docks' gather points near the enemy Docks, so your vessels automatically head to the battle. If you happen to destroy an enemy Dock, prevent the enemy from building a new one. Remember that Egyptian Fishing Ships can build their own Docks.

- Protect your own Docks with Towers (although siege ships with Naval Oxybeles can target them safely). Remember that you can garrison Fishing Ships in your Docks for safety.

- If you have lost the ocean, remember that naval mythological units train quickly and are useful for getting back in the game.

On water maps, be sure to scout out your opponent's coastline before building a large navy. Boats are expensive, and building more than you need might cause you to lose the land-based battles. Don't build a huge navy unless you see that your opponent has a large investment in the sea.

—Kevin "The_Sheriff_" Holme

Battling Effectively

This section includes a variety of important tips to help you become a better commander. Combine these techniques with the other tactics you've learned in this chapter (and in Chapter 11) to improve your play.

Know Your Enemy

In an *Age of Mythology* game, whether single-player or multiplayer, strategy begins even before you've moved your first unit. It's vital to know your enemy! No, not personally, but you must understand the enemy's chosen culture and Major God. Study the culture chapters in this strategy guide, and learn each Major God's benefits. Strong players will exploit those benefits to their advantage.

Gauge the strengths and weaknesses of your enemy by using the following tips:

◈ Learn the benefits of each culture and Major God. Expect, but don't count on, your opponent to exploit those benefits. Scouting can help you determine if your opponent is doing this!

◈ Know the Minor Gods as intimately as the Major Gods. Take note of which Minor God the enemy chooses to worship at each Age-advance. Expect to be on the end of your enemy's new god power sooner or later! Also, the enemy could be choosing the Minor God for a particular improvement to his military units.

◈ Knowing your enemy also means scouting. Monitor your opponent's progress by scouting his resource camps and military structures early and often. By scouting, you can discern your opponent's focus, such as playing defensively, building up the economy, or preparing to attack early in the game.

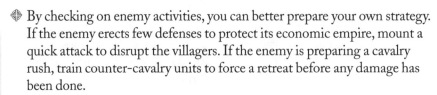

ES TIP

Scout, scout, scout! It's extremely important to know where your next supply of gold or food is, and what kind of units your enemies are making, so you know what units to spend your own resources on!

—Nate "Redline" Jacques

◈ By checking on enemy activities, you can better prepare your own strategy. If the enemy erects few defenses to protect its economic empire, mount a quick attack to disrupt the villagers. If the enemy is preparing a cavalry rush, train counter-cavalry units to force a retreat before any damage has been done.

◈ Think like your enemy. Scout all around his base so you can anticipate where and how he will try to expand. If you can commandeer the settlement or gold pit he's likely to go to next, you can trap him in his own corner of the map, depriving him of resources.

◈ Remain flexible. Base your economic and military decisions on current conditions: You might really love creating big cavalry armies, but if you see that your enemy has a ton of Camelry, and you don't change your military focus, you're doomed!

Offensive Tips

Shrewd unit selection, selective researching, and wise organization: These are the extremely important concepts discussed earlier in this chapter. Use the following offensive tips in combination with those techniques to enhance battle success.

◈ Don't think "successful offense" requires you to knock out your opponent's military units or town structures. An attack on villagers, especially in the early parts of a game, can be very effective. Disrupting an enemy's economy often proves even more valuable then knocking off a few military units. Forcing your opponent to reorganize, or to make new villagers while your resource gatherers work steadily along, can give you a devastating advantage. Just the distraction of having to react to your early-game attack can force your opponent to get behind economically.

- Use your offense to serve expansion. Control valuable resource positions with your military, and starve your enemy of gold or food. Control more settlements than your enemy, which can enable you to increase your population cap to a level your enemy can't attain.

- Disguise the might and nature of your offensive forces by keeping them away from nosy enemy scouts. Keep your opponent guessing, which could force him or her to spend resources on unnecessary improvements.

- Keep the fighting on your opponent's side of the map. Apply offensive pressure at your opponent's resource camps. Constant harassment can really distract your opponent from executing his strategy.

- If you're reinforcing your troops during the battle, set the gather points of your military structures close to the front lines, so you don't train units that remain in your base doing nothing. Even better, forward-build: Put up military structures near your opponent's town so you can quickly reinforce your attackers.

- Retreat, instead of fighting a losing battle. If you can't win, don't lose all your units in a landslide—and especially don't fight against counter units. Your Town Center and Towers can attack; retreat to those structures and adjust your strategy to meet the new demands.

- Try deception. For instance, attack early with cavalry. As your foe starts spending resources on anti-cavalry units, switch your focus to an attack force of archers and infantry.

- God powers can be used only once, so don't waste them! Don't invoke Dionysus' Bronze as you approach the battle; wait until the battle already rages. If you show your cards too soon, the enemy can simply retreat, and the god power will be wasted.

- Each culture offers a method of healing units. Follow a god path to Apollo, and research Temple of Healing or worship Athena for her Restoration god power; the Egyptians use the Pharaoh and Priests; and the Norse have Forseti's Healing Spring god power and Freyja's Valkyrie mythological unit. Don't underestimate the power of healing! Restoring a unit's hit points from one to full is like training a whole new unit—yet you saved resources! Only Poseidon has no way to heal his units.

- Support your human units with mythological units. Study the stat Appendix in the back of this guide to determine your best option. If your opponent trains primarily infantry, support your military with mythological units that inflict pierce damage. If your opponent trains primarily archers, support your military with mythological units that inflict hack damage.

- Use unit combinations so that all of your unit types are protected from counters. For example, guard Greek Hippikon with Hypaspists, which counter infantry (typical cavalry counters). Protect Egyptian Catapults with Spearmen, which counter cavalry.

◆ Don't forget about your mythological units' charged attacks. Nearly all mythological units feature a special attack that slowly recharges after each use. These attacks inflict more damage than standard attacks, or cause specific events, such as the freezing of enemy units by Skadi's Frost Giant. Micromanage your mythological units to maximize the potential of these charged attacks: Use them on the enemy's toughest troops.

Defensive Tips

A sturdy defense provides more time to focus on the economy or plan assaults. The less time you worry about an exposed resource camp, the more time you can devote to creating an efficient economy or utilizing the offensive tips illustrated earlier. Use the following tips to augment defense:

◆ Effective defense begins as soon as you build your first House. Survey the area around your base and consider your placement of structures carefully. Use natural boundaries, such as impassable rock or forests, as makeshift walls. Build Houses or other structures adjacent to these boundaries, creating barriers and forcing your enemy to enter your base in specific areas that you can protect with Towers and other defenses.

◆ Protect resource camps with walls and Towers to make it difficult for your enemy to disrupt your economy. As the enemy weaves through the Towers and walls, flank the position with your military units.

◆ Assign a few cavalry units to their own group for base defense. That way you can quickly recall these cavalry units to counter approaching siege weaponry, which can quickly topple your structures.

◆ Build Towers and Heroic Age defensive structures (Fortress, Migdol Stronghold, Hill Fort) near the enemy's base. Once your offense is counterattacked, retreat to these defenses. Garrison units in the Towers and structures for added attack.

◆ Spread out Towers and walls to avoid losing your defenses in a single invocation of a god power. Heimdall's Undermine and Artemis' Earthquake demolish Towers, walls, and buildings. Protect yourself with careful defensive placement before paying the price against these powers.

◆ Although you're clumping defenses (which is fine if your enemy doesn't have Undermine or Earthquake), build a wall around a Tower to force the enemy to destroy the wall to reach the Tower. You still must defend the defenses against siege weapons, however. Research Burning Oil if enemy units attack your Towers at close range.

Greek Culture

This chapter covers the Age of Mythology's Greek culture. There are important differences between the Greeks and the Egyptians or Norse, and we'll explore how those differences influence strategy. We'll also analyze the complete list of Greek Gods, both major and minor, and their god powers, mythological units, and technological improvements. Finally, we detail all the Greek military units. After studying this chapter, check out Chapter 12 for advanced Greek strategies, straight from the Ensemble Studios test team.

Cultural Differences

The Greek culture is easiest to learn of the three in *Age of Mythology*. Villagers construct buildings and gather resources in a straightforward manner; the Greeks' diverse military arsenal offers a counter for each unit type; the Greeks are the only culture to have direct control over the rate at which they gain favor; and mighty Greek Heroes provide strength against mythological units. But "easy to learn" doesn't mean "weak." Though expensive to produce, Greek human and mythological units are strongest of any in the three cultures. In this section, you'll learn the primary differences between the Greeks and the Egyptians and Norse.

Resource Gathering

The Greeks need a balanced supply of the basic resources food, wood, and gold. They lack the early farming ability of the Egyptians, and the faster gold mining of the Norse Dwarves. Also, Greek structures require wood—plenty of wood—so you must constantly monitor a four-resource economy (including favor). The Greeks can construct Storehouses, used to deposit gold and wood, and Granaries, to drop off food from farms, berry bushes, or domestic and wild animals.

The Greeks can save time and wood by placing the multipurpose resource depository, the Storehouse, between a forest and a gold mine. As long as villagers at both the gold mine and the forest have quick access to the Storehouse, the resources will continue to flow in. Trees disappear relatively quickly, however, and what once was a conveniently placed Storehouse might not be any longer, after a couple of advancements in Age. Be prepared to replace a Storehouse, moving the new one closer to the wood gatherers.

> **TIP**
>
> The Greeks begin the Archaic Age with a free cavalry scout unit, a Kataskopos. At the beginning of a scenario or skirmish, start moving this unit in an ever-widening spiral to uncover gold mines, settlements, the enemy's location, likely attack paths and choke points, and new food sources. You may even be able to steal some domestic animals from your enemy!

Worshipping the Gods

The Greeks are the only culture to have direct control over the rate at which they can gain favor from the Gods. After erecting a Temple, they send villagers to worship there. The more worshippers, the faster the Greeks gain favor (see Figure 3.1). Direct control over the gain of favor can pay off if you just need a bit more favor to pay for researching an important improvement or producing a new mythological unit. Villagers can be moved temporarily off their current duty and sent to the Temple.

Although for the Greeks, gaining favor appears to simply require the 50-food price of producing a villager, remember that while a villager worships at the Temple, he can't accomplish other tasks, such as gathering resources or constructing buildings. Don't overload the Temple at the expense of other resources. Mythological units and improvements do require favor, but they also require large amounts of food, wood, or gold.

Assign enough villagers to the task of worship (usually two or three is enough) to gain a steady supply of favor. Assign more if you require a quick burst of favor to reach a particular requirement. To save food for faster Age-advancement, don't spend the food to train villagers and assign them to at the Temple until the Classical Age.

Greek Heroes

Each Major Greek God gives a follower four (or in the case of Poseidon, five) unique Heroes. A Hero can be built at the Town Center, starting in the Archaic Age; a new Hero is added after each Age-advance. Once you reach the Heroic Age, you also can produce Heroes at the Greek Fortress. You can only have one of each Hero in use at any time. Should the Hero perish in battle, you can produce the Hero again at the appropriate structure.

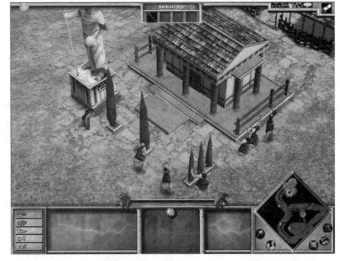

Figure 3.1 *The Greeks can gain favor more quickly by sending more villagers to worship at the Temple.*

> **TIP**
> The Greeks receive three special favor benefits should they choose to worship Zeus, the God of the Olympians: start with favor, faster favor gain, and an increased favor cap of 200.

Heroes are an invaluable asset to the Greek military and an essential counter for enemy mythological units. All Greek Heroes include bonus damage against mythological units. While human soldiers are the best counter for Greek Heroes, there's no *true* counter. There's no single Greek, Egyptian, or Norse unit that inflicts bonus damage against the mighty Greek Heroes. Keep Greek Heroes grouped separately from your other forces and send them into battle specifically against mythological units.

The following chart shows the Greek Heroes, the Major God to whom they are faithful, and the age in which the Hero can be produced. The Heroes are fairly similar for each age. For instance, Odysseus, Hippolyta, and Chiron (all available in the Classical Age) are ranged Heroes. There are some intriguing differences, though. Bellerophon rides a Pegasus and

> **TIP**
> Learn more about the mythology behind each Greek Hero by using the detailed help within Age of Mythology.

leaps into battle; Polyphemus is a lumbering Cyclops Hero with a special bash-attack; and Perseus carries a Medusa's head that periodically can turn enemy human units into stone.

GOD	ARCHAIC AGE	CLASSICAL AGE	HEROIC AGE	MYTHIC AGE
Zeus	Jason	Odysseus	Heracles	Bellerophon
Poseidon	Theseus	Hippolyta	Atalanta	Polyphemus, Argo
Hades	Ajax	Chiron	Achilles	Perseus (with Medusa's head)

Major Gods

In the single-player campaign, your Major God is chosen for you. However, in an *Age of Mythology* Random Map or Multiplayer game, you get to choose. Your selection will frame your strategy, and guide your selection of Minor Gods, until the end of the game.

This section covers the Greek Major Gods by describing their culture benefits, and offers strategic suggestions for exploiting their characteristics for maximum effect. The following chart reveals the possible Minor Gods for each Major God at each Age-advance.

MAJOR GOD	CLASSICAL AGE	HEROIC AGE	MYTHIC AGE
Zeus	Athena, Hermes	Apollo, Dionysus	Hephaestus, Hera
Poseidon	Ares, Hermes	Aphrodite, Dionysus	Artemis, Hephaestus
Hades	Ares, Athena	Aphrodite, Apollo	Artemis, Hephaestus

The following chart offers strategic suggestions on particular God paths, depending on what element of *Age of Mythology* you plan to emphasize.

FOCUS	ARCHAIC AGE	CLASSICAL AGE	HEROIC AGE	MYTHIC AGE
Economy	Poseidon	Hermes	Aphrodite	Hephaestus
Infantry	Zeus	Athena	Dionysus	Hephaestus
Archers	Hades	Ares	Apollo	Artemis
Cavalry	Poseidon	Hermes	Dionysus	Hephaestus
Mythological Units	Zeus	Athena	Apollo, Dionysus	Hera
Naval Units	Poseidon	Hermes	Dionysus	Artemis
Defense	Hades	Athena	Apollo	Hephaestus

Zeus

Zeus, the supreme God of the Olympians, was God of the Sky. Zeus had two brothers, Poseidon and Hades, who are *Age of Mythology*'s other two Greek Major Gods. Zeus' generosity with favor toward those faithful to him (see below) provides the perfect opportunity for a strategy heavy in mythological units and technology. Notice Zeus' bonuses to infantry units.

Zeus' unique civilization benefits include:

◈ **Favor benefits.** Worship Zeus and you start with 15 favor, gain favor faster (25% faster), and have an increased favor cap of 200. Because of these benefits, Zeus offers the best opportunity for a strategy heavy on mythological units. (Follow a God path to Hera if you plan to focus on mythological units.) The favor possessed at starting can be used to research an improvement earlier. The faster gain in favor means you can assign fewer worshippers to that resource, freeing others for other tasks.

◈ **Hoplites move faster (12% faster).** Speedier Hoplites (which also receive 50% bonus damage against buildings) could be used to harass enemy economic sites, particularly their resource-camp structures. Hoplites in general are useful against cavalry, and the increased speed of Zeus' Hoplites makes them even better able to intercept cavalry units.

⬦ **Infantry do more damage to buildings.** Hoplites, Hypaspists, and Myrmidons receive Zeus' benefit of double bonus damage to buildings. As mentioned in the previous benefit, use infantry to pummel resource-camp structures. Research Athena's Aegis Shield to improve infantry further, making them more resistant to pierce, or arrow, attacks.

Bolt God Power

Zeus' god power calls a lightning bolt from the heavens to destroy a single unit. However, you can't use Zeus' Bolt on transports (which would kill multiple units) or a Norse Ox Cart. To invoke Bolt, you must have line of sight on the target unit. Use Bolt to eliminate a powerful enemy unit—such as a Hero or mythological unit—during a crucial battle, or to disrupt an enemy's economy with the destruction of a key villager. For example, scout the enemy quickly with your Kataskopos and use Bolt on an enemy villager to gain an early resource-gathering edge. One of the most beneficial uses of Bolt is to use the god power against the Norse Nidhogg or the Egyptian Son of Osiris—both extremely powerful late game units. By saving Bolt, you're gambling that your opponent will choose to worship Osiris or Hel. They may not simply to avoid your Bolt.

Olympic Parentage Improvement

The blood of Zeus fuels the Olympic Parentage improvement, which causes Greek Heroes to have more hit points. Greek Heroes (a new Hero can be built at the Town Center or Fortress with each Age-advance, for a total of four) are essential units offering bonus damage against mythological units. Olympic Parentage can help in any Age, but offers the greatest rewards in the Mythic Age, when Zeus' mighty Bellerophon can be produced.

Poseidon

Poseidon, the brother of Zeus and Hades, is known primarily as God of the Sea, but was also ruler over horses and earthquakes. Poseidon's affinity for horses and the sea is reflected in his culture benefits. Poseidon's cheaper cavalry provides an instant focus for your tactics. Worship Minor Gods offering other cavalry bonuses to maximize Poseidon's initial benefit. When his worshippers build a Dock, Poseidon spawns the Hippocampus, a free naval scout.

Poseidon's unique civilization benefits include:

⬦ **Militia appear at destroyed buildings.** Followers of Poseidon gain unique Militia units, which appear at destroyed buildings. If Poseidon loses a building, including a Tower, Militia appear in the rubble. While Militia units aren't particularly strong, they will inflict damage to enemy units, and can buy extra time to bring in reinforcements. The larger the destroyed building, the more Militia appear.

Figure 3.2 *Worship Poseidon if you plan to create large cavalry armies.*

⊕ **Using the Market costs less (10% cheaper).** Poseidon offers two economic benefits, including a cheaper Market. Construction of a Market is required to advance to the Mythic Age. The Market also can be vital when you are trading resources to meet certain needs or when you need a Donkey Caravan to accumulate gold in late-game situations.

⊕ **Cavalry (10% cheaper) and Stable (50% cheaper) cost less.** This is Poseidon's primary benefit. His followers should not neglect cavalry (see Figure 3.2). Follow the God path through Hermes and Dionysus to gain additional cavalry bonuses.

⊕ **Free naval scout and unique Mythic Age naval Hero.** When followers of Poseidon construct a Temple and Dock, a free naval scout, the Hippocampus, appears. Half horse, half dolphin, the Hippocampus can be used to monitor enemy naval units and fishing operations. Also, when Poseidon's followers reach the Mythic Age, a unique Hero Trireme, the Argo, can be built at the Dock.

Lure God Power

Poseidon's god power Lure is emitted by a mythical stone that attracts animals both herdable (such as pigs and goats) and huntable (such as elk, caribou, and boar). Monitor the approaching animals carefully, though. Lure can also attract predatory animals, such as wolves, that can attack your villagers. Lure remains active until it attracts a certain amount of food. The closer the animals are to the stone, the faster the food will arrive. Even if you invoke Lure in a spot far from animals, the God power will remain active until the animals arrive. The effect will take much longer than if the stone was placed closer to animals. It's wise to invoke the God power near animals. If Lure takes too much time, your enemy may clear the map of herdables, leaving you with fewer food options!

Lord of Horses Improvement

Research Poseidon's Lord of Horses improvement to increase the line of sight of your cavalry and scout units. This is a further improvement to Poseidon's cheaper cavalry. The added line of sight will make it easier to scout enemy positions for hit-and-run cavalry harassment.

Hades

Hades, brother of Zeus and Poseidon, was the Greek God of the Dead and ruler of the Underworld. Precious minerals came from Hades' realm, which is reflected in his Vault of Erebus improvement. Also from the Underworld come the Shades. Hades favors archers, as can be seen both in the increased damage of his building and archer attacks, and in his Minor God path, which can further increase archers' advantages.

Hades' unique civilization benefits include the following.

⬥ **Dead troops may regenerate as Shades (20% chance).** When the followers of Hades fall in battle, some of the dead may return to the world as undead Shades—empty, ghost-like shadows of their former selves. Shades appear at Hades' Temple and can be sent back into battle as additional warriors, though they are certainly not as strong as they were when alive.

⬥ **Buildings have more hit points (+25% more hit points).** A defense-minded player should follow Hades for his benefit of increased hit points on buildings, walls, and Towers. Furthermore, Hades' god power Sentinel provides added defense to one of your—or an ally's—Town Centers (meaning an original or expansion settlement).

⬥ **Increased building (+20% pierce attack) and archer attack (+10% pierce attack).** Hades adds additional defensive benefits by increasing the attack damage done by buildings, including Towers, Town Centers, and Fortresses. Hades' Toxotes, Peltasts and Gastraphetes also do more damage. Follow a God path through Ares and Apollo to research other archer improvements that add to attack damage.

Sentinel God Power

Invoke Hades' Sentinel god power to cause four stone guardians to arise from the ground around your Town Center or that of an ally. The Sentinels aren't placed directly around the Town Center but rather, approximately two building-lengths at each diagonal. If there's no space for a Sentinel (as when a building is in its way), the Sentinel appears red. You can still invoke the god power, but the red statue won't be created. Remove the obstruction, however, and all four will appear. Sentinels are affected by any improvements that make buildings stronger. Save the Sentinel god power for expansion—invoke the god power around a key new settlement, especially those near valuable gold mines or food sources. Sentinels aren't all-powerful, and can be destroyed by the enemy. Use the Sentinel god power to enhance defense, not to replace Towers or walls.

Vault of Erebus Improvement

Hades' Vault of Erebus improvement provides a slow but steady income of gold. Hades, though known primarily as God of the Dead, was also considered the God of Wealth. Use this improvement to help fund Heroic Age attacks, particularly those featuring Toxotes, as they have increased attack damage, thanks to Hades.

Minor Gods

Each time you advance an Age, you must make a selection between two Minor Gods, depending on which Major God you chose to worship at the beginning of the game. Once you bypass a Minor God, you won't have an opportunity to select that God again during the game.

This section covers the Greek Minor Gods by describing their god powers, mythological units, and unique improvements. We also offer strategic suggestions on exploiting their characteristics to maximum effect.

The following chart reveals all Minor Gods, their Age, and their Major God affiliation.

MINOR GOD	AGE ADVANCEMENT	MAJOR GOD
Ares	Classical Age	Poseidon, Hades
Athena	Classical Age	Zeus, Hades
Hermes	Classical Age	Zeus, Poseidon
Apollo	Heroic Age	Zeus, Hades
Aphrodite	Heroic Age	Poseidon, Hades
Dionysus	Heroic Age	Zeus, Poseidon
Artemis	Mythic Age	Poseidon, Hades
Hephaestus	Mythic Age	Zeus, Poseidon, Hades
Hera	Mythic Age	Zeus

Ares – Classical Age

Ares is the God of Battle and Slaughter. Ares' improvements benefit human soldiers' attacks.

Pestilence God Power

Invoke Ares' Pestilence god power on an enemy town to prevent it from training new military units. Pestilence affects military structures, not economic buildings such as Town Centers. Enemy military structures outside the area of effect can still train new units. Invoke Pestilence to prevent an enemy from reinforcing its army as you mount an assault against a resource position or weak area of the enemy base's defenses.

Cyclops Mythological Unit

The Cyclops were giants with one central eye. They also were the Storm Gods of early Greek mythology. Ares' burly mythological unit offers bonus damage against other mythological units, and also is highly effective against human soldiers. In fact, the Cyclops has the ability to hurl enemy human units at other enemy units. This ability can remove a powerful human unit, such as a cavalry unit, from the battle temporarily, and inflict significant damage. Heroes will inflict bonus damage to the Cyclops. The Cyclops would be better off retreating if attacked by a large number of Heroes.

Will of Kronos Improvement

Research Ares' Will of Kronos to upgrade Cyclops to Elder Cyclops, which train faster and cause more damage. This is certainly an important improvement should you choose to include Cyclops as the backbone of your mythological unit force.

Phobos' Spear of Panic Improvement

Phobos' Spear of Panic improvement increases the attack damage of Greek Hoplites. While you can't couple this improvement with Zeus' faster Hoplites with added building damage, Phobos' Spear of Panic still makes Hoplites a stronger unit, particularly against its counter, enemy cavalry.

Deimos' Sword of Dread Improvement

Research Deimos' Sword of Dread improvement to increase the attack damage of Hypaspists, which are most effective against other infantry units. You won't be able to produce Hypaspists until the Heroic Age, so it's wise to save the resources required for this improvement until you can produce this counter-infantry unit.

Enyo's Bow of Horror Improvement

Ares bestows Enyo's Bow of Horror on Greek Toxotes to increase their attack damage. Followers of Hades will find this improvement most useful—Hades automatically benefits archers with increased attack damage. Stack this improvement with Apollo's Sun Ray, and Artemis' Shafts of Plague, to further increase archer damage.

Athena – Classical Age

Athena is Goddess of Wisdom and of Warfare. Athena's improvements aid infantry defense.

Restoration God Power

Athena's valuable Restoration god power can heal all of your units and repair all of your buildings, siege weapons, and ships. Don't haphazardly use Restoration. For instance, monitor the health of your military units carefully. Invoking this god power will regenerate units even when they are near death, so save Restoration for when you need it most. Restoration does affect allies, but only within its area of effect.

Minotaur Mythological Unit

Half man, half bull, Athena's mighty Minotaur can gore a single enemy unit right out of the battle. Minotaurs are most effective against human soldiers, but also offer bonus damage against mythological units. Steer clear of Heroes, however! If you plan on generating a large Minotaur army, research Athena's Labyrinth of Minos improvement to reduce the cost of this mythological unit.

Labyrinth of Minos Improvement

Athena's Labyrinth of Minos improvement upgrades Minotaurs to Bull Minotaurs—less costly, and even stronger in battle.

Sarissa Improvement

Research Athena's Sarissa improvement to increase Hoplites' hack armor, making the unit more resistant to infantry and cavalry attacks. Combine this improvement with Zeus' benefits to Hoplites, which include increased speed and bonus damage to buildings.

Aegis Shield Improvement

Athena's Aegis Shield improvement increases the strength of infantry units' pierce armor, making them more resistant to archer attacks. Combine this improvement with Zeus' gift to his infantry of bonus damage against buildings to make infantry more resistant to Town Center and Tower attacks.

Hermes – Classical Age

Hermes is the God of Messengers. Hermes' improvements benefit your cavalry.

Ceasefire God Power

Hermes' Ceasefire god power prevents all combat on the entire map for a short time. During Ceasefire, no one can damage units or buildings (see Figure 3.3). This god power also prevents the construction of any building that can attack, such as Tower, Greek Fortress, Egyptian Migdol Stronghold, or Norse Hill Fort (though settlements can be built). Ceasefire has many varied uses. For instance, invoke Ceasefire if an enemy overwhelms a lightly defended resource camp. Ceasefire will buy enough time to send reinforcements to the area. Or use Ceasefire to stop combat while your military structures or Temple complete powerful units capable of reinforcing your defenses once the god power expires.

Centaur Mythological Unit

The Centaur has the head and torso of a man and the body of a horse. Hermes' Centaur is a fast cavalry archer with a special accurate-shot attack that regenerates over time. This quick-ranged unit is perfect for hit-and-run attacks against enemy resource positions. If you plan to use Centaurs, consider Hermes' Sylvan Lore improvement, which increases Centaur speed and hit points. Worship Apollo at the Heroic Age and research Sun Ray to increase the Centaur's attack damage.

Sylvan Lore Improvement

Research Sylvan Lore to improve Centaurs to Centaur Polemarchs, with improved speed and hit points. Improved speed to this ranged mythological unit can help Centaurs escape counter-archers such as cavalry units.

Spirited Charge Improvement

Hermes' Spirited Charge improvement increases the speed and attack damage of Greek cavalry. Stack this improvement with Poseidon's cheaper cavalry benefit to create cheaper, faster, and more damaging cavalry than those available on other God paths. Follow the God path to Dionysus and research the Thracian Horses improvement to increase cavalry hit points.

Figure 3.3 *Invoke Hermes' Ceasefire to buy extra time for reinforcements to reach a critical position.*

Winged Messenger Improvement

Researching Hermes' Winged Messenger improvement reduces the food cost of the Greek Pegasus scout to zero. Winged Messenger also causes Pegasi to train faster and improves the creatures' line of sight. This improvement will serve you best on island maps where scouting by land is impossible.

Apollo – Heroic Age

Apollo is the God of the Sun, and of Music. Apollo's improvements benefit archers.

Underworld Passage God Power

Invoke Apollo's Underworld Passage god power to create two locations on the map—an entrance and an exit. Place the entrance first, by placing the structure on the map. Click on a second map location to place the passage's exit. You must have line of sight on both places to invoke Underworld Passage. The passage is permanent until destroyed. (If either end is destroyed, the passage becomes useless.) You can use Underground Passage to aid in defense, such as placing the entrance in your town and the exit in an ally's town so you can easily reinforce each other's bases. Or invoke the god power for offensive purposes, such as evading wall or Tower defenses, or staging a surprise attack on a new settlement, resource area, or weak area of an enemy's base. The enemy can't use the passage, but can destroy the entrance or exit.

Manticore Mythological Unit

 Apollo's mythological unit, the Manticore, has the body of a red lion, a human face (blue eyes and human ears), three rows of teeth, and the ability to fire poisonous spines from its tail. The Manticore is most effective against human soldiers, but includes bonus damage to mythological units. As with any ranged unit, support the Manticore with a melee force to prevent enemy Heroes from attacking the Manticore at close range.

Oracle Improvement

 The Oracle improvement increases the line of sight of all units and buildings. Use this improvement both as a defensive and scouting aid: Your expansion settlements and defensive Towers will spot enemy units earlier. Your scout units will uncover enemy resource camps and settlements more quickly, allowing you time to plan for an attack.

Temple of Healing Improvement

 Apollo's Temple of Healing improvement turns the Greek Temple into a means of healing your wounded units, and those of allies. Stationary units will heal much faster than those moving or engaged in combat. The Temple of Healing does not affect certain units, such as the undead or the Norse dragon unit, Nidhogg. If you choose to worship Apollo, plan ahead by placing your Temple in an open, convenient area so you can surround the structure between battles with stationary units to be healed. Combine the improvement with the Underground Passage to help get retreating troops, or units from an ally's camp, to the Temple for healing. Unlike the Norse Healing Spring, this improvement can only heal units one at a time.

Sun Ray Improvement

 Research Apollo's Sun Ray improvement to increase the attack damage of Toxotes, Peltasts, Gastraphetes, Manticores, and Centaurs. Stack this improvement with other improvements to archers, including Hades' benefits and Ares' improvement, Enyo's Bow of Horror. Follow a God path that includes Hermes to increase the attack of Centaurs and Manticores for a lethal combination of ranged mythological units.

Aphrodite – Heroic Age

Aphrodite is Goddess of Love and Beauty. Aphrodite's improvements aid your villagers.

Curse God Power

Invoke Aphrodite's god power, Curse, to turn enemy units to pigs. Curse affects only a small area, and not all enemy units within that area will be transformed. After the units have been turned into pigs, the herdable animals can be led back to your town and used as a food source. Disrupt an enemy's economy by invoking Curse on a resource camp. You will interrupt your enemy's economy by decreasing villagers, and you can improve your own economy with added food.

Nemean Lion Mythological Unit

The Nemean Lion, a large, ferocious lion that lived on the plains of Nemea, was slain by Heracles, according to Greek mythology. Heracles is often depicted wearing the Nemean Lion's coat as a symbol of his victory. The Nemean Lion has the ability to roar, which can inflict damage to all enemy units in its area of effect. Like other Greek mythological units, the Nemean Lion is effective against human soldiers, and has bonus damage to mythological units.

Roar of Orthus Improvement

Research the Roar of Orthus improvement to increase the armor of your Nemean Lions. The more resistant the Nemean Lion is to enemy attack, the most opportunities you will have to utilize its potent roaring ability.

Golden Apples Improvement

Aphrodite's Golden Apples improvement causes villagers to generate favor from Temples faster. Aphrodite isn't in Zeus' God path, so you can't stack Zeus' favor benefits with the Golden Apples improvement. Greeks have direct control over the rate of favor generation (the more villagers worshipping, the faster the favor gain), and Golden Apples can increase the rate, allowing you to assign villagers to other resource tasks.

Divine Blood Improvement

Aphrodite's Divine Blood improvement is an all-encompassing upgrade of your villagers' abilities (although it doesn't benefit favor gain). They'll move faster, build faster, and carry more resources. The benefits can be far-reaching: Villagers can erect defenses or expansions faster, and return more resources more quickly to the respective resource camps. Divine Blood is a Heroic Age benefit that can help fund a Mythic Age military strike.

Dionysus – Heroic Age

Dionysus is the God of Wine and of Celebration. Dionysus' improvements aid your cavalry and navy.

Bronze God Power

Dionysus' Bronze god power temporarily transforms your human units and ships (and those of your ally within the area of effect) into bronze. The metal makes your human units nearly invulnerable to enemy weapons. Bronze can be invoked offensively or defensively: Use it just before assaulting an enemy base or expansion, or—in a defensive position—invoke Bronze as the enemy begins to attack your human units. Bronze is a timed god power. After the time expires, your units return to their normal selves and become vulnerable again to enemy attacks.

Hydra Mythological Unit

The Hydra is a large land unit: a serpent with multiple heads and poisonous breath. Like the fire-breathing Chimera, it's an offspring of Echinda and Typhon. The Hydra grows additional heads as it fights in battle. The longer the Hydra fights and survives, the more heads the creature grows (see Figure 3.4). The number of heads is based on the number of units killed by the Hydra. Additional heads allow the Hydra to attack multiple (adjacent) units. Use the Hydra against human and mythological units.

Figure 3.4 *Preserve your Hydras because the creature grows—literally—more useful after fighting.*

Scylla Mythological Unit

A sea monster with six serpent heads and a ring of barking dogs around its waist, the Scylla originally was a beautiful nymph, but was transformed by the jealous sorceress Circe. The Scylla is essentially the nautical equivalent of Dionysus' Hydra. It grows additional heads as it fights in battle. The longer the Scylla battles and survives, the more heads (up to six) the creature grows. With additional heads, the Scylla can attack multiple units at once. Use the Scylla against ships—except ramming ships, which counter the Scylla's attack effectively.

Bacchanalia Improvement

 Research Dionysus' Bacchanalia improvement to increase hit points of all your units by a small amount. Use this improvement in the late game when both you and your enemy have maximized the population cap and boast nearly equal armies. Dionysus' small benefit to hit points could provide the edge required to gain the upper hand.

Thracian Horses Improvement

 Dionysus offers your civilization Thracian Horses, which will improve cavalry hit points. Research this improvement and combine it with Poseidon's cheap cavalry as well as Hermes' Spirited Charge improvement, which increases cavalry speed and attack. Acquire all three for cheap, fast, stronger, and more durable cavalry units.

Anastrophe Improvement

 You'll have a better chance at ruling the seas with Dionysus' Anastrophe improvement, which upgrades the attack damage, swiftness, and training speed of the Greek Pentekonter hammer ships.

Artemis – Mythic Age

Artemis is Goddess of the Hunt and of Nature. Artemis' improvements benefit archers and the navy.

Earthquake God Power

 Invoke Artemis' wrath on an enemy town! Create an Earthquake to crumble buildings, Towers, and walls, and toss armies to the ground. Although Earthquake will inflict some damage on enemy units, and knock them around, it inflicts much more damage on enemy buildings and walls. Allied units and structures within the area of effect also will be damaged, but not so severely. One special note regarding Earthquake: Enemy farms take very little damage from this god power.

Chimera Mythological Unit

 The Chimera, one of the varied offspring of Echinda and Typhon, was a fire-breathing beast with the body of a goat, head of a lion, and tail of a serpent. Artemis' mythological unit can breathe fire, inflicting damage on multiple nearby enemy units. The Chimera is most effective against human soldiers, and features bonus damage against mythological units. It cannot use flaming breath against Heroes.

Flames of Typhon Improvement

Flames of Typhon improves Artemis' Chimera units, making them Chimera Tyrants, which are more powerful by boosting hit points, hand attack and flame attack.

Shafts of Plague Improvement

With this improvement, Artemis grants Toxotes, Peltasts, and Gastraphetes the Shafts of Plague. Research it to increase the attack damage of the Greek archer and counter-archer units. Follow a God path that includes Hades, Ares, and Apollo for additional benefits and improvements to Greek archers.

Trierarch Improvement

Research the Trierarch improvement to make Greek Triremes more resistant to enemy siege ships. Combine Trierarch with Dionysus' improvements to Pentekonter ramming ships to further aid your naval efforts.

Hephaestus – Mythic Age

Hephaestus is the God of the Forge and of Labor. Hephaestus' improvements benefit human soldiers' armor and weapons.

Plenty God Power

Invoke Hephaestus' god power, Plenty, to erect a great vault that grants a constant flow of food, wood, and gold resources. But Hephaestus favors the strong; you must maintain control of the Plenty vault in order to retain its bounty. If an enemy has more units or buildings around the vault than you, the Plenty vault falls under enemy control, and the enemy reaps its rewards. Place the vault in an easily defended location. Surround the vault with walls and Towers to protect the valuable structure.

Colossus Mythological Unit

Hephaestus' mighty Colossus is a slow but brawny melee unit that can inflict heavy damage against buildings as well as human and mythological units (Colossi feature bonus damage against mythological units). Hephaestus provides two improvements to the Colossus—Hand of Talos and Shoulder of Talos—that must be researched in that order. Both change the metallurgy of the originally bronze Colossus, and increase hit points. The Colossi can also eat resources to replenish their health! Devour a tree or animal to regenerate this powerful mythological unit.

Hand of Talos Improvement

Hephaestus reforges Colossi to Silver Colossi, which possess more hit points.

Shoulder of Talos Improvement

Hephaestus reforges Silver Colossi to Gold Colossi, further increasing hit points.

Forge of Olympus Improvement

Research this improvement to reduce the cost of all Armory upgrades. Save Heroic Age armory improvements until you've reached the Mythic Age and chosen to worship Hephaestus. Then upgrade your military units at their respective military structures before researching Forge of Olympus to follow up with Heroic- and Mythic Age armory improvements. Group this improvement with Hephaestus' Plenty god power to increase income and decrease cost.

Weapon of the Titans Improvement

Hephaestus' Weapon of the Titans improvement improves the attack damage of the Greeks' unique Fortress units, as well as Zeus' Myrmidon, Poseidon's Hetairoi, and Hades' Gastraphetes.

Hera – Mythic Age

Hera is the Goddess of the Home. Hera's improvements benefit buildings and mythological units.

Lightning Storm God Power

Invoke Hera's devastating Lightning Storm against a group of enemy units (see Figure 3.5). All enemy units that remain in Lightning Storm's area of effect could well perish at Hera's hand. The Lightning Storm doesn't move, however, so it's possible for faster enemy units to escape the storm. Hera's god power works best against enemy units, though it may strike trees and buildings to inflict mild damage. Lure an enemy into an ambush, using Lightning Storm. Block the enemy's exit routes with a flanking maneuver so the enemy units have trouble escaping Hera's wrath.

Medusa Mythological Unit

Medusa was one of the three Gorgon sisters, children of Sea Gods, who have live sea snakes for hair, scaly necks, boar-like tusks, golden hands, and bronze wings. Hera's Medusa mythological unit also has the ability to turn enemy human units into stone (the ability slowly recharges after use). Medusa uses a bow and arrow, and should be supported with melee units. Though expensive, a group of Medusa units can quickly turn the tide of battle by eliminating human units from the fight. Stoned units are eliminated instantly, and disappear from the map after a few seconds.

Figure 3.5 *Shock an incoming enemy force with Hera's monstrous Lightning Storm god power.*

Carcinos Mythological Unit

During Heracles' battle with the Hydra, Hera summoned a crab to attack Heracles and aid the Hydra. Heracles managed to defeat both, but as a reward for its efforts, Hera placed the crustacean in the sky as a constellation. The Carcinos fights as a naval unit against enemy ships. As it dies, the Carcinos releases a rush of boiling blood, to further damage any nearby vessels.

Face of the Gorgon Improvement

Research the Face of the Gorgon to improve Medusas, making them Medusa Matriarchs, with increased hit points.

Athenian Wall Improvement

Research Hera's Athenian Wall improvement to increase building hit points. Acquire this upgrade, particularly for defensive Towers and expansions, if you need more protection in the late game.

Monstrous Rage Improvement

Hera's Monstrous Rage increases the damage caused by mythological units using any type of attack, including "hack," "pierce," and "crush." Combine this improvement with Zeus' benefits regarding favor and its gain, and implement a strategy focused on mythological units. Obviously, the more mythological units you have in the field, the more worthwhile Hera's Monstrous Rage will be.

Military Units

This section describes the Greek military units, including siege and naval units. The following charts show where to improve each unit, and how the unit improves after research. Note that all military units can be improved at the facility, such as "Barracks," where they were produced.
Units are first improved to Medium, then to Heavy, then to Champion.

See the Appendix in this strategy guide for Greek unit, building, and improvement stats.

Kataskopos

All Greek civilizations receive a free Kataskopos, a cavalry scout unit that should be used to quickly survey the map, looking for settlements, resources, and enemy positions. The Kataskopos is fast and has excellent line of sight, but will lose in battle against nearly any opponent. You aren't able to train an additional Kataskopos. Should you lose this cavalry scout, no other will appear for the duration of the game. You will have the option to produce Pegasus units at the Greek Temple to continue your scouting efforts.

Hippocampus

Worship Poseidon, and after constructing a Temple and a Dock, you receive this free naval scout. The Hippocampus—known for pulling Poseidon's chariot—is half fish and half horse, with the tail of a serpent or dolphin. Although the Hippocampus can't attack enemy units, it can be used to scout enemy naval positions, strengths, and fishing operations. If the Hippocampus is killed, another is spawned at your Dock after a short time.

Pegasus

All three Major Gods of Greece can produce the winged horse Pegasus as early as the Archaic Age. Pegasus is an inexpensive flying scout, produced at the Temple, that can be attacked only by ranged units. Although the Greeks have a capable land scout in Kataskopos, and worshippers of Poseidon have a free naval scout, there are many scenarios when you might need a Pegasus to explore over water and to check out places inaccessible except by air. Worship Hermes and acquire the Winged Messenger improvement to reduce the cost of the Pegasus unit to zero. The improvement also trains the mythological unit faster, and improves its line of sight.

ES TIP

Pegasi are useful "spotters" to cast god powers against an enemy or to find a good location for an Underworld Passage.

— Greg "Deathshrimp" Street

UPGRADE	IMPROVES
Hermes' Winged Messenger	Cost (only requires favor), Training Rate, Line of Sight

Hoplite

The Greek Hoplite is most effective against cavalry units, such as Greek Hippikon, Egyptian Camelry, or Norse Raiding Cavalry. Steer clear of counter-infantry units or archers, though you can improve your odds against these units through improvements, including Athena's Sarissa and Aegis Shield. Follow Zeus to receive instant Hoplite improvements—Zeus' Hoplites are faster and feature bonus damage against buildings. For an infantry unit, Hoplites are pretty slow without Zeus' benefit.

UPGRADE	IMPROVES
Military Academy	Attack, Hit Points, Training Rate, Line of Sight
Armory	Attack, Armor
Zeus	Swiftness, Damage vs. Buildings
Ares' Phobos' Spear of Panic	Attack
Athena's Sarissa	Hack Armor
Athena's Aegis Shield	Pierce Armor

Toxote

Toxotes are the Greeks' initial ranged units and first counter-infantry units. Although Toxotes are highly effective against infantry, enemy cavalry easily runs down the slow-moving archers. Toxotes also don't fare well against other archers, such as Egyptian Slingers. The Toxote does compete handily against the Norse Throwing Axemen, actually an infantry unit that the Toxotes defeat rather easily. Worship Hades to give your Toxotes instant improvements in attack damage. Follow Hades' God path through Ares, Apollo, and Artemis to research other useful improvements.

UPGRADE	IMPROVES
Archery Range	Attack, Hit Points, Training Rate, Line of Sight
Armory	Attack, Armor
Hades	Attack
Ares' Enyo's Bow of Horror	Attack
Apollo's Sun Ray	Attack
Artemis' Shafts of Plague	Attack

Hippikon

Expensive and slow, but mighty against enemy archers and siege units, Greek Hippikon are best used in flanking maneuvers—to avoid infantry units (particularly Hoplites and Spearmen, which feature bonus damage against cavalry) and to strike enemy range and siege units behind the front lines. Worship Poseidon to benefit from cheaper cavalry. Continue through the God path to Hermes and Dionysus and research their improvements to receive faster, more durable, and more damaging Hippikon.

UPGRADE	IMPROVES
Stable	Attack, Hit Points, Training Rate, Line of Sight
Armory	Attack, Armor
Poseidon	Cost
Poseidon's Lord of Horses	Training Rate
Hermes's Spirited Charge	Speed, Attack
Dionysus's Thracian Horses	Hit Points

Hypaspist

The Hypaspist infantry unit, available in the Heroic Age, excels against other infantry; it has bonus damage against them. Increase the Hypaspist's resistance to archers with Athena's Aegis Shield improvement. Hypaspists also benefit from worshipping Zeus, gaining bonus damage against buildings.

UPGRADE	IMPROVES
Military Academy	Attack, Hit Points, Training Rate, Line of Sight
Armory	Attack, Armor
Zeus	Damage vs. Buildings
Ares' Sword of Dread	Attack
Athena's Aegis Shield	Pierce Armor

Peltast

Defend against archers, including Egyptian Chariot Archers, with the Greek Peltast, which offers bonus damage against archers. The Peltast is weak against other units, however, particularly cavalry (which typically have bonuses against archers). Research Apollo's Sun Ray and Artemis' Shafts of Plague to improve Peltast attack damage.

UPGRADE	IMPROVES
Archery Range	Attack, Hit Points, Training Rate, Line of Sight
Armory	Attack, Armor
Hades	Attack
Apollo's Sun Ray	Attack
Artemis' Shafts of Plague	Attack

Prodromos

Available in the Heroic Age, the Prodromos serve as the Greek's counter-cavalry unit. Although the Prodromos features bonus damage against cavalry (such as Greek Hippikon, Norse Raiding Cavalry and Jarls, and Egyptian Camelry), the unit is relatively weak against other types of unit. Improve Prodromos through Poseidon, Hermes, and Dionysus.

UPGRADE	IMPROVES
Stable	Attack, Hit Points, Training Rate, Line of Sight
Armory	Attack, Armor
Poseidon	Cheaper
Poseidon's Lord of Horses	Line of Sight
Hermes's Spirited Charge	Faster, Attack
Dionysus's Thracian Horses	Hit Points

Petrobolos

These Greek siege weapons are produced at the Fortress. The Petrobolis, similar to the Egyptian Catapult, can assault buildings and Towers at long range. Lacking a close-range attack, the lightly armored Petrobolis must be supported with other units, especially those that counter cavalry. Improve the Petrobolis at the Fortress, with attack-speed and damage upgrades.

UPGRADE	IMPROVES
Fortress	Attack Speed, Attack

Helepolis

The Greek Helepolis is a rolling Tower that can transport units and fire ballista bolts that are strong against enemy buildings. The Helepolis moves very slowly and should be supported by quicker infantry and cavalry units. Surprise an attacker with the Helepolis' transport abilities: Unload units as from a Trojan horse after the enemy has approached with victory in mind. Improve the Helepolis at the Fortress to increase weapon speed and damage.

UPGRADE	IMPROVES
Fortress	Attack Speed, Attack

Myrmidon

Zeus' unique Mythic Age Fortress unit features bonus damage against Norse and Egyptian human units. In a match between Zeus and the Norse or Egyptians, the Myrmidon can provide added military might during Mythic Age battles. Worship Hephaestus instead of Hera at the Mythic Age advancement to research the Weapon of the Titans improvement, which increases the Myrmidon's attack damage.

UPGRADE	IMPROVES
Zeus	Damage vs. Buildings
Athena's Aegis Shield	Pierce Armor
Hephaestus' Weapon of the Titans	Attack
Military Academy	Attack, Hit Points, Line of Sight
Armory	Attack, Armor

Hetairoi

The Hetairoi prided themselves on their horsemanship and made up one of the elite units in the Macedonian army. Poseidon's unique Mythic Age Fortress unit provides bonus damage against enemy buildings. Groups of Hetairoi can make quick work of enemy resource camps and Towers. Support them with counter-infantry units, to prevent units such as Greek Hoplites or Egyptian Spearmen from engaging the Hetairoi. Worship Hephaestus and research the Weapon of the Titans improvement to increase Hetairoi damage.

UPGRADE	IMPROVES
Poseidon's Lord of Horses	Training Rate
Hermes' Spirited Charge	Speed, Attack
Dionysus' Thracian Horses	Hit Points
Hephaestus' Weapon of the Titans	Attack
Stable	Attack, Hit Points, Line of Sight
Armory	Attack, Armor

Gastraphetes

Depending on your point of view, Hades' unique Fortress unit is either an inexpensive siege weapon or an archer that does extra damage to buildings. Protect these unique archers from cavalry counter attack with Hoplites or Prodromos. Worship Hephaestus in the Mythic Age and research Weapon of the Titans to increase Gastraphetes attack damage.

UPGRADE	IMPROVES
Apollo's Sun Ray	Attack
Artemis' Shafts of Plague	Attack
Hephaestus' Weapon of the Titans	Attack
Archery Range	Attack, Hit Points, Line of Sight
Armory	Attack, Armor

Trireme

This oared galley, named because the oarsmen were stationed at three different levels, propelled the classical Greek city states into the status of naval power. The Trireme Archer ship is most effective against hammer or ramming ships. Avoid siege ships, unless you worship Artemis in the Mythic Age and have researched Trierarch, which makes Triremes more resistant to siege ships.

UPGRADE	IMPROVES
Armory	Attack, Armor
Armory's Burning Pitch	Bonus damage vs. buildings
Dock	Hit Points, Range, Attack, Training Rate
Artemis' Trierarch	Resistance to siege ships

Pentekonter

The Greeks developed the "dolphin," which was made of heavy lead or bronze and swung from the boom on a ship's mast to puncture holes in enemy hulls. The Pentekonter hammer ship is most effective against siege ships. Counter the Pentekonter with archer ships. Research Dionysus' Anastrophe improvement to receive upgrades to the Pentekonter in attack damage, swiftness, and training speed.

UPGRADE	IMPROVES
Armory	Attack, Armor
Dock	Hit Points, Attack, Training Speed
Dionysus' Anastrophe	Attack, Swiftness, Training Speed.

Juggernaut

As war ships increased in size, navies began mounting larger weapons, such as Catapults and Ballistae, on the vessels. Siege ships such as the Greek Juggernaut are best used against archer ships and buildings. Avoid hammer or ramming ships, and support with arrow ships or mythological naval units—siege ships can't defend themselves at close range.

UPGRADE	IMPROVES
Armory	Attack, Armor
Dock	Hit Points, Range, Training Speed

The Egyptians

I n this chapter, we discuss the important differences between the Egyptians and the Greek or Norse, and how those differences influence strategy. We also analyze the major and minor Egyptian Gods and their god powers, mythological units, and technological improvements. Finally, we detail the Egyptian military units. After reading this chapter, check out Chapter 13 in our Advanced Multiplayer Tactics section (written by Ensemble Studios experts) for more Egyptian strategies.

Cultural Differences

The Egyptians are a diverse culture, offering several play options. While it's possible to mount an early rush, the Egyptians' unique economic and military benefits are geared more toward a build-heavy, or defensive, strategy. This section covers some of the Egyptian culture's unique features.

Resource Gathering

The Egyptians focus their economy, especially early in the game, on three of the four resources: food, gold, and favor. The Egyptians can largely ignore wood gathering because their structures don't have a wood cost. In fact, many important Egyptian structures (including Houses, resource camps such as Granaries, and the Armory) are completely free. To offset this advantage, Egyptians must build structures more slowly than the other cultures do. (This disadvantage can be offset somewhat by the Pharaoh. More on that later.) Note that naval units, Slingers, Chariot Archers, and Egyptian siege weapons still require wood.

Rebuilding resource camps closer to currently harvested resources is much easier for the Egyptians: Granaries, Lumber Camps, and Wood-gathering Camps don't require resources, only a laborer to erect the building. Laborers build slower than their Greek and Norse counterparts, though you can speed the process by empowering the construction with a Pharaoh (or a Priest, in the case of Ra). Instead of taking the time to try and lure hunted animals to a Town Center or Granary, just build another Granary closer to the herd. You can build a single Granary (especially with multiple laborers on the task) much faster than luring multiple animals to another resource camp or Town Center.

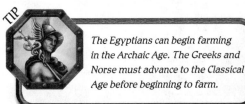

The Egyptians can begin farming in the Archaic Age. The Greeks and Norse must advance to the Classical Age before beginning to farm.

Lacking the need for wood, the Egyptians should focus laborers on food and gold in the early part of the game. Don't produce fewer laborers just because you need fewer types of resources, or it will be difficult to maintain your resource income during the mid- and late game. In fact, Egyptian villagers gather more slowly than Greek ones, making the Pharaoh's empowering critical. In Egypt's early ages, assign most villagers to collect food and gold, and ignore wood until it's needed. Don't completely ignore wood, however, because Tower improvements after the Heroic Age require it, as do ranged units, several mythological units, and very important economic upgrades that benefit gold mining and farming. While the Greeks need 20–30 percent of their villagers collecting wood to build Houses and military structures approaching and entering the Heroic Age, the Egyptians can get by with no wood gatherers until the Heroic Age, when tower improvements and, depending on strategy, ranged units will likely be needed.

One of the most important elements in Egyptian resource gathering is the Pharaoh, described in detail later in this section. You can use the Pharaoh to empower any structure, which enhances the activities of that particular structure. This applies to all resource camps and the Town Center. Any laborer delivering resources to the empowered building will perform duties faster than normal.

Worshipping Their Gods

In order to gain the resource called favor from their Gods, the Egyptians erect a series of five Monuments (see Figure 4.1). Each Monument must be built in its turn. Each subsequent Monument is more expensive and takes longer to build than the last, but each new Monument provides greater gains in favor. Unlike the Greeks, the Egyptians won't have to devote valuable villagers to gaining favor, except when they're building the

Figure 4.1 *The Egyptians must construct Monuments to gain favor from the Gods.*

Monument. The Norse gain favor by hunting animals and attacking enemy units.

There are several ways to enhance the rate at which Egyptians gain favor. When you build a Monument, use a Pharaoh (or, if you are a worshipper of Ra, you can use a Priest) to empower the construction, and the Monument will go up faster. Empower a finished Monument to increase the rate of favor-gain. Finally, worship the Minor God Anubis and choose the Necropolis improvement to further increase the rate at which you gain favor.

The Pharaoh and Priests

The Egyptians have two types of Hero: the Pharaoh and the Priest. Each Egyptian civilization receives one Pharaoh; Priests require gold, and are produced at the Temple or Town Center. The Pharaoh features several unique abilities, the most important being the ability to empower a building. Although the Pharaoh can only empower one building at a time, it's possible to shift the empowerment to another building at any time.

> *Ra's Monuments are cheaper and stronger than those of other Major Gods. Isis' Monuments project an invisible shield that protects an area around the Monument from enemy god powers.*

The results of the empowerment depend on the building: If you empower a Town Center, which also serves as a deposit for food and wood, the structure will research improvements faster. Empowering the Town Center will not speed up villager production or age advancement, though. Also, laborers depositing resources here will work faster than normal. You can empower any building during construction to speed that process. A Monument empowered by a Pharaoh will gain favor at a faster rate.

The Egyptian Pharaoh also is a capable warrior, best used against mythological units. The offensive strength of the Pharaoh increases with each Age-advance. Should the Pharaoh be killed in battle, a new Pharaoh appears at your original Town Center after a minute. The Pharaoh also can heal wounded allied units, but that duty usually falls to the Priests. The Pharaoh is also the only Egyptian unit who can claim relics.

Priests serve primarily to heal wounded allied units; include Priests in all your military groups to heal the wounded. This can save valuable resources that would otherwise be needed to reproduce these units. Priests also boast a moderate attack, which is most effective against mythological units.

Followers of Ra can use their Priests like Pharaohs, to empower buildings. Better yet, you can use multiple Priests to empower multiple buildings (including a Monument, empowering multiple Monuments does not increase favor rate). Followers of Set can use Priests to convert wild animals for use as a unique offensive weapon.

Mercenaries and the Art of Defense

The Egyptians provide several benefits that encourage a more defensive game style. The Egyptians are the only culture with Mercenaries, produced at Town Centers. Mercenaries train very quickly, require only gold, and occupy no population slots. They're effective warriors, but perish automatically after a short time. (Mercenaries are effective against cavalry; Mercenary Cavalry are effective against archers.)

Scouting and line of sight also play important roles. Priests can erect Obelisks, inexpensive but weak structures that allow you to see a long way in all directions. Use Obelisks at the edge of your towns or in choke points to monitor enemy movements. You also can erect them near your enemies to keep an eye on their resource gathering or expansion activities. In fact, Isis' Priests build Obelisks faster. The Lighthouse is another observation structure available only to the Egyptians. Lighthouses are massive structures with no offensive or defensive capabilities beyond their enormous line of sight.

Also befitting their basically defensive posture is that Egyptians receive the first Tower improvement of the Classical Age free, just for advancing. (Subsequent Tower improvements require resources, including wood.) Note that this feature also allows for a sneaky early attack—building forward Towers to pin enemies within their base, hindering their resource gathering and expansion—that is explained in detail in Chapter 13.

Major Gods

In the single-player campaign, your Major God has been chosen for you. In a Random Map or Multiplayer game, however, you choose which Major God to worship. The choice will frame your strategy and affect your selection of Minor Gods throughout the game.

This section covers the Egyptian Major Gods by describing their cultural and military benefits, and offers strategic suggestions on best exploiting their characteristics.

The following chart shows the Minor Gods from which your Major God allows you to choose at each Age-Advance.

MAJOR GOD	CLASSICAL AGE	HEROIC AGE	MYTHIC AGE
Ra	Bast, Ptah	Hathor, Sekhmet	Horus, Osiris
Iris	Anubis, Bast	Hathor, Nephthys	Osiris, Thoth
Set	Anubis, Ptah	Nephthys, Sekhmet	Horus, Thoth

When choosing your Minor Gods in each age, consider the unique improvements they offer, as well as the god power. Although the god power will help you for an instant, the myth improvements might benefit your military or economy more in the long run.

— Justin "GX_Bear" Rouse

The following chart offers strategic suggestions for choosing Gods, depending on what element of *Age of Mythology* you plan to emphasize.

FOCUS	ARCHAIC AGE	CLASSICAL AGE	HEROIC AGE	MYTHIC AGE
Economy	Ra	Bast	Hathor	Osiris
Infantry	Ra, Set	Ptah	Any	Horus
Archers	Set	Ptah	Sekhmet	Thoth
Migdol Stronghold	Ra, Set	Anubis, Ptah	Sekhmet	Osiris, Thoth
Defense	Isis	Bast	Hathor	Osiris
Pharaoh and Priests	Iris, Set	Anubis	Nephthys	Osiris, Thoth
Mythological Units	Ra, Isis	Bast	Any	Osiris
Naval Units	Ra, Isis	Bast	Nephthys, Sekhmet	Osiris, Thoth

Ra

Ra, the most important deity to ancient Egyptians, is known as the God of the Sun. Choosing to follow Ra offers you a diverse set of strategies. Empowering-Priests and faster empowering Pharoahs can help build a strong economy, enabling a strategy heavy on mythological units and Ra's cheap Monuments, or a strategy heavy on Migdol Strongholds, source of Ra's improved Chariot Archers and Camelry.

Ra's unique civilization benefits include:

◈ **Priests can empower buildings.** Other Egyptian Gods allow their single Pharaoh to empower a single building at a time—the exception being Osiris' New Kingdom improvement in the Mythic Age, which lets you have two Pharaohs, each of which can empower a building. Followers of Ra, however, can build numerous Priests and

ES TIP

If you are faithful to Ra, scout with your Pharaoh instead of your Priest, because the Pharaoh has a longer line of sight, and your Priest can empower the economy while he's gone. With luck, the Pharaoh can pick up a relic while he's out there, too!

—Justin "GX_Bear" Rouse

use them to empower all resource centers, drastically increasing the economic boom. Ra's Priests also can empower buildings during construction, speeding the usually slow Egyptian building process.

◈ **Pharaoh empowers faster.** Ra's Pharaoh empowers faster than the other two Egyptian cultures. Combined with Priests that can empower, this makes Ra the best and most versatile Egyptian economy civilization.

◈ **Monuments are stronger (+20% hit points) and cheaper (-25% resources).** Followers of Ra can construct the Egyptian Monuments much more cheaply than followers of the other Major Gods can. Build all five Monuments to enable a favor-heavy strategy for more mythological units and more powerful improvements.

◈ **Chariot Archers and Camelry possess more hit points (+20% hit points) and are faster (+10% speed).** This allows a strong late-game Migdol Stronghold strategy from followers of Ra. Worship Sekhmet (whose Bone Bow gives Chariot Archers longer range) and Osiris (Desert Wind increases Camelry speed and attack) to further improve Ra's strong Migdol Stronghold units. Ra's Chariot Archers and Camelry also move faster.

Rain God Power

Ra's god power Rain invokes a rainstorm, causing all farms to produce food at a faster rate (as long as a laborer is working on the farm). No other allied or enemy god powers may be used on the map during Rain. Save Rain until the Classical or Heroic Age, after heavy farming has begun, but keep in mind that the god power affects enemy farms as well. Coordinate with your allies in a team game, to ensure maximum food output from Rain. Ra's god power affects everyone on the map, but affects the invoker more than enemies or allies.

Skin of Rhino Improvement

Skin of Rhino improves the hack-and-pierce armor, and the hand attack, of your laborers. For instance, you could use this improvement to hunt wild animals better (or to counter Set's converted-animals attack—see Chapter 13), or to help defend against very early rushes.

ES TIP

Use Locust Swarm against an enemy before using your Rain power, so the enemy does not benefit from the improved food gathering.

—Chris "Swinger" Rupp

Isis

Isis, the wife of Osiris and mother of Horus, is a protective Goddess, and her benefits reflect this. Her benefits include Monuments that block enemy god powers, and fast-building obelisks to provide a long line of sight. Choose to worship Hathor in the Heroic Age, and research Sun-Dried Mud Brick to decrease the cost of buildings, complementing Isis' improvements. Consider Thoth in the late game: The Book of Thoth improvement increases resource gathering to further fund defensive tactics.

Isis' unique civilization benefits include:

◈ **Monuments block enemy god powers.** Spread Isis' Monuments throughout your main town, as a shield against enemy god powers such as Thoth's devastating Meteor. Build a Monument on the outskirts of an enemy base and keep your assault group close, to prevent an enemy from attacking them with a god power.

◈ **Cheap technology improvements (-10% off food, wood, and gold requirements).** All of Isis' technology improvements are cheaper, including Age advancement. This helps save valuable resources to fund military units or even additional improvements.

◈ **Priests build obelisks faster (+60% build rate). Obelisks are also cheaper (-60% resources).** Use Isis' Priests to quickly erect obelisks around the map. Use their height to scout the enemy's whereabouts and activities.

◈ **Town centers add +3 to population cap.** Isis' Town Centers provide an additional +3 to the Egyptian population cap. This allows production of a couple more laborers early in the game, to begin gathering resources before Houses are needed. Additional Town Centers built on settlements also provide +3 to the population cap.

Prosperity God Power

Invoke Isis' Prosperity god power to cause your laborers to gather gold at double their normal rate (even if you have already researched gold-mining improvements) for a short time. Maximize this god power by sending a majority of your laborers to mine gold before invoking Prosperity.

Flood of the Nile Improvement

Flood of the Nile must be researched at a Granary. Isis causes the Nile River to provide free food for your town. There's nothing to do other than research the improvement. The free food automatically begins to trickle into your coffers.

Set

Set is the God of Evil and of Chaos, the Desert, and Foreign Lands. Set also had an affinity with animals, which is reflected in this Major God's cultural benefits. Use Set's Priests and Pharaoh abilities to convert or summon wild animals, respectively. Complement Set's bonuses to Egyptian ranged units and Migdol Stronghold units by worshipping Ptah, Sekhmet, and Thoth.

Set's unique civilization benefits include:

◈ **Begin with a Hyena and extra animals appear at Temple on Age advancement.** Set's followers begin with a Hyena, which can be used to scout or attack enemy villagers. Upon each age advancement, a batch of additional animals spawn at Set's Temple.

◈ **Priests can convert wild animals.** Set's Priests can approach any wild animal and put it under your control (just select the Priest and right-click on the animal). You can use this power to create an animal army and harass enemy villagers at resource positions. Combine this benefit with Set's Feral improvement to increase the wild animals' attack.

◈ **Pharaohs can summon wild animals.** Set's Pharaoh, at the cost of favor, can summon various wild animals (including apes, giraffes, crocodiles, and more) to use either as food or used as an army (see Figure 4.2). The Pharaoh receives more animal options as you advance through Ages.

Figure 4.2 *Use Set's Pharaoh to summon wild animals, which can be converted into offensive units or slaughtered for food.*

◈ **Slingers and Chariot Archers train faster (+20 faster training rate).** The Egyptian military's ranged units train faster under Set's control. Combine this benefit with those of Minor Gods who also benefit Slingers and Chariot Archers (such as Ptah's Electrum Bullets or Sekhmet's Bone Bow).

◈ **Slingers have more hit points (+10% hit points) and hack armor.** In addition to training faster, Set's Slingers also have 10% more hit points and resistance to infantry attacks. Combine with other Slinger benefits, such as Ptah's Electrum Bullets, to increase the power of Set's stronger Slingers.

Vision God Power

Invoke Set's god power of Vision to gain the brief ability to see any part of the map, including unexplored areas. You can use Vision to scout the enemy's activities and abilities, or to prepare for an attack using a more powerful god power, such as Horus' Tornado or Thoth's Meteor.

Feral Improvements

Research Set's Feral improvement to increase the damage caused when your converted animals attack. Research this improvement if you plan to use Priests to convert wild animals for an attack on an enemy's laborers, or in conjunction with a military rush in the Classical Age. When Set converts or summons an animal, it has less food than a wild animal. Researching Feral also restores this food loss to wild animals, so it is useful economically as well.

Minor Gods

Each time you advance an Age, you must choose between two Minor Gods for worship. Your options depend on which major God you chose to worship at the beginning of the game. The Gods are very proud and jealous: Once you bypass a Minor God, you will never have the opportunity to select that God again, for the duration of the game.

This section covers the Egyptian Minor Gods, describing their god powers, mythological units, and unique improvements. Here you'll find strategic suggestions for exploiting their characteristics to maximum effect.

The following chart shows the Minor Gods, their Age, and their Major God affiliation.

MINOR GOD	AGE ADVANCEMENT	MAJOR GOD
Anubis	Classical Age	Isis, Set
Bast	Classical Age	Ra, Isis
Ptah	Classical Age	Ra, Set
Hathor	Heroic Age	Ra, Isis
Nephthys	Heroic Age	Isis, Set
Sekhmet	Heroic Age	Ra, Set
Horus	Mythic Age	Ra, Set
Osiris	Mythic Age	Ra, Isis
Thoth	Mythic Age	Isis, Set

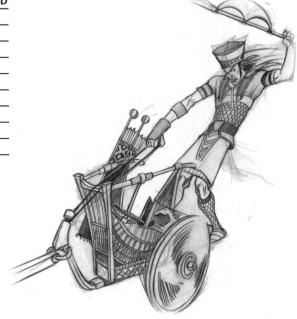

Anubis – Classical Age

Anubis is the God of Judgment (and, logically, of the Dead). Anubis' improvements benefit Spearmen and mythological units.

Plague of Serpents God Power

Invoke Anubis' Plague of Serpents god power by targeting an area on the map. Serpents will appear and defend the area. You can't control them; they won't leave the area into which they're summoned even to pursue fleeing enemies. The serpents remain in the area until killed, aren't very strong against laborers, and won't attack buildings. If the god power is invoked over water, sea serpents appear. They will attack only warships, not fishing ships. Use the god power as a defensive measure to help protect a town or resource-gathering area from enemy attack.

Anubite Mythological Unit

The Anubite is a fast-moving mythological infantry unit that possesses the ability to leap into combat. When the Anubite nears the enemy, the unit jumps toward the enemy, covering the distance faster than any other unit could. This provides both advantages and disadvantages. Avoid leaping into combat too far in front of your other troops, or the Anubites may be overmatched until your other units enter the battle. However, the Anubites can quickly reach enemy ranged units that are far from the fight. Use Anubites against human soldiers rather than Hero units, and improve them with the Feet of the Jackal improvement.

Feet of the Jackal Improvement

This improvement boosts Anubite hit points, attack power, and jumping distance. Research this improvement if you plan a Classical Age (or early Heroic Age) strike with a squad of Anubites.

Serpent Spear Improvement

Research this improvement to increase the attack of Egyptian Spearmen, which are most effective against enemy cavalry units. Anubis grants the Spearmen weapons coated with venom to increase damage. This is certainly a mandatory improvement should your enemy send massed cavalry units against you. Combine this improvement with others, including Horus' improvements called Spear on the Horizon and Greatest of Fifty.

Necropolis Improvement

The Necropolis improvement increases the rate at which your civilization gains favor. If you plan a heavy mythological-unit strategy, research this improvement to help fund your plan. Make sure you have all five Monuments to maximize the benefit of this improvement.

Bast – Classical Age

Bast is the Goddess of Fertility. Bast's improvements aid farmers and wood gatherers.

Eclipse God Power

Invoke the Eclipse god power to cause the day to immediately turn into night for a short time. During the Eclipse, all of your mythological units receive attack and speed bonuses. Obviously save Eclipse for when you possess a large amount of mythological units and are prepared to mount an assault. Eclipse only affects the invoker and also blocks other god powers, keeping your improved mythological units safe from enemy deity counterattack.

Sphinx Mythological Unit

The Sphinx is a fast unit that turns into a sand vortex when attacking. Use the Sphinx against human soldiers and buildings. Bast offers two Sphinx improvements—Criosphinx, which improves hit points and attack damage, and Hieracosphinx, which improves speed and attack damage. You must research Criosphinx before Hieracosphinx becomes available.

Criosphinx Improvement

Bast's first Sphinx improvement turns Sphinxes into Criosphinxes, which increases the mythological unit's hit points and attack damage.

Hieracosphinx Improvement

Bast's second Sphinx improvement turns Criosphinxes into Hieracosphinxes, which increases the mythological unit's speed and attack damage.

Sacred Cats Improvement

Research the Sacred Cats improvement to cause farms to produce food faster (as long as a farmer works the farm). Bast's cats protect the farms from vermin, which increases the amount of food produced. Save the resources required for this improvement until you've begun heavy farming. Combine this with Ra's god power Rain for a big increase in farm production.

Adze of Wepawet Improvement

Bast's Adze of Wepawet enables laborers to knock down trees and gather wood faster. Egyptians aren't as dependent on wood as other cultures, at least in the early ages. But if you plan to improve Towers in the Heroic or Mythic Ages, acquire certain improvements (such as improvements to gold and farming), or produce certain mythological units and ranged units (such as Chariot Archers), consider this improvement in the Heroic Age. It will increase wood gathering to fund these improvements or units.

Ptah – Classical Age

Ptah is the God of Creation. Ptah's improvements benefit farms, Axemen, Slingers, and Spearmen.

Shifting Sands God Power

Invoke Ptah's Shifting Sands god power to teleport allied or enemy units from one location to another (see Figure 4.3), either as an offensive or defensive tactic. Shift allied units beyond enemy defenses to conduct an attack, or teleport an enemy invasion away from your units. You must be able to see both areas (for instance, with the assistance of Set's Vision god power) to invoke the god power successfully. Shifting Sands teleports all allied units, but only a random sampling of enemy units will be affected. Land units can't be teleported into the sea and naval units can't be teleported onto land.

Figure 4.3 *Teleport a group of enemy villagers into an ambush, with Ptah's Shifting Sands.*

Wadjet Mythological Unit

Named for the Serpent Goddess who appears in snake form on the Pharaoh's crown, the Wadjet mythological unit spits venom from long-range. Use the Wadjet against human soldiers; beware of enemy Heroes, who are most effective in countering the Wadjet.

Shaduf Improvement

Ptah's invention, the Shaduf, decreases the cost and build-time of farms. Research this improvement after you've exhausted other food sources and have begun farming. After constructing your cheaper farms, invoke Ra's god power Rain to increase food production.

Scalloped Axe Improvement

Research the scalloped axe improvement to increase the attack damage of your Axemen. Egyptian Axemen are most effective against infantry units, so if your enemy concentrates on infantry, research this improvement. Combine this improvement with Horus' Axe of Vengeance improvement to add bonus damage vs. buildings to your improved Axemen.

Electrum Bullets Improvement

Ptah's Electrum Bullets improvement increases the attack damage of Slingers. Egyptian Slingers are most effective against enemy ranged units. Research this improvement if you need to do more damage to an enemy with a heavily ranged army. To add bonus damage against infantry units, combine Electrum Bullets with Sekhmet's Slings of the Sun. Combine this improvement with Set's stronger Slingers, which boast more hit points and hack armor…plus they train faster!

Leather Frame Shield Improvement

The Leather Frame Shield improvement augments the pierce armor of Spearmen, making them more resistant to ranged attacks. Spearmen have bonus damage against cavalry but can be countered with enemy ranged units. Stack Ptah's Leather Frame Shield with other improvements for Spearmen, including Horus' Spear on the Horizon and Greatest of Fifty.

Hathor – Heroic Age

Hathor is Goddess of the Sky. Hathor's improvements benefit Mercenaries and buildings.

Locust Swarm God Power

Invoke Hathor's Locust Swarm god power to summon a plague of locusts upon enemy farms or fishing boats. You can really set back an enemy who's heavily dependent on those resources. You also can use Locust Swarm as a diversionary tactic, following the swarm with an offensive at a weak area or expansion of the enemy base. While they're busy mending their farms or boats, you're applying further pressure with an attack.

Petsuchos Mythological Unit

Hathor offers two mythological units. Her offensive unit is the Petsuchos, a bejeweled crocodile that fires a focused ray of sunlight. The Petsuchos is effective against human soldiers, and features bonus damage against other mythological units. (As usual, steer clear of Hero units.) You must support Petsuchos with melee units; the Petsuchos is a ranged unit ineffective at close range.

Roc Mythological Unit

Use this mythological unit to transport troops from one area of the map to another, including over water and other impassable terrain. The Roc can't attack, but it can be damaged by enemy ranged units, including Towers and other defensive structures.

Crocodopolis Improvement

Research the Crocodopolis improvement to increase the range of your Petsuchos units. Increased range certainly helps, by giving them more firing opportunities before an enemy can reach them, but don't fail to support them with melee units. Even with this improvement, the Petsuchos is still ineffective at close quarters.

Medjay Improvement

The Medjay improvement boosts the lifespan of Egyptian Mercenaries and Mercenary cavalry. Research this improvement if you need added defense for your town while your main army is exploring or seeking to attack another position. Be careful, however. Mercenaries produce fast and don't occupy population slots, but they are expensive and can drain your gold coffers quickly.

Sun-Dried Mud Brick Improvement

Research this improvement to increase building hit points, and lower the cost of construction. Combine this improvement with Isis' improvements for cheaper technologies and buildings. Maximize the benefits of this improvement before creating multiple Migdol Strongholds. Since many Egyptian buildings are free (resource structures, Houses, etc.), reaping the rewards of this improvement could be difficult unless you plan ahead.

Nephthys – Heroic Age

Nephthys is the Goddess of Night and of Death. Nephthys' improvements are to Pharaohs and Priests.

Ancestors God Power

Invoke Nephthys' Ancestors god power to summon an army of dead soldiers to rise and fight again. Unlike Anubis' Plague of Serpents, the Ancestors can be controlled just like normal military units. However, your dead soldiers will only come back for a short time, and can disappear even before being slain again. This god power can be stacked with Plague of Serpents for added defense at an important map position. If invoked on water, Ancestors summons ghost ships instead.

Leviathan Mythological Unit

Leviathan, also "Twisted Animal" in Hebrew, generally refers to any gigantic animal. In *Age of Mythology*, the Leviathan is a living naval transport that can counterattack enemy ships and defend itself. If you're facing Leviathan, counter it with ramming ships.

Scorpion Man Mythological Unit

Scorpions had a large influence on Egyptian mythology. Nephthys' offensive mythological unit attacks with a sword and a venomous stinger. The Scorpion Man has a devastating attack against human soldiers but is weak against Hero units, such as the Norse Hersir, Egyptian Pharaoh, or Greek Heroes. The Scorpion Man's venom affects several units at once, who will continue to take damage for a few seconds.

Spirit of Ma'at Improvement

Research Nephthys' Spirit of Ma'at improvement to reduce the cost of Priests and improve their healing rate. If you plan to support your army with healing Priests, this improvement will prove both economic and militarily useful. You can produce more Priests for less gold, and they'll heal your wounded faster between battles.

Funeral Rites Improvement

Nephthys' Funeral Rites improvement increases the attack damage done by the Pharaoh and Priests to mythological units. The Pharaoh, a Hero, is already powerful against mythological units, and after each Age-advance, the Pharaoh becomes even stronger. Keep in mind, however, that if the Pharaoh joins your military, he won't be available to empower buildings. For added benefit, combine this improvement with Osiris' New Kingdom improvement, which provides an extra Pharaoh.

City of the Dead Improvement

 Research the City of the Dead improvement to make Pharaohs stronger and help them return from the dead more quickly—as in under a minute. Stack this improvement with Funeral Rites and Osiris' New Kingdom to further increase the power of the Egyptian Pharaoh. This is a mandatory improvement if you plan to shift the Pharaoh from an empowering unit to an offensive power against enemy mythological units.

Sekhmet – Heroic Age

 Sekhmet is Goddess of Warfare and of the Desert. Sekhmet's improvements benefit Slingers, Chariot Archers, Catapults, Siege Towers, and War Barges.

Citadel God Power

 Sekhmet's god power can transform your Town Center or that of an ally into a defensive Citadel, with increased hit points and attack. You can invoke Citadel on any allied Town Center, even if it is Greek or Norse. Consider using this god power on a second or third settlement, which will likely have fewer defenses.

Scarab Mythological Unit

 The ancient Egyptians considered the scarab beetle sacred; it is often used in art to represent Ra. Sekhmet's Scarab mythological unit is a living siege weapon, a lumbering insect with immense power (bonus damage) against buildings and towers. Support your Scarabs as you would any siege weapons, with melee and ranged forces to protect them (see Figure 4.4.) The Scarab also spews corrosive blood as it dies, damaging any enemy unit next to it. Keep this in mind if attacking a Scarab. It's best to let ranged units finish off the beast.

Bone Bow Improvement

Increase the range of Chariot Archers by researching Sekhmet's Bone Bow improvement. Protect your Chariot Archers, highly vulnerable to cavalry attacks, with melee units. Combine this improvement with Ra's benefit of increased hit points for Chariot Archers to further increase this ranged weapon's potency. You could also combine this improvement with Set's faster training Chariot Archers.

Figure 4.4 *Treat Scarabs like other siege weaponry—protect them with units that counter cavalry!*

Slings of the Sun Improvement

Sekhmet can give your Slingers burning slings, enabling extra damage to infantry units. Slingers are most effective against enemy ranged units, and this improvement could prove valuable should your opponent shift to the use of infantry against them. Combine this improvement with other benefits to Slingers such as Set's Slingers, who train faster and have more hit points and increased hack armor.

Stones of Red Linen Improvement

Stones of Red Linen allows Sekhmet's Catapults and War Barges to inflict increased damage to buildings. Both units already offer bonus damage against buildings. This improvement increases it. If you plan a massive siege assault, consider this improvement so you can quickly topple defensive Towers and other structures.

Rams of the West Wind Improvement

Sekhmet's Rams of the West Wind grants increased hit points and attack damage to your Siege Towers. You will likely only need to research either Rams of the West Wind or Stones of Red Linen, depending on your selection of siege weaponry, but if have both types, you can certainly improve both.

Horus – Mythic Age

Horus is God of Vengeance. Horus' improvements benefit Axemen and Spearmen.

Tornado God Power

Horus unleashes his wrath with his Tornado god power, a twisting funnel-cloud that can sweep up entire armies and crush buildings into dust. Once invoked, the Tornado moves around randomly (its path can't be controlled) and can damage even allied units and buildings, although the damage is greater to enemy units and buildings. To invoke Tornado, you must have line of sight on the area where you wish to unleash Horus' wrath.

Avenger Mythological Unit

Horus' Avenger is a fast-moving mythological unit that can attack multiple enemy units at once with its whirlwind attack (periodically used automatically). The Avenger is deadly against human soldiers. If you are facing the Avenger, it's best to assault it from a distance with ranged human or mythological units (and certainly Heroes).

Axe of Vengeance Improvement

Research Horus' Axe of Vengeance to increase the damage Axemen can do to buildings and walls. To produce strong Axemen effective against both infantry and buildings, combine this improvement with Ptah's Scalloped Axe.

Greatest of Fifty Improvement

Horus' improvement called Greatest of Fifty improves the pierce armor of Spearmen (making the units more resistant to archers) and adds bonus damage against enemy archers. Combine this improvement with Ptah's Leather Frame Shield, which also strengthens the Spearman's pierce armor.

Spear on the Horizon Improvement

Research the improvement called Spear on the Horizon to increase the hit points of Spearmen and improve their attack damage. For even stronger armor and more bonus damage to archers, combine this improvement with Greatest of Fifty and Leather Frame Shield.

Osiris – Mythic Age

Osiris is God of Judgment in this Age. His improvements benefit Camelry, Pharaohs, and archer ships.

Son of Osiris God Power

Osiris' unique god power, Son of Osiris, can transform a single Pharaoh into a new Hero, the aptly named Son of Osiris. This new Hero offers greater empowerment ability (the effects are even greater than the Pharaoh's) and an impressive chain-lightning attack, particularly damaging against mythological units. You can research Osiris' New Kingdom improvement to gain a second Pharaoh, but only one of the two can be transformed into the Son of Osiris. The Son of Osiris cannot be healed by Priests or any ally means. If killed, a normal Pharaoh will respawn to take his place.

Mummy Mythological Unit

Osiris commands undead Pharaoh units called Mummies. The attack of these mythological units can convert enemy human units into minions, which can be controlled and used against your enemy (although they perish automatically after a short time). Mummies are very expensive but can turn the tide in a battle by converting tough enemy units. As with other mythological units, steer clear of Hero units. Improve the Mummies by researching Osiris' Atef Crown, which increases the lifespan of your minions.

Atef Crown Improvement

This improvement boosts the strength of your Mummies and increases the lifespan of their minions. Get the most from this expensive tactic by supporting your human units with a gang of Mummies, which can transform enemy units into allied minions.

Desert Wind Improvement

Osiris' Desert Wind improves Camelry units by increasing their speed and the strength of their attack. Combine this improvement with other Camelry and Migdol Stronghold benefits, including Ra's increased Camelry hit points.

New Kingdom Improvement

Research this improvement to create a second Pharaoh, which can be used to empower additional buildings or to replace the Pharaoh transformed into the Son of Osiris. Stack this improvement with Nephthys' excellent Pharaoh improvements to possess two combat units highly effective against mythological units. The secondary Pharaoh will continue to respawn, like your original Pharaoh, so you will have two for the rest of the game.

Funeral Barge Improvement

Osiris can boost your naval dominance with the Funeral Barge. Research this improvement to give your Kebenit warships bonus damage against other archer ships.

Thoth – Mythic Age

Thoth is the God of Wisdom. Thoth's improvements benefit laborers and Migdol Stronghold units.

Meteor God Power

Invocation of Thoth's Meteor brings a barrage of flaming meteors upon a designated area (see Figure 4.5). You must have line of sight on the targeted area to invoke the god power. Meteor is strongest against enemy buildings, but inflicts moderate damage on enemy units. Nearby allied units and buildings will also take damage, although the allied units tend to get thrown, rather than sustaining significant damage.

Phoenix Mythological Unit

The Phoenix is a slow-moving air unit that can only be countered with ranged units. If a Phoenix is killed in battle, it reverts to egg form, which remains at the site where the creature was killed. You can retrain the Phoenix from the egg for the same cost as a new Phoenix. The benefit is that the slow-moving unit will typically be closer to the battle once retraining is complete. Furthermore, you won't have to tie up a temple to produce a replacement. No egg is created if the Phoenix dies over impassable terrain, such as rocks or water. Use the Phoenix primarily against human soldiers or buildings.

Figure 4.5 *Ruin your enemy's day with a barrage of flaming meteors from the hand of Thoth.*

Sea Turtle Mythological Unit

The Egyptians considered the turtle a creature of night and dark water, and typically associated it with Set, God of Evil and enemy of Ra. Thoth's Sea Turtle mythological unit is a ship-killing specialist. Enemy ships are literally flung out of the water. Support a naval offensive with the Sea Turtle.

Book of Thoth Improvement

The Book of Thoth offers a potential late-game resource explosion. Research this improvement to allow your laborers to gather food, wood, and gold faster. With Book of Thoth, the out-classed Egyptian Villagers can catch up or surpass the Greek or Norse ones. Stack this improvement with other resource-gathering improvements to fund Thoth's Migdol Stronghold units and their improvements.

Tusks of Apedemak Improvement

Tusks of Apedemak increases the hit points and attack damage of War Elephants. If you worship Set you can use this improvement to build even cheaper, stronger Elephants. You also can research Thoth's companion improvement, Valley of Kings, to speed the production of these great beasts.

Valley of the Kings Improvement

Research this improvement to train Camelry, Chariot Archers, and War Elephants faster. The difference is dramatic. Migdol Stronghold units appear almost as fast as Egyptian Mercenaries!

Military Units

This section describes the Egyptian military units, including siege and naval units. The following charts reveal where to upgrade each unit and how the unit improves after research. Note that all military units can be improved at the facility at which they're produced (such as "Barracks," for instance). Units are first improved to Medium, then to Heavy, then to Champion.

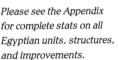

Please see the Appendix for complete stats on all Egyptian units, structures, and improvements.

Axeman

The Egyptian Axeman is most effective against other infantry units. Avoid cavalry, ranged, and mythological units. Researching improvements will increase both the attack and defense of Axemen, and Horus' Axe of Vengeance adds bonus damage against buildings. The Axeman will lose to the Throwing Axeman, who is the best counter-infantry.

UPGRADE	IMPROVES
Barracks	Attack, Hit Points, Training Rate, Line of Sight
Armory	Attack, Armor
Ptah's Scalloped Axe	Damage
Horus' Axe of Vengeance	Damage vs. Buildings

Slingers

Slingers are the initial ranged unit of the Egyptians and one of their few technology-tree items that requires wood. You'll need to stretch the Egyptian economy to include wood if you plan to fund an army of Slingers, which are most effective against enemy archers. Support Slingers with melee units to defend them against cavalry. This is the only ranged unit Egypt has until the Chariot, so use them against archers or counter-infantry units.

UPGRADE	IMPROVES
Barracks	Attack, Hit Points, Training Rate, Line of Sight
Armory	Weapon, Armor
Set	Training Rate, Hit Points, Hack Armor
Ptah's Electrum Bullets	Damage
Sekhmet's Slings of the Sun	Damage vs. Infantry

Spearman

The Egyptian Spearman is most effective against cavalry units and vulnerable to infantry, ranged, and mythological units. The Egyptian technology tree offers many Spearman improvements to increase their power against cavalry units and archers. Early on, Spearmen are the best counter against Slingers. Slingers are better at beating other archers.

UPGRADE	IMPROVES
Barracks	Attack, Hit Points, Training Rate, Line of Sight
Armory	Attack, Armor
Anubis' Serpent Spear	Damage
Ptah's Leather Frame Shield	Pierce Armor
Horus' Spear on the Horizon	Damage, Hit Points
Horus' Greatest of Fifty	Pierce Armor, Bonus Damage vs. Archers

Chariot Archer

A ranged unit as mobile as cavalry, the Chariot Archer is better than the slow Slinger at hit-and-run tactics. Still, support this mobile unit with melee units to protect the fragile chariots from cavalry or counter-cavalry units. Chariot Archers are good against infantry but not very effective against buildings or siege weaponry. The Chariot Archer also requires wood to build. If you plan to use this versatile unit, adjust your economy accordingly.

UPGRADE	IMPROVES
Migdol Stronghold	Attack, Hit Points, Training Rate, Line of Sight
Armory	Attack, Armor
Ra	Hit Points, Speed
Set	Training Rate
Sekhmet's Bone Bow	Range
Thoth's Valley of the Kings	Training Rate

Camelry

Camels form the backbone of the Egyptian cavalry. Steer clear of enemy units that are effective against cavalry, such as Greek Hoplites, Egyptian Spearmen, Norse Ulfsarks, and mythological units. Mobilize Camelry against siege weaponry, archers, and cavalry (Camelry boasts bonus damage vs. cavalry units). Stack improvements to build stronger, faster Camelry that can be trained faster.

UPGRADE	IMPROVES
Migdol Stronghold	Attack, Hit Points, Training Rate, Line of Sight
Armory	Attack, Armor
Ra	Hit Points, Speed
Osiris' Desert Wind	Speed, Damage
Thoth's Valley of the Kings	Training Rate

War Elephant

The Egyptian's most powerful non-mythological unit is the War Elephant, produced at the Migdol Stronghold. The Elephant is a strong, slow, and expensive unit that's most effective against enemy buildings (though it will certainly defeat many things standing in its path). Protect these expensive units well! Losing a War Elephant would be a waste of extremely valuable late-game resources. Counter the War Elephant with infantry units or counter-cavalry such as the Camel or Prodromos.

UPGRADE	IMPROVES
Migdol Stronghold	Attack, Hit Points, Training Rate, Line of Sight
Armory	Attack, Armor
Thoth's Tusks of Apedemak	Hit Points, Attack
Thoth's Valley of Kings	Training Rate

Pharaoh

The Pharaoh, the Egyptian Hero unit, appears automatically at the start of a mission or multiplayer game. You can only possess one Pharaoh at a time (unless you choose Osiris' New Kingdom improvement). Pharaohs have multiple uses. The Pharaoh can empower a building, increasing build rate, resource gathering, favor-gain—any activity focused on the building. The Pharaoh also is an effective fighter against mythological units and the only Egyptian unit that can collect relic. The Pharaoh improves as you advance through the Ages, and can further be improved through Nephthys' improvements and Osiris' Son of Osiris god power. The Pharaoh also can heal wounded allied units. If killed, the Pharaoh returns to the Town Center after remaining dead for a minute.

UPGRADE	IMPROVES
Armory	Attack, Armor
Ra	Faster Empowering
Set	Summon Animals
Nephthys' City of the Dead	Stronger, Faster Resurrection
Nephthys' Funeral Rites	Damage to Mythological Units
Osiris' Son of Osiris	Transformation, Greater Power
Osiris' New Kingdom	Second Pharaoh

ES TIP

Research Nephthys' City of the Dead improvement to turn your Pharaoh into a powerful warrior. Combine that with Osiris' New Kingdom improvement later on to give you a second Pharaoh. Now you will have two powerful ranged units that come back for free if they're killed, and do not count against your population limit.

—Kevin "The_Sheriff_" Holme

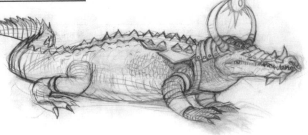

Priest

The Egyptian Priest is a secondary Hero unit that can heal wounded allied units. It's wise to include a couple of Priests in all of your offensive military groups! Ra's Priests also can empower buildings, just like the Pharaoh (enabling followers of Ra to empower multiple buildings). Set's Priests can convert animals, which can be used to attack the enemy. Priests can be used on offense but aren't as strong as normal combat units. Use Priests against mythological units. You can increase their strength by researching Nephthys' Funeral Rites. Priests are weak in the Classical Age, but automatically get better in later ages.

UPGRADE	IMPROVES
Armory	Attack, Armor
Ra	Can Empower Buildings, Faster Empowering
Set	Can Convert Animals
Nephthys' Funeral Rites	Damage to Mythological Units
Nephthys' Spirit of Ma'at	Healing Rate, Lowers Cost

Mercenary

Mercenaries are created at Town Centers. Mercenaries train quickly, require no population space, and cost only gold, but live only a short time. You will use Mercenaries to defend against an early rush or to protect a newly created settlement from counterattack. Use Mercenaries with caution, because it's very easy to expend all your gold reserves. Mercenaries are most effective against cavalry units. Mercenaries also get better in later ages automatically.

UPGRADE	IMPROVES
Armory	Attack, Armor
Hathor's Medjay	Lifespan

Mercenary Cavalry

Reaching the Heroic Age rewards you with a new type of Mercenary, Mercenary cavalry, which is most effective against archers. Use infantry units to counter Mercenary cavalry. Mercenary cavalry functions in the same way as the original Mercenaries. They are very useful at defeating enemy siege weapons advancing on your town. The Mercenary Cavalry also get better in later ages automatically.

UPGRADE	IMPROVES
Armory	Attack, Armor
Hathor's Medjay	Lifespan

Siege Tower

The Egyptian Siege Tower can transport units and ram enemy buildings, but its lack of speed leaves the unit vulnerable to cavalry. This siege weapon has a moderate arrow-attack defense, but it is still wise to support a group of Siege Towers with forces that counter cavalry. Improve the Siege Tower at the siege works, or by worshipping Sekhmet and researching Rams of the West Wind.

UPGRADE	IMPROVES
Siege Works	Attack Speed, Damage
Sekhmet's Rams of the West Wind	Hit Points, Crush Attack

Catapult

The staple of the Egyptian siege force is the Catapult, a long-range weapon most effective against towers, walls, and buildings. Unlike the Siege Tower, the Catapult has no defense, so it must be protected. Position anti-cavalry units near the Catapult. Improve the Catapult at the Siege Works or by researching Sekhmet's Stones of Red Linen improvement.

UPGRADE	IMPROVES
Siege Works	Attack Speed, Damage
Sekhmet's Stones of Red Linen	Bonus Damage vs. Buildings

Kebenit

The Egyptians' cheapest warship is the Kebenit, an archer ship that's good against hammer or ramming ships. Research Osiris' Funeral Barge to improve the Kebenit's attack damage against other archer ships. Counter Kebenits with siege ships such as the Egyptian War Barge, or mythological naval units.

UPGRADE	IMPROVES
Dock	Attack, Hit Points, Range
Armory	Attack, Armor
Osiris' Funeral Barge	Bonus Damage vs. Archer Ships

Ramming Galley

The Egyptian Ramming Galley, or Hammer Ship, rams enemy vessels at close range. It's most effective against siege ships and can be countered by using archer ships.

UPGRADE	IMPROVES
Dock	Attack, Hit Points
Armory	Attack, Armor

War Barge

The War Barge is an Egyptian naval siege weapon that boasts excellent damage against buildings and archer ships. Counter these siege ships with Ramming Galleys. Research Sekhmet's Stones of Red Linen to increase the War Barge's bonus damage against buildings. Like all siege ships, the War Barge will not be able to outrange Towers and Fortresses until it has research its Mythic War Barge upgrade, Naval Oxybeles.

UPGRADE	IMPROVES
Dock	Hit Points, Range
Armory	Attack, Armor
Sekhmet's Stones of Red Linen	Bonus Damage vs. Buildings

Norse Culture

This chapter covers Age of Mythology's Norse culture. There are important differences between the Norse and the Greeks or Egyptians, and we'll explore how those differences influence strategy. We'll also analyze the complete list of Norse Gods and their god powers, mythological units, and technological improvements. Finally, we detail the Norse military units. After studying this chapter, check out Chapter 14 for advanced Norse strategies, written by Ensemble Studios' expert players.

CHAPTER 5

Cultural Differences

The Norse are quite different from *Age of Mythology*'s other two cultures. Two distinct units—gatherers and Dwarves—are used to collect resources of food, wood, and gold; the Norse infantry not only wages war but also constructs all structures except farms; favor can be gained from the Norse Gods only through hunting and combat; and the Norse Hero unit, the Hersir, can be produced in mass quantities. Norse armor, including building strength, is weaker than that of other cultures, but their warriors' attacks are more punishing. In this section, you'll learn the primary differences between the Norse and the Greeks and Egyptians.

Resource Gathering

The Norse use two separate units, gatherers and Dwarves, to collect resources. Although either can collect food, wood, or gold, each has a specialty: Gatherers are more proficient at hunting, farming, and collecting wood, and Dwarves are best at mining gold.

> **TIP**
>
> Worship Thor and benefit from cheaper Dwarves that gather wood and food faster than other Norse Dwarves. When following Thor, use the Dwarf as your primary resource collector to exploit its cheaper cost and save the food resources required to use gatherers.

Instead of building stationary structures to serve as resource-collection camps, the Norse deposit their resources in movable Ox Carts. This saves resources and time. Since Ox Carts can be moved, it's to your advantage to place them midway between multiple resources—a gold mine and a clump of trees, for instance—to save the resources and time required to construct another cart. Resources deposited in the cart automatically reach your coffers; you don't have to move the Ox Cart to a Town Center.

Worshipping the Gods

The Norse gain favor from their Gods by engaging in war. All damage dealt to opposing units and buildings adds to favor. Hunting animals for food also generates a small amount of favor. The Hero unit, the mighty Hersir, gains favor faster than other units. Norse mythological units never gain favor.

Because favor is generated through combat, it's important for the Norse to engage in battle early in their development. Favor funds mythological units and unique God improvements, which often prove vital in late-game situations. The Norse can generate a lot of favor in a hurry, through battle. Advancing quickly to the Classical Age and mounting a rush against an enemy will certainly add favor, and it may provide an early advantage that spells victory (see Chapter 14 for strategic examples).

The Norse have only one Hero unit, the Hersir, but it can be produced in mass numbers—the only restriction is the population cap. Production of Hersir—at the Longhouse and Temple—does not require favor, only food and gold. Hersir also gain favor in combat at a rate double that of other human units, so it's wise to mix them in with your other units. In fact, Hersir generate a small amount of favor for simply being on the map. Like Greek and Egyptian Heroes, Hersir are most effective against mythological units.

Infantry Focus

Like the Greeks and Egyptians, the Norse have ranged units, cavalry, and siege units in their military, but the Norse focus on their infantry (see Figure 5.1). Not only do Norse infantry units fight, but they're also required to build Norse structures and defenses. (Farms are built only by gatherers.) When you begin a Random Map or Multiplayer game as the Norse, you're provided with a single Ulfsark (the infantry unit best used against cavalry) to use for building structures. To build faster, assign multiple infantry units to the task.

Figure 5.1 *The Norse use infantry to construct new buildings and defenses.*

The Norse focus on infantry goes even further than construction: The Ulfsark is one of the more versatile units, with many potential improvements throughout the Norse god paths; Norse gatherers can be instantly trained to become Ulfsarks; the Hersir Hero is an infantry unit, and can build structures, in addition to its Hero duties; and the Norse have the only infantry unit best used against enemy archers, the Huskarl.

Major Gods

In a single-player *Age of Mythology* campaign, your Major God is chosen for you. In a Random Map or Multiplayer game, however, you choose which Major God to worship. The selection will frame your strategy, and your Minor God selections, from beginning to end.

This section covers the Norse Major Gods. We describe their culture benefits and suggest ways to best exploit their characteristics. The following chart reveals the Minor Gods from which you must choose, according to your Major God, at each Age-advance.

MAJOR GOD	CLASSICAL AGE	HEROIC AGE	MYTHIC AGE
Odin	Freyja, Heimdall	Njord, Skadi	Baldr, Tyr
Thor	Forseti, Freyja	Bragi, Skadi	Baldr, Tyr
Loki	Forseti, Heimdall	Bragi, Njord	Hel, Tyr

The following chart offers strategic suggestions on particular god paths, depending on which element of Age of Mythology you plan to emphasize.

FOCUS	ARCHAIC AGE	CLASSICAL AGE	HEROIC AGE	MYTHIC AGE
Economy	Thor	Forseti, Freyja	Skadi	Tyr
Ulfsarks	Thor	Forseti	Bragi	Tyr
Throwing Axemen	Thor	Forseti, Freyja	Skadi	Baldr, Tyr
Cavalry	Odin	Freyja	Njord	Baldr
Hersir	Loki	Forseti	Bragi	Hel
Mythological Units	Loki	Forseti	Bragi	Hel
Naval Units	Odin	Heimdall	Njord	Baldr, Tyr
Defense	Odin	Heimdall	Njord, Skadi	Baldr, Tyr

Odin

Odin, Thor's father, is the God of War and of Poetry, Wisdom, and Death. Odin grants his followers bonuses to human units, scouting, hunting and the Hill Fort. Odin's unique civilization benefits include:

- **Human regeneration.** Odin's most important benefit is that human units can recover their health. Stationary units regenerate faster than moving units. Since all idle units will regenerate over time, Thor's gift is better than the ministrations of Egyptian Priests or Norse Valkyrie, who can heal only one or at best a few units at once.

- **Respawning Raven scouts.** After reaching the Classical Age, you can use Odin's two free Ravens to scout. Seek out huntable and herdable animals (you must use land units to retrieve them). Search for gold mines, settlements, key defensive positions, and the enemy's location. Use the Ravens to gain line of sight on an area to invoke a god power. If either Raven dies, it is respawned at Odin's Temple after a short time.

- **Greater hit points for Hill Fort units.** Followers of Odin are granted a 20 percent increase to the hit points of any unit produced at the Hill Fort, which include Jarl and Huskarls. Combine this with God improvements that improve Jarl, such as those of Freyja and Njord.

- **Faster hunting, more favor.** Hunting is important to the Norse—gatherers gain small amounts of favor by hunting and killing animals for food. Because Odin grants you the ability to hunt 10 percent faster, choose hunting as your primary food source. Use Odin's Ravens to find more wild animals to hunt.

Great Hunt God Power

Odin is a master of the hunt, and his god power reflects this. The Great Hunt god power can be invoked to increase the size of a herd of animals in the area. Great Hunt is best used on the greatest number of animals possible. For instance, move your herdable animals next to a group of huntable animals before invoking Great Hunt. This god power increases both food income and favor income, since the Norse gain favor from hunting. An Odin player teamed with Poseidon can combine Great Hunt with Lure, but multiple Odin players will not be able to exponentially increase the amount of animals with multiple casts of Great Hunt.

Lone Wanderer Improvement

 Odin imbues Ulfsarks with the spirit of the Lone Wanderer, which increases their speed. Ulfsarks are best used against cavalry units, and Lone Wanderer can help them intercept enemy cavalry packs sooner, protecting more vulnerable Norse units such as Throwing Axemen and Portable Rams. Lone Wanderer is also great for early scouting! With increased speed, the Ulfsark can reveal more unexplored territory in less time.

Thor

Thor, God of Thunder and son of Odin, provides his worshippers with a special Armory, and with cheaper Dwarves who gather food and wood faster than other Dwarves. Thor's special Dwarven Armory grants followers an additional weapon and armor improvement. Thor also grants his followers a shortcut to wealth— his Dwarven Mine god power creates a gold mine anywhere on the map.

Thor's unique civilization benefits include:

◈ **Thor's Armory available in all Ages; improvements are cheaper.** You can construct Thor's Dwarven Armory as early as the Archaic Age, giving you a military head start in the Archaic and Classical Ages. You can research weapon and armor improvements sooner than your enemies (unless they're worshipping Thor, too), providing an edge in early attacks. And even better, the Armory improvements are cheaper! Additionally, the Thor Armory is cheaper to build than a normal Armory.

◈ **Starts with Dwarves, who gather food and wood faster.** Since Thor's Dwarves gather food and wood faster than Dwarves serving other Gods, you can save the food you would otherwise need to train gatherers, and use the resource on military units, mythological units, or other improvements.

◈ **Dwarves are cheaper.** As well as gathering food and wood faster, Thor's Dwarves are also 10 percent cheaper than those of other Norse civilizations. Focusing on gold gathering, and sticking with Dwarves as your gathering unit in the mid and late game, is a sound Thor strategy.

Dwarven Gold Mine God Power

Thor's Dwarven Gold Mine god power can create a special gold mine on any terrain that can accommodate structures. (For example, you can't place the Dwarven Gold Mine in the middle of the sea, on impassable terrain, or on a building.) This mine actually holds different amounts of gold depending on the Age in which you invoke the power: The Dwarven Gold Mine is worth 250 in the Archaic Age, 1,000 in the Classical Age, 3,000 in the Heroic Age, and 6,000 in the Mythic Age. Withholding the power until the map has been exhausted of other gold mines is a sound strategy, should the game last that long. But sometimes it's wise to use the mine early. When you don't want to shift gatherers, Dwarves, and an Ox Cart to a new site after they've cleared a mine, for instance, you might drop the Dwarven Gold Mine and continue mining.

Pig Sticker Improvement

Thor offers his gatherers and Dwarves the Pig Sticker improvement. Research Pig Sticker to increase attack damage for gatherers and Dwarves, and to increase the rate of gathering when hunting animals—which also increases the rate of favor gain.

Loki

Loki, blood brother to Odin, offers his followers benefits to mythological units and to Ox Carts. Heroes loyal to Loki can summon mythological units while in combat. Mythological units cost less favor, and Ox Carts cost less and move faster (but are weaker) under Loki.

Loki's unique civilization benefits include:

- **Hersir move faster and summon mythology units during combat.** In combat, Loki's Hersir suddenly will be aided by mythological units that appear alongside them. These Hersir generate favor in combat faster than other units—favor that can be used to create more mythological units, which are cheaper under Loki. Exploit Loki's benefits by using a combo strategy involving a Hersir and a mythological unit. (An example of such a strategy is explained in Chapter 14.) Worship Forseti in the Classical Age and research Hall of Thanes to further increase Hersir speed and hit points.

- **Mythology units require less favor.** Loki's mythological units require 10 percent less favor than those of other Norse civilizations. This certainly encourages a heavy mythological unit strategy (see Chapter 14 for an example). Follow a god path through Bragi, for the Thurisaz Rune improvement (which increases the speed of mythological units), and Hel, for Rampage (allowing mythological units to train almost instantly).

- **Longhouse units train faster.** Under Loki, Longhouse units train 10% faster so mounting a Classical Age attack could prove successful. Build multiple Longhouse structures to take advantage of this benefit.

◈ **Ox Carts are cheaper and faster, but weaker.** Ox Carts are inexpensive, which is good because you'll likely need more than one to gather resources efficiently. And, being faster, Loki's Ox Carts can be used to scout or to reach resource more quickly. Protect them well, however: Loki's carts are much weaker than those of other Norse civilizations!

Spy God Power

Loki's intriguing Spy god power permits you to permanently tap into the line of sight of one enemy unit—to see what that unit sees. The enemy has no way to know that the unit is being used as a spy. Should the enemy unit perish, the god power is exhausted. Your allies also can share the enemy's line of sight. A Laguz rune, the symbol for Loki, marks the affected enemy unit (see Figure 5.2). You must have line of sight on the enemy unit to invoke the Spy god power.

Figure 5.2 *Invoke Loki's Spy to share an enemy unit's line of sight. Excellent for covert scouting!*

Since you must scout the enemy, don't make it obvious that you are scouting just to invoke Spy. The enemy may deduce which unit is being used, and stuff him in a corner—or send him into your town to his death. Some good uses of Spy include invoking the power on a villager to monitor resource gathering and expansion; using it on a military unit to gauge military maneuvers and if (and where) the enemy is mounting for an attack—just don't kill that unit!; and invoking Spy on an Egyptian Pharaoh, to see which of his structures is currently empowered.

Eyes in the Forest Improvement

Research Loki's Eyes in the Forest Improvement to increase the line of sight of all current and future infantry units. Increasing line of sight can help your military units spot the enemy sooner, allowing you to adjust your attack depending on the enemy's unit mix. It also aids in scouting both for enemy expansions and for your own expansion or resource options.

ES TIP

Try casting Loki's Spy god power on an enemy Ox Cart, then send forces in to destroy the surrounding gatherers (but leave the cart alone). Your enemy will eventually send new villagers to work at that Ox Cart, and as long as you leave the Ox Cart alone, you will know exactly when and where to attack. The best part is, your opponent will never know how you keep getting so "lucky"!

—Matt "Maimin_matty" Scadding

Minor Gods

Each time you advance in Age, you must choose between two Minor Gods, whose identities depend on which Major God you chose to worship at the beginning of the game. Once you bypass a Minor God, you won't have the opportunity to select that God again for the duration of the game.

This section covers the Norse Minor Gods—their god powers, mythological units, and unique improvements—and offers suggestions on strategic exploitation of their characteristics. The following chart shows the Minor Gods, their Ages, and their Major God affiliations.

MINOR GOD	AGE	MAJOR GOD
Forseti	Classical Age	Thor, Loki
Freyja	Classical Age	Odin, Thor
Heimdall	Classical Age	Odin, Loki
Bragi	Heroic Age	Thor, Loki
Njord	Heroic Age	Odin, Loki
Skadi	Heroic Age	Odin, Thor
Baldr	Mythic Age	Odin, Thor
Hel	Mythic Age	Loki
Tyr	Mythic Age	Odin, Thor, Loki

Forseti – Classical Age

Forseti is the God of Justice. His improvements benefit Ulfsarks and Hersir.

Healing Spring God Power

Invoke Forseti's Healing Spring god power to create a pool of healing water on any place that can accommodate a building (for example, not on water, impassable terrain, or on an existing building). The Healing Spring is fairly large, so you will need ample space to place the new structure. Maneuver any of your units or allied units near the Healing Spring to mend wounds. Idle units heal much faster than units that are moving or in battle. Although the Healing Spring can't be destroyed, it can be captured. If the enemy has more units around the Healing Spring than you do, the enemy captures the structure, and receives healing from the spring. The Healing Spring can be recaptured.

Placement of the Healing Spring can be a double-edged sword: Putting it safely in your defended base could keep it from the enemy but requires a long trek back from the front lines for your wounded forces. Putting it closer to enemy territory might make it vulnerable to capture. Wherever you place the Healing Spring, protect the structure with Towers and walls.

Troll Mythological Unit

Trolls, allies of the Giants, were dim-witted, man-eating creatures that lived in caverns beneath hills and caves. Forseti's mythological unit is a slow but capable ranged unit that's most effective against human soldiers. Because of its sluggishness, be careful around enemy Heroes, which dominate the slow Troll at close range. Upgrade Forseti's Troll with the Hamarrtroll improvement.

Hamarrtroll Improvement

Research Forseti's Hamarrtroll improvement to upgrade Trolls to Hamarrtrolls, with increased hit points, range, and attack damage. And it even gives Trolls two heads—though this doesn't do anything special.

Hall of Thanes Improvement

Hall of Thanes improves the Norse Hersir's speed and hit points. The Norse Hero unit, while powerful against enemy mythological units, is quite slow. Research this improvement and Forseti's Hersir can intercept powerful mythological units faster than standard Hersir, with more hit points for increased durability.

Mithril Breastplate Improvement

Forseti's Mithril Breastplate improvement makes Ulfsarks more resistant to hack attacks, such as those employed by other infantry units. While Ulfsarks offer bonus damage against cavalry, the Norse warrior is vulnerable to infantry and archers. Research this improvement to upgrade the Ulfsarks' defense against counter-infantry units—though it's still wiser to employ the Ulfsarks primarily against cavalry.

Freyja – Classical Age

Freyja is the Goddess of Beauty. Her improvements benefit your cavalry.

Forest Fire God Power

Invoke Freyja's Forest Fire god power to burn a group of trees into ashes, completely destroying a chosen forest. You can use this god power to deny an enemy access to wood, or to remove a forest that provides a natural barrier to an enemy town or expansion. Any unit or structure adjacent to the burning forest also sustains damage. You must have line of sight on at least part of the forest to invoke the power. Against a Norse player, Forest Fire won't prevent the enemy from simply seeking a

new source easily with a movable Ox Cart, but it will slow down income for a short period of time. A Greek player will be forced to move and expend wood on another storehouse. An Egyptian player will lose gathering time, but can place another lumber camp for free. For added effect, attack while burning down a forest that's being harvested by villagers. Your enemy will need to decide quickly to micromanage the battle or save the villagers from a fiery death. This small distraction could provide an edge in the battle.

Valkyrie Mythological Unit

In Norse mythology, the Valkyries were blond, blue-eyed warrior maidens who assisted Odin by selecting which recently slain warriors would enter Valhalla. The Valkyries often rode through the air and served as messengers for Odin. It's been said that the Valkyries' glistening armor creates the atmospheric phenomenon known as the "Northern Lights." In combat, Valkyries are best used against human soldiers and can be countered by Hero units. Their most important characteristic is that they automatically generate a healing aura that mends the wounds of your nearby warriors, including those of your allies. Support military efforts with Valkyries. If your enemy has no way to heal units, he must use resources to replace slain troops, while you can save resources by healing injured units.

Aurora Borealis Improvement

Research Freyja's Aurora Borealis improvement to increase Valkyrie hit points and healing rate. This is certainly a valuable improvement if you plan on supporting your military with Valkyrie mythological units. It's a sound alternative to Forseti's Healing Spring, particularly with increased healing rate.

Thundering Hooves Improvement

Freyja's Thundering Hooves improvement increases the speed and hit points of Raiding Cavalry and Jarl. Both of these cavalry units are effective against archers, but Jarl also feature bonus damage against mythological units. With this improvement, your cavalry can reach enemy ranged and (in the case of Jarl, mythological units) quicker. The increased hit points allow the cavalry units to survive longer in battle. Combine with Njord's Ring-Giver improvement, which further increases Jarl hit points. Thundering Hooves also benefits Valkyries, increasing the speed and hit points of Freyja's mythological unit.

Heimdall – Classical Age

Heimdall is the God of Vigilance. His improvements benefit your buildings.

Undermine God Power

Heimdall's god power, Undermine, can reduce enemy walls and Towers to rubble. The god power inflicts some damage on other defensive buildings (such as Town Centers, Hill Forts, Fortresses, and Migdol Strongholds), but absolutely destroys multiple walls and Towers within its area of effect. Only fully improved walls and Towers will remain standing after you invoke Undermine, but they'll be significantly weakened. Follow up use of this god power with a Portable Ram attack to finish them off. Defend against this god power by spreading out your Towers and walls. Clumping defenses together will only lead to clumped rubble (see Figure 5.3). Scout an enemy's base to discover the best area to invoke the god power. Follow up Undermine with an attack, or the enemy will simply replace the destroyed walls and Towers as resources become available.

Einherjar Mythological Unit

The Einherjar were the dead warriors, gathered by Valkyries, who were taken to Asgard to live with Odin. In Asgard, the Einherjar battled all day and feasted all night. Wounds were magically healed so the Einherjar could repeat the routine day and night until Odin called them to fight with the Gods at Ragnarok. Einherjar are slow-moving mythological units, strong against buildings and human soldiers, with bonus damage against other mythological units. The Einherjar can boost the effectiveness of nearby allied units with their special horn-blast attack, which improves morale.

Figure 5.3 *If your enemy worships Heimdall, don't clump Towers and walls together, or they'll crumble when he invokes Undermine.*

Elhrimnir Kettle Improvement

Heimdall feeds the Einherjar from the Elhrimnir Kettle to increase the Einherjar's attack damage and hit points. Research this improvement to upgrade your Einherjar, making them stronger in battle. Added hit points mean the Einherjar can last longer, with more time to utilize their special horn blast ability.

Safeguard Improvement

Research Heimdall's improvement, Safeguard, to make walls and Towers stronger, and Towers cheaper. Defensive-minded players should certainly consider Safeguard. The cheaper Towers save wood and gold that can be used for military units or additional Towers. Exploit all benefits of this improvement by adding walls, as well as Towers, to your defense. Norse walls and Towers are generally inferior to Greek and Egyptian defenses, but researching Safeguard can even the odds.

Arctic Wind Improvement

Heimdall's Arctic Wind improvement increases the swiftness and hit points of his Norse Longboats. Naval strategists should follow a god path through Heimdall for the Arctic Wind improvement. Longboats generate added favor in combat and are best used against enemy hammer ships and buildings. Improve the Longboat further at your Dock, which increases range, attack damage, and hit points.

Bragi – Heroic Age

Bragi is the God of Poetry and of Skalds. His improvements help your Ulfsarks.

Flaming Weapons God Power

When you invoke Bragi's Flaming Weapons god power, your human soldiers' weapons burst into flame. That's a good thing: It adds extra damage to their attacks. Flaming Weapons also affects allied units in its area of effect. Flaming Weapons also affects projectiles, including siege weapon and ship shots. This god power affects all of your units on the map, but no allies. You must target it on a valid target. This prevents you from wasting the god power in the mistaken belief that it might help allies. Invoke Flaming Weapons in offensive or defensive situations (including key naval battles). Invoke it during the early moments of an engagement so the enemy can't run and avoid all of your attacks.

Battle Boar Mythological Unit

 Two boars, Gullinbursti and Slidrugtanni, pulled the chariot of Freyr (Freyja's brother). The boars weren't living animals, but were manufactured by the Dwarf Heroes Brokk and Eitri. Bragi's Battle Boar mythological unit is a speedy melee unit that periodically goes berserk and bucks at any nearby enemy units (the effect recharges after each use). Use the Battle Boar against human soldiers, but avoid enemy Hero units.

Call of Valhalla Improvement

 Bragi's Call of Valhalla improvement increases Ulfsark hit points. Combine the improvement with Bragi's Swine Array (which increases bonus damage against cavalry) and Forseti's Mithril Breastplate (which increases hack armor) to further increase the strength of your Ulfsark units.

Swine Array Improvement

 Research the Swine Array improvement to increase Ulfsark bonus damage against cavalry. Ulfsarks are already the Norse counter-cavalry unit. This improvement increases their abilities and should be combined with other Ulfsark benefits, including Forseti's Mithril Breastplate improvement. Swine Array cannot be combined with Odin's Lone Wanderer improvement, which increases Ulfsark speed.

Thurisaz Rune Improvement

 Bragi's Thurisaz Rune improvement brands mythological units with the Thurisaz Rune, which increases their speed. Combine this improvement with Loki's cheaper mythological units and Hel's Rampage improvement, which causes mythological units to be trained almost instantly.

Njord – Heroic Age

Njord is the God of the Sea and of Storms. His improvements benefit ships and hill forts.

Walking Woods God Power

 Invoke Njord's Walking Woods god power to animate a group of trees, which will attack nearby enemy units and buildings (the trees are stronger against buildings than units). It's best to target Walking Woods on a group of trees; if you target a tree that's not closely surrounded by others, the god power will animate only that single tree (see Figure 5.4). The fighting trees can't be controlled, but will persist in

Figure 5.4 *Invoke the Walking Woods god power on forests adjacent to enemy buildings.*

attacking the enemy until they're killed. They won't leave the general area in which they were summoned, so scout the enemy carefully to find the most suitable spot for the power (a forest near groups of buildings, particularly Houses or military structures, is ideal). You must have line of sight on at least one tree to invoke the power.

Kraken Mythological Unit

In Norse mythology, the immense Kraken sea serpent was often mistaken for a chain of islands. Norse warriors would camp unknowingly on a Kraken only to drown when the beast submerged. The Kraken features large tentacles covered with suckers, with which it seizes large ships and drags them under, destroying them nearly instantly. This ability recharges, and while waiting to use it again, the Kraken thrashes at enemy ships with its tentacles. When assaulting a naval group using Krakens, target separate ships with each beast to utilize its abilities faster. The Kraken is effective against all ships, but can be countered by ramming ships. The Kraken's special ability can also be used to throw—and kill—shore units that get too close to the Kraken's tentacles.

Mountain Giant Mythological Unit

Mountain Giants, also known as Jotun, were known for their great strength and stupidity. The Jotun were antagonistic and destructive. Njord's Mountain Giant is most effective against humans and buildings but also features bonus damage against mythological units. It also has a stronger bash attack, which recharges over time. The bash attack only works against buildings. The Mountain Giant is terribly slow, however, and should be supported by human units when facing Heroes.

Wrath of the Deep Improvement

Research Njord's Wrath of the Deep improvement to upgrade Krakens to Trench Krakens, which increases hit points. In a naval war, any edge could mean the difference. If you plan on adding Krakens to support your Norse vessels, research this improvement as soon as possible.

Long Serpent Improvement

Njord's Long Serpent improvement upgrades both the offensive and defensive capabilities of the Norse Longboat. Long Serpent improves attack damage and makes the Longboats more resistant to their counter-units, siege ships.

Combine this improvement with Heimdall's Arctic Wind, which increases Longboat speed and hit points. The improvements complement each other well, and create a well-rounded attack vessel. Improve Longboats further at the Dock and Armory.

Ring-Giver Improvement

Research Njord's Ring-Giver improvement to grant Jarl the Lore of the Rings, which increases the cavalry unit's hit points. Jarl are most effective against enemy mythological units. Ring-Giver essentially helps them last longer in tough fights. Combine this improvement with Freyja's Thundering Hooves, which increases Jarl speed as well as hit points.

Skadi – Heroic Age

Skadi is Goddess of Winter, and of Hunting. Her improvements aid your Throwing Axemen.

Frost God Power

Skadi's Frost god power can freeze an enemy army for a short time. The units are frozen within solid ice and can't move, attack, or be significantly damaged (it is possible to damage units in ice but it's extremely difficult). You won't be able to eliminate an enemy army using Frost, but the god power can buy you time to add reinforcements, erect more defenses, retreat, or reorganize your units to battle more effectively.

Frost Giant Mythological Unit

According to Norse mythology, Frost Giants, also called Thurses or Rime Giants, were among the first of the giants created when the world began. Skadi's Frost Giant, most effective against human soldiers, features a (recharging) icy-breath attack that can freeze an enemy unit for a short period. As with the Frost god power, the unit frozen by the Frost Giant can't move, attack, or be damaged. In an equal battle, however, if you can freeze a unit out of a fight, it could provide the edge you need. Send the Frost Giant against the largest perceived enemy threat.

Rime Improvement

Rime improves Frost Giants by increasing their hit points and attack damage.

Winter Harvest Improvement

Skadi offers an improvement for your economy: Winter Harvest. Research Winter Harvest to increase the speed of Norse farmers. Save the improvement until you have a network of farms built and being farmed. Save the resources required for the improvement if you're still hunting animals or obtaining food by other means.

Huntress's Axe Improvement

Research Skadi's Huntress's Axe improvement to increase the attack damage of Throwing Axemen. Combine this improvement with infantry improvements at the Longhouse and Hill Fort to further increase the Throwing Axemen's attack and hit points.

Baldr – Mythic Age

Baldr is the God of Beauty. His improvements benefit siege weapons and cavalry.

Ragnarok God Power

Baldr can begin "the end of the world" by invoking the Ragnarok god power. Cast Ragnarok anywhere on the map to turn all of your Norse gatherers and Dwarves into "Heroes of Ragnarok." This readies your entire empire for a final assault on the enemy. Your gatherers and Dwarves can't revert to their previous form, so your economy will suffer greatly after you invoke Ragnarok. Prepare ahead by researching any last improvements you wish to add to your units.

ES TIP

Before casting Ragnarok, be sure you have the food available to quickly replace your gatherers and resume the operation of your economy, just in case.

—Chris "Swinger" Rupp

Fire Giant Mythological Unit

The Fire Giants, or Muspilli, are eager participants at Ragnarok; they believe in the fiery destruction of the cosmos. The most famous Fire Giant was Surtr, a Jarl with burning hair, skin of boiling lava, and a flaming sword. Baldr's Fire Giants are extremely powerful beasts that hurl fireballs—best used against buildings and human units. Fire Giants have additional bonus damage against mythological units. They also possess a recharging attack that hurls multiple fireballs at the target. Support the ranged Fire Giant with melee units to protect the beast from close-range attack, particularly by Heroes.

Arctic Gate Improvement

Baldr's Arctic Gate improvement increases the speed of Norse Dragon Boat siege ships and makes the vessels more resistant to their counter-vessels, hammer ships. Follow the god path through Heimdall and Njord for additional naval improvements.

Sons of Sleipnir Improvement

Research the Sons of Sleipnir improvement to increase the Raiding Cavalry's bonus damage against archers and Throwing Axemen. Raiding Cavalry and Huskarls are the Norse's counter for ranged units. Huskarl units are strong but slow. Raiding Cavalry are weaker, but fast.

Dwarven Auger Improvement

Baldr enhances the Norse Portable Ram with Dwarven Auger, which increases the training speed of the siege weapon, as well as its swiftness and attack damage. Research other improvements at the Norse Hill Fort to further improve the Portable Ram's speed and attack damage. Combining improvements will create siege weapons capable of leveling Towers, walls, and buildings in short order.

Hel – Mythic Age

Hel is Goddess of the Underworld. Her improvements benefit mythological units.

Nidhogg God Power

Invoke Hel's Nidhogg god power to summon the mighty Norse dragon, Nidhogg, from his delve beneath the Earth. The Nidhogg uses its fiery breath to attack units from the air. Most effective against groups of human units, the Nidhogg can be countered only with ranged units, so steer clear of them. Support the Nidhogg with counter-archer units, such as Raiding Cavalry or Huskarls. The Nidhogg has a lot of hit points, but when they're gone, they're gone: It cannot be healed by any method.

Fire Giant Mythological Unit

Hel can produce Baldr's mythological unit, the Fire Giant. Fire Giants are extremely powerful beasts that hurl fireballs, best used against buildings and human units, with additional bonus damage against mythological units. The Fire Giants also possess a recharging attack that hurls multiple fireballs at the target. Support the ranged Fire Giant with melee units to protect the beast from close-range attack, particularly by Heroes.

Frost Giant Mythological Unit

Hel also can produce Skadi's mythological Frost Giant—most effective against human soldiers—featuring a recharging frozen-breath attack that can freeze an enemy unit for a short period. A unit frozen by the Frost Giant can't move or attack. Frozen units also can't be damaged, but in an equal battle, temporarily removing an enemy from the fight could give you the edge. Send the Frost Giant against the largest perceived enemy threat.

Mountain Giant Mythological Unit

Hel can produce Njord's mythological unit, the Mountain Giant. Most effective against humans and buildings, the Mountain Giant also features bonus damage against mythological units. Like those produced by Njord, this Giant has a stronger bash attack, which recharges over time. The Mountain Giant is terribly slow, and should be supported by human units against faster Heroes.

Rampage Improvement

Research Hel's Rampage improvement, which allows you to train mythological units almost instantly. Build multiple Norse Temples to enhance this valuable improvement. Rampage can aid in reinforcing an offense quickly or in defending a town or expansion. To worship Hel, you must have selected Loki as your Major God, and Loki reduces the favor cost of mythological units. These combined benefits are extremely valuable in late-game situations.

Granite Blood Improvement

Hel's Granite Blood improvement increases the hit points of Frost, Fire, and Mountain Giants. Combine with her Rampage improvement to create tougher giants almost instantly.

Tyr – Mythic Age

Tyr is God of Warfare. His improvements benefit your infantry.

Fimbulwinter God Power

Tyr can invoke Fimbulwinter, which darkens the sky, summons a blizzard, and creates wolves near enemy Town Centers and settlements (the wolves appear at four Town Centers regardless of the number of opponents in the game). You can target Fimbulwinter anywhere on the map; the wolves will attack the enemy Town Centers and any surrounding units. The wolves can't be controlled and will disappear once the god power ends (see Figure 5.5). You will also receive line of sight on the enemy town for the duration of the god power and should follow up Fimbulwinter with a military assault on enemy Town Centers or resource positions

Fenris Wolf Brood Mythological Unit

The original Fenrir (this brood is just the offspring) was the product of Loki and the giant Angrboda. The Gods raised Fenrir in Asgard but only Tyr had the courage to feed the beast. Tyr's Fenris Wolf Brood mythological unit becomes even stronger in packs—the more Fenris Wolves in the pack, the more damage *each* can inflict. Instead of expending resources on other mythological units, consider creating a pack of Fenris Wolves

Figure 5.5 *Invoke Tyr's Fimbulwinter to summon packs of wolves to assault enemy towns.*

to exploit this damage bonus. Use the Fenris Brood against human units and other mythological units.

Jormund Brood Mythological Unit

The original Jormungard (the Jormund Brood are akin to the Jormungard's babies) was a monstrous sea serpent, offspring of Loki and the giant Angrboda. Odin tossed Jormungard into the seas of Midgard. The Jormund Brood is a slithering naval unit that breathes steam as a ranged attack. Use the Jormund Brood against archer- and siege ships. Beware of ramming ships, however, which can damage the Jormund Brood just as a melee unit or cavalry unit would damage an archer at close range. Follow a god path through Heimdall and Njord for other naval improvements, which should be used to support the Jormund Brood.

Berserkergang Improvement

Tyr's Berserkergang improvement upgrades your Ulfsarks' attack damage and hit points. You should combine this improvement with the many Ulfsark improvements available (don't neglect the infantry improvements at the Longhouse and Armory). Follow a god path through Forseti and Bragi to research Mithril Breastplate and Swine Array.

Bravery Improvement

Research Tyr's Bravery to improve your Huskarls' damage vs. buildings.

Military Units

This section describes the Norse military units, including siege and naval units. A chart included with each unit describes the possible improvements for each unit type. Note that all military units can be improved at the facility where they were produced (shown in the accompanying chart). Units are first improved to Medium, then to Heavy, then to Champion.

Ravens

Odin, the chief God of Asgard, is blind in one eye. To compensate and stay aware of all that's happening in the nine worlds, Odin sends out his two Ravens—Huginn ("thought") and Munnin ("memory")—each morning.

You must follow Odin to receive the two Ravens, which will grace your village starting in the Classical Age. Use Odin's Ravens to quickly scout unexplored areas for animals (huntables and herdables), gold mines, settlements, enemy locations, and choke points where

TIP

See the Appendix in this strategy guide for Norse unit, building, and improvement stats.

you can position your defenses. Ravens also can be used to gain line of sight on a position so you can invoke a god power. Although they can be harmed only by ranged units and structures, Ravens have no attack and are very weak. Should a Raven be killed, however, it is respawned at Odin's Temple after several minutes of game time.

Ulfsark

Vikings who wore wolfskins into battle were known as Ulfsarks. These Norse warriors were lightly armored and wielded mainly axes and swords. The Ulfsarks' varied improvement potential makes them a wise choice for the backbone of your Norse army. Ulfsarks are best used against enemy cavalry units; they should avoid archers and counter-infantry units. Keep in mind that you can train an Ulfsark immediately from a gatherer. This method requires the cost of a gatherer and an Ulfsark, so it's not resource-friendly, but the Ulfsark instantly appears in a pinch (like when a group of defenseless gatherers is being attacked).

UPGRADE	IMPROVES
Longhouse	Attack, Hit Points, Training Rate, Line of Sight
Armory	Attack, Armor
Odin's Lone Wanderer	Speed
Loki's Eyes in the Forest	Line of Sight
Forseti's Mithril Breastplate	Hack Armor
Bragi's Swine Array	Bonus Damage vs. Cavalry
Tyr's Berserkergang	Attack, Hit Points

Throwing Axeman

The strong weapon of the Norse Throwing Axeman makes the unit one of the best counter-infantry units in the game. Despite using a ranged weapon, the Throwing Axeman is considered an infantry unit, and receives benefits from the infantry improvements at the Longhouse and Armory (as well as Loki's Eyes in the Forest). Throwing Axemen have bonus damage against infantry, but should avoid archers and cavalry. For example, support Throwing Axemen with Raiding Cavalry and Ulfsarks. If you plan on using groups of Throwing Axemen, follow a god path through Skadi to research Huntress's Axe.

UPGRADE	IMPROVES
Longhouse	Attack, Hit Points, Training Rate, Line of Sight
Armory	Attack, Armor
Loki's Eyes in the Forest	Line of Sight
Skadi's Huntress's Axe	Attack

Raiding Cavalry

Norse Raiding Cavalry units are fast, but lack the strength of more expensive cavalry units such as Greek Hippikon or Egyptian Camelry. Use Raiding Cavalry against enemy archers, and avoid infantry and counter-cavalry units. The Norse offer a second counter-archer unit, the Huskarl, upon reaching the Heroic Age. Because of their speed advantage over Huskarl, though, Raiding Cavalry are still an effective answer to archers. Worship Baldr in the Mythic Age and research Sons of Sleipnir to increase Raiding Cavalry damage against archers and Throwing Axemen.

UPGRADE	IMPROVES
Longhouse	Attack, Hit Points, Training Rate, Line of Sight
Armory	Attack, Armor
Freyja's Thundering Hooves	Speed, Hit Points
Baldr's Sons of Sleipnir	Bonus Damage vs. Archers and Throwing Axemen

Hersir

The Norse Hero unit is the Hersir. Originally, Hersir—independent landowners comparable to medieval knights in rank and influence—were the commanders of the Viking raids. The Hersir had better equipment than most of his fellow warriors, including possibly heavy chain mail. Unlike the Greeks and Egyptians, the Norse can produce as many Hersir as resources and the population cap will allow. Like other Heroes, Hersir can grab and carry relics, and are best used in combat against mythological units. Hersir generate favor in combat faster than other units. In fact, Hersir generate a small amount of favor just from being on the map. Improve Hersir with Forset's Hall of Thanes improvement, which increases Hersir speed and hit points.

UPGRADE	IMPROVES
Armory	Attack, Armor
Loki	Summons Myth Units, Speed
Loki's Eyes in the Forest	Line of Sight
Forseti's Hall of Thanes	Speed, Hit Points

Huskarl

Huskarls, which were the elite household guards of a Viking Lord, are unique infantry units, because they're best used against archers. Typically, archers are counter-infantry units, but Huskarls possess strong pierce armor, making them more resistant to archers and even buildings that shoot arrows. In general, though, the Huskarl is weaker than other infantry and cavalry units, although it requires more resources. Avoid infantry and counter-infantry units. Improve the Huskarl with Loki's Eyes in the Forest for line of sight, or worship Odin for greater hit points.

UPGRADE	IMPROVES
Hill Fort	Attack, Hit Points, Training Rate, Line of Sight
Odin	Hit Points
Loki's Eyes in the Forest	Line of Sight
Tyr's Bravery	Bonus Damage vs. Buildings

Jarl

The Norse Jarls were high-ranking Vikings who owned substantial land. Because of their wealth and status, the Jarl used excellent equipment. The Jarl cavalry unit is best against mythological units, though it's not as strong as the Norse Hersir in this regard. Jarl are slow for cavalry, but it's possible to research Freyja's Thundering Hooves to improve speed as well as hit points. Worship Njord and research Ring-Giver to increase hit points even further. Protect the expensive Jarl from infantry and counter-cavalry units.

UPGRADE	IMPROVES
Hill Fort	Attack, Hit Points, Training Rate
Odin	Hit Points
Freyja's Thundering Hooves	Speed, Hit Points
Njord's Ring-Giver	Hit Points

Portable Ram

To take down an enemy town quickly, Vikings often cut down a strong tree, trimmed the trunk, attached some handles, and used the new weapon to bash a gate, wall, or structure. The Norse Portable Ram is similar to the Greek Helepolis and Egyptian Siege Tower in that it must attack from close range, putting the unit within range of Towers and defensive buildings. Improve the Portable Ram at the Hill Fort, and research Baldr's Dwarven Auger to improve attack damage, unit speed, and training rate.

UPGRADE	IMPROVES
Hill Fort	Attack, Weapon Speed
Odin	Hit Points
Baldr's Dwarven Auger	Attack, Speed, Training Rate

Ballista

The Ballista was a pre-gunpowder artillery weapon, used mainly against men in formation. The Ballista was a large crossbow that required the use of a winch and ratchet to draw the bow. A large metal or metal-headed bolt served as the missile. The Norse Ballista is strong against units and naval units (the Ballista launches from the shoreline). Although a decent weapon against buildings, the Ballista is much stronger against tight formations of enemy units. Research improvements at the Hill Fort to improve this weapon's attack damage and firing speed. The Ballista is one of the few ranged units the Norse have, and the only one (aside from the Troll) to do pierce damage.

UPGRADE	IMPROVES
Burning Pitch	Attack
Hill Fort	Attack, Weapon Speed
Odin	Hit Points

Longboat

Vikings had a long history of naval trading, which eventually developed into coastal raiding. The Viking Longboat was a fast warship about 80 feet long. Its maneuverability, high speed, and shallow draught allowed the ship to penetrate rivers and beach on shores. The Longboat, an archer ship, is best used against hammer ships, but also features bonus damage against buildings. Plus, the Longboat generates bonus favor during combat, definitely encouraging naval aggression on water maps. Follow a god path through Heimdall and Njord and research their Longboat improvements to upgrade speed, hit points, attack, and resistance to siege ships.

UPGRADE	IMPROVES
Armory	Attack, Armor
Burning Pitch	Attack, Bonus Damage vs. Buildings
Dock	Attack, Hit Points, Range, Training Rate
Heimdall's Arctic Wind	Speed, Hit Points
Njord's Long Serpent	Attack, Resistance to Siege Ships

Drakkar

The Viking Drakkar is a hammer or ramming ship, best used against enemy siege ships. Counter the Drakkar with arrow ships such as the Greek Trireme, Egyptian Kebenit, or Norse Longboat. Protect your Drakkar by supporting the vessel with Norse Dragon Ships or naval mythological units such as the Kraken or Jormund Brood. Drakkar are also the Norse response to enemy naval mythological units.

UPGRADE	IMPROVES
Armory	Attack, Armor
Dock	Attack, Hit Points, Training Rate

Dragon Ship

The Norse Dragon Ship is a siege ship that carries a mounted ballista effective against arrow ships and buildings. Counter the Dragon Ship with ramming or hammer ships. Follow a naval god path to Baldr and research Arctic Gate to improve the Dragon Ship's speed and resistance to hammer ships.

UPGRADE	IMPROVES
Armory	Attack, Armor
Dock	Attack, Hit Points, Training Rate
Baldr's Arctic Gate	Speed, Resistance to Hammer Ships

Missions 1–8 Walkthrough

Mysterious hordes of pirate invaders, along with powerful sea creatures called Kraken, have breached the shores of Atlantis. The Hero Arkantos must successfully defend his homeland from attack. This is just the beginning of a perilous epic journey for Arkantos, who is faithful to Poseidon, god of the sea, of earthquakes, and of horses. Over the course of the first eight missions in Age of Mythology's single-player campaign, Arkantos must assist the Greeks in their military struggle with Troy, unravel the mystery behind the pirate attacks, and eventually discover a passage into the dangerous Underworld.

Following is the Age of Mythology walkthrough for the first eight missions of the game. Each walkthrough includes the mission's objectives, an overview of the map (including the locations of important resources and the positions of enemy units), and a suggested battle plan.

Omens

Initial Objective

◈ Protect Atlantis by killing the Kraken.

Map Highlights

You begin with your Hero Arkantos in the seaside city of Atlantis. The mainland occupies the north and northwestern sections of the map; open sea lies to the south and southeast. Atlantis' resources—farms, gold mines, and forests—can be found on the western side of the city. The Military Academy and Archery Range lie along the western and eastern shorelines. Incoming pirate ships and Kraken arrive from the southeast—advancing from a small shore in the southeast corner of the map.

Battle Plans

As the mission begins, a Kraken is attacking your Dock and other units along the shoreline of Atlantis. Gather Arkantos and your initial forces—ranged archer units called Toxotes and stone-throwing siege weaponry called Petroboli—and target the Kraken as quickly as possible. You also possess several Watch Towers to assist in the city's protection. Defeat the Kraken to receive the next mission objective.

◈ **New Objective:** Train reinforcements and defend the harbor until the Atlantean army arrives.

Additional Kraken and transport ships carrying pirate invaders will continue arriving from the southeast corner of the map. Although it's possible to survive the Kraken and pirate assault with your Watch Towers and initial units, the mission becomes much more manageable if you utilize Atlantis' ample resources to bolster your ground army and Tower defenses.

Two god powers are included to assist in the mission: Use Rain to hasten food gathering by Atlantis' farmers, and use Restoration to heal all units, buildings, and siege units. Observe the southeastern corner of the map and watch the mini-map carefully to spot incoming enemies (marked with red on the mini-map) as early as possible.

Maneuver your Petroboli siege weapons east toward the shoreline to target incoming pirate ships and Kraken. Place Arkantos and your archer units near a Watch Tower—the Tower defends your units against invading pirates. Shift your attention to your military structures. The military academy can produce Hoplites, heavily armed infantry units effective against enemy cavalry; your Archery Range can produce Toxotes, units of ranged archery effective against enemy infantry.

Heroes

In the single-player game, Heroes such as Arkantos are immortal. Should a Hero be killed, the scenario doesn't end, and the Hero's body remains on the map. If you use other units to hold position around the dead body, the Hero revives—although initially with only one hit point left. Gradually the Hero's hit points will return to full strength. Don't thrust the Hero immediately back into battle; allow time for healing. Heroes are most effective against mythological units.

Concentrate at first on producing archery units, in preference to Hoplites. Queue up several of these Toxotes (leave yourself at least 400 wood for additional Towers) and set their gather point near Arkantos and your other defenders. You may need to shift villagers from the production of food to that of wood to increase production of the Toxotes. Make sure your Toxotes remain at a distance from the sea, because the Kraken can grab units who stray too close to the shore! Produce a couple of villagers and use them to build two additional Watch Towers near the Atlantis Dock (see Figure 6.1). Construct another on the shore northeast from the Dock to add to the city's defense. Towers and Toxotes are the best method to holding off the incoming enemies because you can't train any ships during the mission.

TIP

Several upgrades are available at the Military Academy, Archery Range, and Armory. Choose the Archery Range and Armory upgrades first. These weapon and armor upgrades will cost you resources, so keep villagers busy on the western side of the city.

There will be brief intervals between the attacks by Kraken and pirate ships, but after the first few strikes, the frequency and strength of the attacks becomes stronger. Use the precious time between attacks to regroup your army, produce additional Toxotes, and position your Petroboli to pour deadly fire on the next wave of pirate ships and Kraken to reach the shoreline.

The pirate transport ships unload progressively more powerful troops. Send your Hero, Arkantos, into play against any mythological units

Figure 6.1 Bolster the defense of Atlantis by adding Watch Towers along the shoreline.

and lure enemy groups within range of your defensive Watch Towers and Petroboli siege weapons. Also, don't forget to use the god power Restoration to heal your units, buildings, and siege weapons should the need arise.

The Atlantean army will arrive after defeating a large wave of pirates. You gain control of the Atlantean army once it arrives. Use the army to eliminate the invasion force to complete the mission.

Consequences

Objective

⊕ Advance to the Classical Age and explore the island.

Map Highlights

You begin with a Town Center and a small group of villagers on the map's western shoreline. Berry bushes lying just east of the Town Center will provide your first source of food. Explore north of town to discover an additional food source—a herd of pigs—and south of the Town Center to reveal another: a flock of chickens. Search south of the Town Center to uncover two gold mines to help fund your military campaign. Just off shore, two of your Triremes battle two pirate ships.

Battle Plans

After defending Atlantis from invading pirates and Kraken, you and the Hero Arkantos must turn to building a base and organizing an attack against a pirate camp. You have a Town Center, and arrayed on your side are Arkantos and an army of Toxotes, a Kataskopos (scout), and a small group of villagers to gather resources and build the structures required both to advance to the Classical Age and to mount an assault against the pirates.

Gather all villagers except one and order them to the berry bushes just east of the Town Center. The remaining villager must construct a House. You need houses immediately to raise the population cap. Raising the population cap allows you to produce additional villagers, hasten resource gathering, and develop an economy. While the other villagers forage for berries, construct houses as you need them until you've reached the population cap. Queue up 10–15 additional villagers as the population cap increases.

> **TIP**
>
> Because of Arkantos' faithfulness, Poseidon grants you the god power Lure, which erects a stone (at a spot you designate) that beckons wild animals. Use Lure to draw the deer grazing on the hill east of Town Center.

Meanwhile, send the Kataskopos—a fast-moving but weak cavalry unit best used as a scout—north to reveal a group of pigs just outside your line of sight. Move the pigs toward your Town Center to use as a food source once the berry bushes have been depleted. Search south of the Town Center to reveal a group of chickens, which can also be hunted for food. Continue to scout along the northern shore to uncover a couple of enemy Spearmen. Lure these Spearmen back to town and eliminate these enemies with Arkantos and your Toxotes.

All the House building has likely depleted your wood supply, and you'll need additional wood to construct your Greek Temple—a prerequisite for advancement to the Classical Age. Assign five or six villagers to chop and gather wood, keep another five or six villagers on slaughtering and gathering meat from the pigs and chickens, and assign remaining villagers to the two gold mines just south of the Town Center. Construct a Storehouse between the forest and gold mines to provide a drop-off point for your gatherers.

As soon as enough wood becomes available, construct the Greek Temple. Once you meet the prerequisites to advance to the Classical Age, return to your Town Center and engage your first age-advancement.

When you advance ages in *Age of Mythology*, you're presented with an important decision: You must choose which of two Minor Gods your villagers will worship. Each Minor God offers its own unique god power, mythological unit(s), and various upgrades to military and economic power.

A good bet would be to worship Ares instead of Hermes, to gain Ares' powerful military upgrades and lumbering mythological unit, Cyclops. Ares also bestows the unpleasant but effective god power Pestilence, which can be used on enemy structures to prevent unit building for a period of time. You'll need a new resource, favor, to build new mythological units and to acquire your god's unique upgrades. Produce three to four additional villagers and set their gather point on the Temple. As your villagers worship their gods, you gain important favor.

Advancing to the Classical Age also permits you to produce Greek Heroes from your Town Center, adding their powers to that of Arkantos. Theseus, a mighty infantry Hero, and Hippolyta, a sturdy archer, can be added to your military groups. You can't mass produce them—you can have only one of each Hero at any single time. Like Arkantos, they are most effective against other Heroes and mythological units. Advancing to the Classical Age initiates a new mission objective.

◈ **New Objective:** Train an army and destroy the pirate Town Center.

Note on the mini-map that the pirate Town Center has been revealed on the eastern side of the map. Construct a Military Academy and Archery Range immediately and start producing Hoplites

TIP

Should your Kataskopos perish, produce another scout—a Pegasus—at the Greek Temple. Pegasus is an effective scout: a fast, flying horse that can only be attacked by ranged units. Send either type of scout south of your Town Center toward the southern shore to discover more pigs and a gold mine.

and Toxotes. The discovery of the pirate Town Center also triggers the beginning of enemy attacks—pirate Axemen and Slingers (ranged units) arrive and attack north of your Town Center. Defend the region using Arkantos, upgraded Towers, and your military units. As food and wood become available, upgrade your Hoplites and Toxotes at their respective production centers.

Build a couple of Towers on the eastern hill overlooking your Town Center. Pirate Slingers tend to migrate to this hill and use their long-range weapon to attack your villagers gathering wood and gold below. A couple of Towers should end this threat before it becomes a problem.

TIP

Use your Kataskopos or Pegasus to scout the northeastern shoreline and sea in search of a damaged ship. Finding it adds wood and gold to your resources. Use the additional resources to fund your military campaign against the pirates. There's also another gold mine in the northeast corner, but it's protected by a pirate ship.

Also, the pirates possess a Dock just below their Town Center. You may wish to construct four or five Triremes at your own Dock and maneuver them just south of the pirate Town Center to destroy any

Figure 6.2 *You can use Triremes crammed with archers to assault the pirates' Dock, just south of their Town Center.*

ships and the Dock (see Figure 6.2). Approach the Dock from the eastern side to avoid a nearby Watch Tower.

Before mounting your assault on the pirate Town Center, make sure to protect the northern and southern entrances of your own base with several Towers. You may also wish to keep four to seven Toxotes and Hoplites near in your Town Center to repel any late pirate attacks. Leave a small force behind in your town and position these units along the southern edge of your base to protect against pirate incursions. Send the fast Kataskopos or Hoplites against the Catapult to prevent extensive damage to your Towers or structures.

Once you have two groups of 10–15 Hoplites and Toxotes, two or three Cyclops, and your Heroes, move the army along the northern shore to the far eastern side. You may notice several paths leading south into the pirate town but these are blocked by Watch Towers. Use the hill on the eastern side of the map to begin your assault; position your Toxotes on this hill and your archers will fire at the pirate structures and units below. Cast Ares' god power Pestilence on the military structures within the pirate camp.

Your primary target is the pirate Town Center. You can leave all other pirate structures intact and still complete your mission if the Town Center falls. Beware of the Pharaoh lurking in the pirate base: On sight, the enemy invokes the god power Plague of Serpents, summoning several serpents to attack your army. Send your Toxotes to fend off the serpents, while pummeling the Town Center with your Cyclops, Heroes, and Hoplites. A new objective appears when the pirate Town Center has nearly fallen.

◈ **New Objective:** Corner and attack Kamos the Minotaur.

Three Anubites appear to help defend the pirate Town Center. Locate Kamos—the Minotaur donning the steel armor—and maneuver all your troops toward him. Attack Kamos to complete the mission successfully.

Scratching the Surface

Initial Objective

◈ Lead your soldiers to the unclaimed settlement.

Map Highlights

You begin on the western shore. The unclaimed settlement lies along the shoreline to the south. You're very close to mighty Troy, which lies in the northeast. Once you reach the unclaimed settlement, food sources can be found north (chickens) and northwest (gazelle) of the location. Search north of the settlement for a gold mine. The Trojan docks, an important objective later in the mission, lie north and east of the unclaimed settlement.

Battle Plans

As the mission opens, you possess a sizeable group of units. You have three Heroes at your disposal—Arkantos is joined by Ajax and Agamemnon—as well as Hypaspists, Toxotes, and Hoplites. You'll face many attacks during the course of the mission.

Organize these troops into four groups: Use the Heroes primarily against mythological units, the Hypaspists against other infantry, the Toxotes primarily against infantry, and the Hoplites primarily against enemy cavalry. Although these should be your primary targets, make sure all of your units are participating in the battle so enemy units are vanquished as quickly as possible.

After organizing your troops, send them south toward the unclaimed settlement revealed on the mini-map. A small enemy group guards the path to the settlement. Eliminate these enemy troops with your organized army. A new objective appears once you maneuver within range of the unclaimed settlement.

◈ **New Objective:** Build a Town Center.

You're given villagers to claim the settlement and build a Town Center. Use all villagers to build the structure to quicken the process.

As the Town Center goes up, send your Heroes to search the area around the settlement. North of the settlement they can find a gold mine, some goats, and a herd of gazelle. Hunt the gazelle for your first food source. A pack of chickens wandering north of the settlement can be processed for food. A new mission objective appears once the Town Center is finished.

◈ **New Objective**: Destroy the two Trojan docks.

Enemy siege ships begin assaulting Agamemnon's small village to the north-east. To stop the enemy naval units, destroy the Trojan docks now high-lighted on the mini-map—one to the north and another to the east. Sink any enemy Triremes offshore with your

> *There's another valuable source of food on the map. Search the area northwest of your settlement to discover a large herd of deer. Build a Granary, used to deposit collected food, near the deer. Use Poseidon's gift of Lure, placing the stone next to the granary to lure the nearby wildlife toward it.*

Toxotes. Start construction of a Dock. Queue 14 villagers and begin collecting wood and gold to fund a naval fleet. Keep at least six to eight villagers on food (research Husbandry before processing the goats). You need the food to meet the requirements to advance to Classical Age. You'll also need to erect a Temple as soon as possible.

Advance to the Classical Age. As always, you must choose between Minor Gods at advancement. Select Ares because he has more options for the military and offers you the chance to produce the mighty Cyclops. Attacks arrive from north of your town. Protect the area with upgraded Towers and your Heroes. Build military structures to create Hoplites and Toxotes to help guard your town.

You could assault the docks or gather the resources required to advance to Heroic Age. Advance first! Build an Armory and continue to gather food (the goats should be fattened by now). Upon advancing to the Heroic Age,

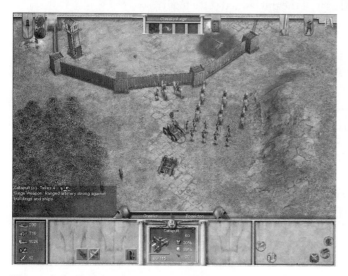

Figure 6.3 *Use Agamemnon's Catapults to batter the Towers.*

worship Dionysus for the Bronze god power and the Anastrophe improvement.

Train about eight Triremes (and two Pentekonters to remain for defense) and upgrade them to Heavy Triremes; apply Armory upgrades if the resources are available. Head to the eastern Trojan Dock. Sink any enemy ships along the way.

Assault the Dock with your naval fleet. When it has been destroyed, Agamemnon sends transports to unload troops (Hippikon and Catapults) to assault the small village north of the Dock. Command these troops. Bombard the Tower and Town Center with the Catapults (see Figure 6.3). After crushing the town, send Agamemnon and his army into your town for added defense.

◈ **New Objective**: Destroy the last Trojan Dock.

After tasking the Catapults on the Tower and Town Center, shift focus back to your original town. Defend against enemy siege ships (with your Triremes or Pentekonter ramming ships) and an attack from the west. Use available resources to bolster your defenses with Hoplites, Toxotes (upgrade them) and Towers.

Add to your naval units with some Juggernaut siege ships. Send the fleet to the northern Trojan Dock. Eliminate any defenders and bombard the Dock with your fleet. Maintain defense in your base and repel any enemy attacks (mostly mythology units, which you can counter with your Heroes and cavalry, which you can counter with Hoplites). When the second Trojan Dock is destroyed, the mission ends in victory.

A Fine Plan

Initial Objective

◈ Find and take a Gold Mine from the Trojans.

Map Highlights

You begin this mission on the southern edge of the map. The imposing city of Troy sweeps along the northern edge of the map. There are goats in your town ready to be slaughtered for food and a herd of deer west of your town. Troy's rich gold mines can be found just northwest and north of your city. Another Trojan gold-mining operation—a small camp supplying gold to Troy by donkey caravan—is situated in the northwestern area of the map.

Battle Plans

This time, your mission begins in the Classical Age. You already have a sizable army, including Hoplites, Hippikon, and a Helepolis Siege Tower. The Helepolis is a mobile weapon—a rolling Tower that can transport units and fire ballista bolts at buildings. Most of the structures required to enhance your well-established army are already in place. Instead of bolstering your military, spend the mission's opening minutes improving your economy.

Select your Town Center and use all your initially available food to produce additional villagers. Use one villager to build Houses (to support the population cap), and order the remaining villagers to harvest food from the herd of western deer. You'll use most of your initial wood on Houses and eventually structures, improvements, and farms, once the supply of animals runs dry. You could also build fishing boats if you wish to collect food from the sea (you already have a couple fishing boats).

Build a Granary near the herd of deer west of your city. Send most of your villagers there to harvest food (leave three to five for wood) as you wait to conquer a Trojan gold mine.

> **WARNING**
>
> The first Trojan attacks come from the area north of your city. Position your initial army to quickly intercept the attacks. For additional protection, build defensive Towers along the northern edge of your base.

Group your available military units and head northwest from your town to locate the nearest Trojan gold mine. Accompany the Helepolis with your units and use the siege weapon to topple the enemy mining camp there. Send the Hippikons against defending Toxotes and eliminate all enemy villagers. Move up your own villagers, build a Storehouse, and begin mining gold. You should use gold stolen from the Trojan mine to erect a Tower. When resources become available, upgrade the Tower.

After using your initial food stores, produce about eight more villagers. Although you possess a Military Academy, Stable, and Temple, you still lack an Archery Range (which you need to produce Toxotes and Peltasts) and an Armory, needed to advance to the Heroic Age. Build each as soon as possible and, as the resources become available, purchase the upgrades at each of the military structures.

> **TIP**
>
> A second enemy, in the northeastern part of the map, sends Trireme ships to pester your naval fleet and attack your Dock. Protect your Dock with ships or Towers. You could even attack this enemy's mainland if you wish (sending troops over with transports). There's a relic available in the enemy town!

If you've established a significant defense of Towers, consider remaining inside the safe confines of your base while you continue gathering resources to advance into the Heroic Age, which, depending on your use of resources, shouldn't take more than 20–30 minutes from the mission's start. You'll want to produce a mixed group of forces, including Hoplites to counter Trojan cavalry, Hippikon to counter Trojan archers, and Toxotes to counter Trojan infantry. Don't forget to support your forces with mythological units, including the Cyclops, available since the beginning of the mission.

Don't leave your base unguarded as you explore and assault the Trojan gold mine. Towers can help hold off a Trojan assault, but it's wise to leave a small, mixed group behind to defend the town long enough for your main army to return. When you reclaim the Trojan gold mine, a new objective appears.

New Objective: Train an army and destroy the Trojan West Gate.

It's the age-old question: Dionysus or Apollo? You must choose between them for worship upon advancing to the Heroic Age. Dionysus' Bronze god power could provide an added armor bonus to your human units during the critical battles near the Trojan base. Apollo's Underground Passage god power could be used to quickly maneuver troops near the Trojan gate (see Figure 6.4). Plus, Apollo's Temple of Healing improvement can regenerate your units' health in between battles.

Figure 6.4 *Loyalty to Apollo will give you the Underground Passage to maneuver troops quickly between two areas on the map.*

After advancing to the Heroic Age, build a Greek Fortress for additional town defense and the ability to build Petroboli siege weapons. Continue to monitor your resources, purchase new upgrades at your military structures, and add troops to your current military groups. Begin to maneuver your troops west and around to the north toward the main gate of Troy. Place scouts around the perimeter of your base to monitor any Trojan assaults, and bring troops home to assist in town defense as needed.

Advance to Troy across the northern edge of the map. Advance slowly and beware of counter attacks, especially those supported by god powers (Troy doesn't hesitate to use Bolt or Bronze). Use your siege weapons, including the Helepolis Siege Tower provided at the beginning of the mission, against the Tower defenses and gates. Defend your siege weaponry against counterattack. Group your units according to type and counter the Trojan forces with the appropriate units. Utilize the god powers you have gained or been provided to assist in the battle.

You'll discover a Troy Market and caravans south of the Troy gate. Destroying the Market and caravans reduces Troy's ability to reinforce its army and produce more units. Task the Petroboli on the Market and eliminate the donkey caravans with your military units. It's also possible to cut Trojan production temporarily by using the god power Pestilence. Scout the northwestern side of the Trojan base with a Pegasus to discover the Military Academies. After obtaining line-of-sight, invoke Pestilence to cause

Trojan Trade Caravan

Thorough investigation of the western corner of the map reveals another Trojan gold operation. A Town Center protects a small gold-mining camp, which sends gold to Troy via donkey caravan. Upon its discovery, Arkantos alerts you to its presence. He wants to destroy the camp. A couple of siege weapons can obliterate the Trojan trade caravan but must be supported by strong military forces. After you breach the camp and begin razing structures, Troy will send a heavy retaliation force spearheaded by tough cavalry. Make sure you send plenty of upgraded Hoplites with the siege weapons, to counter the powerful Trojan cavalry. Eliminating this Troy trade caravan weakens Troy's attacks.

production to stop for a short period of time. Topple the nearby Towers, gate, and Fortress before advancing near the Trojan gate.

If necessary, it's possible to advance to the Mythic Age by building a Market and gathering the required food and gold resources. At advancement, two more gods become available for your worship. Choose Hera for her Lightning Storm god power, which should be saved for the climatic battle near the Trojan main gate; or choose Hephaestus for his god power of Plenty, with which you can erect a vault that continually pours additional resources into your coffers to fund your military campaign.

It's possible to win the mission in the Heroic Age, though the Mythic Age gods and upgrades offer additional powers that are fun to wield. The mission ends immediately once the main gate of Troy falls to your forces. You aren't required to destroy all of the enemy buildings in the city. Simply eliminate the gate to complete the mission.

> TIP
>
> Berry bushes in the northeastern corner of the map could provide another source of food for your town. Simply construct a granary nearby and assign several villagers to forage for berries. Also, there are two relics nearby. Search the northwestern corner of the map for a relic protected by a Medusa. Search an alcove just west of Troy to uncover another relic. To gain their benefits, use a Hero to garrison the relics in your Temple.

Just Enough Rope

Initial Objective

⊕ Destroy the cavalry attacking Ajax.

Map Highlights

You start the mission just north of the city of Troy, which lies along the southern edge of the map. The Trojan cavalry assaults Ajax and his small army just north of your start position.

Battle Plans

At the beginning of the mission, you're provided with a nearly fresh batch of Hippikon and Hoplites, under the command of Arkantos. Group them by type. Send the Hoplites into battle first, as these units possess a bonus against cavalry. Follow with your own Hippikon, and Arkantos, and attack any Trojan units assaulting Ajax directly (see Figure 6.5). If Ajax dies, the mission ends immediately in failure. A new objective appears once all the Trojan cavalry perish.

⊕ **New Objective:** Bring Arkantos and your army to Ajax's Town Center to the southwest.

Ajax's camp is revealed on the mini-map just southwest of your current position. Move your entire army into Ajax's camp to receive the next objective.

⊕ **New Objective:** Build up a stronger army and destroy all the buildings in the Trojan forward military base area.

Figure 6.5 *Assist Ajax quickly by attacking any Trojan cavalry near him. Save Ajax or fail in your mission!*

The Trojan outpost Town Center appears on your mini-map in the northeastern corner of the map. Scan your new town and locate villagers adjacent to various resources. Put villagers to work collecting wood. Build a Granary and research Husbandry to quicken the pig fattening process (the town has several pig pens). You also can spot the area south of your town to discover a donkey caravan trading with Agamemnon's Town Center—this provides extra gold for your town. Hunt deer south and north of town (on the hill) for your initial food source. Your new town contains plenty of living quarters but lacks military structures and Tower upgrades. As soon as possible, upgrade your Towers to Watch Towers to aid in town defense, and construct a Military Academy, Archery Range, Armory, Stable, and Temple. Produce six to eight more villagers as food becomes available. Use these additional villagers on your biggest resource needs, including favor, gained by worshiping at the Temple. Once you have depleted your food sources, build farms surrounding your Town Center.

The Trojan outpost throws increasingly difficult armies at your town. Protect your settlement with plenty of Watch Towers, and spend what resources you must to acquire the Burning Oil Tower upgrade, so the structure can defend itself against close-quarter attacks. Continue to add to your army with mixed groups of infantry, archers, cavalry, and mythological units, and acquire various upgrades as resources become available.

TIP

Explore the area just east of your town to locate a small alcove containing a relic. To gain its bonus, place a Hero to garrison the relic in your Temple.

Monitor the area east of your town with scouts. You're warned that a team of Trojan villagers will attempt to build a Stable somewhere just outside your town's line of sight. Scouting and a couple of Towers on the eastern side of your base should eliminate the threat without consequence.

You'll likely need more gold, particularly if you plan to advance to the Mythic Age. Search the area north of your base to discover a cluster of gold mines. Build a couple of Towers north of the gold mines before you begin collecting resources. The Towers will eliminate any enemy threats in the area.

TIP

A small Trojan farming area can be found due north from your camp along the northern edge of the map. Eliminate the farmers and steal the farms for your own use. There are also several berry bushes nearby. Construct a Granary and begin foraging for the extra food.

You can choose to attack in the Heroic Age or continue gathering resources (while effectively defending your town) and advance to the Mythic Age. Select Hera upon advancing to the Mythic Age and gain her Lightning Storm god power. Lightning Storm's ability to decimate an enemy army could provide the upper hand in the mission's climactic battle. Following up Lightning Storm with Dionysus' power of Bronze adds a powerful one-two punch.

Assemble an assault team of 15–20 infantry (predominately Hoplites to counter Trojan cavalry), 12–15 Hippikon, 12–15 Toxotes, and several mythological units, including Minotaurs, Hydra, and (thank Hera!) Medusa. Don't forget to spend resources on military upgrades to improve the offensive and defensive capabilities of your troops.

There are several routes into the Trojan outpost. One way is to head due north from your base and follow the northern area of the map toward the outpost. This route is tougher—there are more Trojan defenses to combat. You could also head north just before the gate and discover a small back entrance; it's a hill overlooking the town, perfect for Petroboli. Finally, also consider moving east from your Town Center until you find the small valley just south of the Trojan outpost. A group of villagers gather in front of a gate that leads directly to the Trojan outpost.

Expect a heavy counterattack to any route you take. Use Hera's Lightning Storm to bombard the Trojan army. Use Athena's Restoration (available from the beginning of the mission) to regenerate your troops during the battle. Position Minotaurs and Hydras near the front lines to pummel the gate and intercept any Trojan forces that emerge.

Once inside the gate, use the god power Bronze to enhance your human units' armor. Avoid the Fortress just north of the Trojan Town center until you've moved siege weapons into position. Beware of Poseidon's militia, which appear at destroyed buildings. Destroying all Trojan forward base structures completes your mission.

I Hope This Works

Initial Objective

◈ Accumulate 1,000 wood to build the Trojan Horse.

TIP

A large supply of food can be found within the rubble of Troy in the southern corner of the map. Navigate through the main gate and head south. Several Towers guard this route, however; safely maneuvering your villagers into the ruins will prove very difficult. Send at least six if you plan to just scurry beyond the Towers. At the southern end, you'll find a herd of cows and goats. Build a Granary and start collecting additional food.

Map Highlights

You begin on the western side of the map. The intimidating city of Troy can be found on the eastern side of the map. There are three gold mines around your base camp—two to the north and one to the south. A search of the area north of your town will reveal an additional food source, a herd of deer. Search the area around your initial start position for a hidden relic.

Battle Plans

This is a unique mission, because it is possible to complete it without significant base building or bolstering of your military numbers. So far, Troy is unaware of your plans to build a huge horse and sneak a small force into the city.

Trojan scouts, however, roam throughout the area. If a scout spots the Trojan Horse, the unit will head back to Troy to alert the military to your presence. You must kill any such scouts before they can reach the city, or you will have to defend your town against Trojan attack. If you can stop every scout who attempts to intervene, you can build the Trojan Horse undetected and complete the mission without the need for a military force. The Trojan scouts are Hetairoi, which are slower than the normal Kataskopos scout. However, the Hetairoi are stronger in battle

The faster you can collect 1,000 wood and build the Trojan Horse, the better. You begin, however, with only three villagers. Send them immediately to the goats just north of your Town Center and begin collecting food to fund additional villagers. Select the Town Center and produce four additional villagers immediately (using up available food) and set their gather point at the trees near the storehouse just east of the Town Center. Troy invokes the Forest Fire god power on the thicker woodlands west of your Town Center.

Continue to produce more villagers as food continues to come in from the goats. Send them to chop wood. If you aren't collecting food fast enough to maintain constant villager flow, send one or two villagers to assist in the slaughtering of goats.

You are provided with four Prodromos at the beginning of the mission. Split them into two groups of two. Position one group in the clearing north of your Town Center and another group in the clearing east of your Town Center. Spread them out a bit to maximize your line of sight, and monitor the mini-map carefully. As soon as you spot a red blip, toggle the correct grouping of Prodromos and attack the scout. You should also support with your Heroes. Your Prodromos will take damage from the scouts, so it may be necessarily to build additional units to keep the Trojan Horse undetected. If an emergency arises—an enemy scout escapes your Prodromos and begins to return to the enemy base—use a god power to eliminate the unit.

Continue to produce villagers, and assign them to collect wood (though save food for the Hand Axe improvement). It's viable to assign as many as 80% of your villagers to that task. Hunt the deer north of the Town Center (there are more deer southeast of town but it's safer to hunt the northern herd) and pick berries in the bushes to the northwest. Explore the far northern corner of the map to discover more deer and some goats. Spend food on more villagers, especially after the Trojan Horse begins construction.

If you're countering the scouts, additional military units are unneeded. You do lack vital military structures, however: If you are detected, you must immediately build a Military Academy, Archery Range, Stable, and Temple to produce combat units. It also would be wise to use the wood stores to build defensive Towers (and upgrade them) to help protect the city. You could consider producing some military units even if you haven't been spotted. Order these military units to assist the Heroes in intercepting Trojan scouts.

Once you collect the total of 1,000 wood, a new objective appears. Don't consider assaulting Troy. The purpose of the mission is to build the Trojan Horse to sneak into Troy. Attacking Troy would result in heavy casualties and likely make the mission impossible, or at minimum much harder, to complete.

New Objective: Build the Trojan Horse.

> TIP
>
> *If you build a Temple, purchase the Olympic Parentage upgrade, which gives your Heroes more hit points. These Heroes will be the units hiding inside the Trojan Horse and invading Troy. They'll need to fight, and the extra hit points could prove invaluable in combat.*

Completing the Trojan Horse automatically finishes the base-building portion of the mission. It's to your advantage to finish building this equine troop-transport as quickly as possible. Order all or most of your villagers to assist in the construction of the horse. Depending on your need (for instance, you might be producing military units to aid in defense), you may need to leave some villagers on food, wood, or gold. But the more villagers you have assisting in the construction of the Horse, the faster the transport will be built (see Figure 6.6).

As soon as the villagers complete the Trojan Horse, a cut-scene reveals the completed covert transport. Arkantos, Ajax, and Odysseus automatically board the horse and order Agamemnon to pull back and wait until nightfall. After sneaking the Trojan Horse inside Troy, Arkantos, Ajax, and Odysseus will open the southern gate to open a passage for Agamemnon's reinforcements. Night falls and a new objective appears as the three Heroes disembark from the Trojan Horse, now safely inside Troy's city walls.

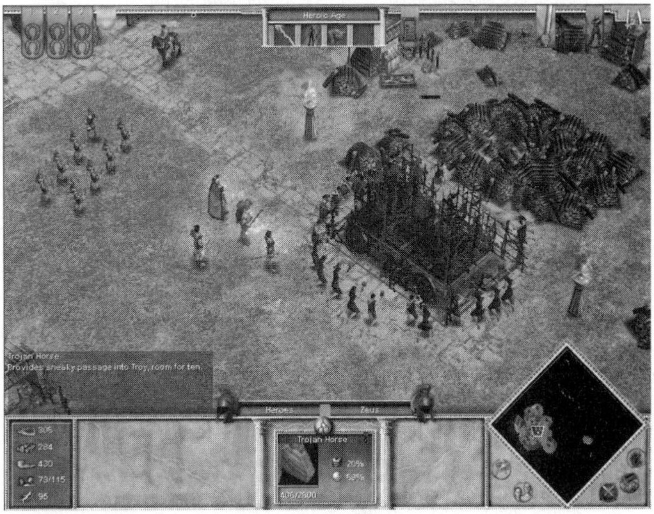

Figure 6.6 *Time is of the essence! Put all or most of your villagers to work on the Trojan Horse.*

New Objective: Sneak your Heroes through Troy toward the Trojan Gate and find a way to destroy it.

Group Arkantos, Ajax, and Odysseus together and cautiously move south. If you've saved your god powers, use them (especially Bolt) against the mythological creatures you will encounter in Troy. Move slowly to the south until you spot the patrol, led by a Trojan Cyclops. A new objective appears.

New Objective: Avoid being seen by the Trojan patrols.

Don't attack the Cyclops patrol. Wait for the patrol to head west and through the gate. Continue south until you reach an intersection patrolled by a Colossus. You can invoke Bolt against the Colossus, or just wait for the creature to patrol west and out of the way. A new objective appears when you reach the intersection.

New Objective: Kill the Cyclops guard to capture the Siege Towers.

Just east of the path, two Trojan Cyclops guards protect four Helepoli. Your Heroes can handle the two Cyclops rather easily. If they need assistance, invoke the Bolt god power to defeat one of the monsters.

New Objective: Use the Helepolis Towers to destroy the Gate of Troy.

Group the Siege Towers and continue south toward the south gate. Order the Siege Towers to attack the gate. Some enemy units attempt to defend the area. Use your Heroes to protect the Towers from counterattack, and Watch out for the Colossus you bypassed at the intersection. When the south gate falls, a new objective appears, along with Agamemnon's huge reinforcement party.

◈ **New Objective:** The gate is down, use Agamemnon's reinforcements to destroy three Trojan Fortresses.

The Gods reward your invasion of Troy with a gift: two uses of the god power Meteor. The Petroboli can make short work of the Fortresses, so consider using Meteor on any remaining Troy defenders, especially those guarding the two Fortresses to the west of the main gate.

Agamemnon's massive group of reinforcements may be difficult to control at first. The most important unit in the group comprises the Petroboli, which can knock out the Trojan Fortresses rather quickly. Apart from the Petroboli, the reinforcement party includes Hypaspists (to use against Hoplites), Hoplites (for use against cavalry), and several Colossuses. Protect the Petroboli and captured Helopoli with the bulk of the reinforcements.

Two Trojan Fortresses can be found west of the main gate. The third is located on the eastern side of the city. Group the siege weapons and maneuver within range of the Fortresses. Protect the Petroboli with Agamemnon's reinforcements and your Heroes. The mission ends with success once all three Fortresses have been destroyed.

More Bandits

Initial Objective

◈ Bring Arkantos and Ajax to the prison area to rescue the hostages.

Map Highlights

You begin along the southern edge of the map. The Ioklos hostages are to the northwest. A bandit wall lies to the north of your start position so it would be wise to heed what the Ioklos villager reports and use the western road. You can find three unclaimed settlements on the map—one in the northwest, a second in the map's center, and a third just beyond the wall north of your start position. An important Ioklos fortress can be found in the southeastern corner of the map.

Battle Plans

When you gain control of Arkantos and Ajax, an Ioklos villager approaches your position and suggests taking the western road toward the hostages. Follow his suggestion and maneuver your Heroes toward the west. A couple of Spearmen will engage your Heroes along the path—these troops should provide little challenge for Arkantos and Ajax. Face a couple groups of Wadjet as you continue toward the prison area. Defeat them all before continuing down the path.

Follow the road northwest and arrive at the prison area, guarded by another Wadjet. Defeat the mythological unit and approach the Centaur hostages enclosed in the pen. The

Centaurs reveal the location of more prisoners as well as Chiron and provide a new mission objective.

◈ **New Objective**: Defeat the bandits guarding the prison to free the prisoners.

Head northeast toward the new location revealed on the mini-map. There are many enemy Spearmen guards patrolling the area around this adjacent prison. You'll even find

Search the eastern side of the prison area for a relic. Grab this relic with a Hero and save it for the Temple you'll convert later in the mission. When you can train units later in the mission, check to see what your relic enhances and consider producing that unit type!

a Wadjet or two attacking the Ioklos houses and militia. Defeat all of the enemy Spearmen in this prison area to free the next set of prisoners. When you save fleeing militia, they become converted to your cause and under your control. A new objective appears after rescuing these prisoners.

◈ **New Objective**: Destroy the enemy Watch Towers and Barracks.

You also receive access to two Military Academies upon rescuing the prisoners. If you wish to add additional troops to your army (you have resources now), select Hypaspists, which are counter-infantry unit and effective against these bandit Spearmen. You're also given a Helepolis Siege Tower. Use it against the bandit gate south of the prison then start advancing to the map's revealed center—that's where the Watch Tower and Barracks are.

Head southeast into the map's center. Combat the bandit Spearmen and Anubites with your now impressive army. Order the Helepolis to assault the Tower adjacent to the enemy Barracks. The bandits, worshippers of Set, won't sit back and allow you to topple their structures. Expect more Spearmen, Slingers, a Pharaoh, and converted animals to assault your army from the northeast. Intercept them while the Helepolis crushes the Tower, walls, and enemy Barracks. After toppling both the Tower and the Barracks, a new objective appears and a new location appears on the mini-map.

◈ **New Objective**: Destroy the enemy Watch Tower and Barracks.

There's another Tower and Barracks complex to the east that's waiting to be destroyed. You've now converted several Ioklos structures, including Archery Ranges, Stables, Armory, and a Temple. Your coffers are also filled with resources.

It's time to start producing some units. Add Hippikon, more Centaurs, and Hydra to your army. You could also train Toxotes and Peltasts depending on need and desires. Don't forget the Military Academies back at the prison area (the Hypaspists are valuable against the Spearmen) or the Armory—you can research its technologies to improve your units' attack and armor.

Attack the eastern gate with the Helepolis and Hydra. Defeat these units from bandit counter attack with your formidable army. Continue east taking the lower route toward the Tower and Barracks complex. Counter the enemy Slingers with either Peltasts or Hippikon. Support your attacks with your Centaurs (upgrade them to Polemarches if you have the resources).

Don't forget your god powers! Zeus, Hermes, and Dionysus have provided Bolt, Cease Fire, and Bronze. Use Bolt to instantly terminate a single enemy unit; invoke Cease Fire to provide extra time to train reinforcements to defend against an attack; and cast Bronze during your final assault on the Migdol Stronghold at the end of the mission.

Maneuver the Helepolis to the Watch Tower and Barracks and begin your assault. Maintain defense of the area by intercepting any incoming bandit attackers. When the two structures fall, a new objective appears.

◈ **New Objective**: Destroy the Migdol Stronghold to free Chiron.

A new location appears on your mini-map: The bandit Migdol Stronghold guarding the

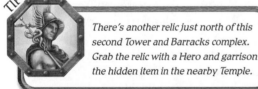

captured Chiron. After toppling the Tower and enemy Barracks, more resources are added to your reserves. Also, the Ioklos structures in the area are converted to your side. Search east for a Fortress, southeast for a Market and more military structures, and northeast for even more military structures.

Enemies are assaulting the area. Intercept them with your army and start producing new units. Train two or three Petroboli from the Fortress; more Centaurs and Hydras from the Temple; and additional Hippikon and Hypaspists from the Stable and Military Academy (see Figure 6.7).

You can advance toward the Migdol Stronghold from either a left or right side route. An elevated Tower defends the right route, though it's possible to eliminate this structure with Petroboli. Choose either

Figure 6.7 *Your siege weapons provide the punch you'll need to invade the bandit base and rescue Chiron. Guard them well!*

route, just don't advance your army until your Petroboli have toppled all Towers and gates.

A fierce counterattack arrives as you begin bombarding the Towers and walls near the Migdol Stronghold. Invoke Bronze to help protect your human units. Keep the siege weaponry targeted on Towers and the Migdol Stronghold while your other units combat the

bandit Anubites, Slingers, and Spearmen. Send your Heroes, mythological and human units to rampage through the bandit town while your siege weapons finish off the Towers and Migdol Stronghold. The mission concludes in victory when the Migdol Stronghold falls and Chiron is rescued.

> **TIP**
> There's another relic just north of this second Tower and Barracks complex. Grab the relic with a Hero and garrison the hidden item in the nearby Temple.

Bad News

Initial Objective

◈ Build up Ajax and Arkantos' bases and fight your way to the mine.

Map Highlights

Your forces begin in two locations—on the western and eastern sides of the map, with a rugged mountain between them. It's impossible to combine the forces until much later in the mission. Resources vary on the two sides of the mountain, so it's important to scout quickly to discover them. The western side offers goats near the Town Center and berries south and northwest of the Town Center. You'll also find two gold mines in the southern corner of the west side and another to the northwest. Gather food and gold from the western side. On the eastern side, the large forest in the southern corner promises a steady supply of wood.

> **TIP**
>
> Gargarensis isn't enthused about your invasion of these mines and will invoke the Meteor god power as you begin to advance north. Spread out structures and farms as much as possible and keep buildings and gatherers away from your Town Centers. After the attack, shift units back toward your Town Center to combat the Cyclops dropped by Gargarensis' Roc transport.

Battle Plans

As your mission begins, your forces find themselves on two sides of the map—the western and eastern sides of the southern corner. Arkantos and Chiron occupy the eastern side; Ajax commands in the west. Your first task should be to begin collecting resources on both sides. Each side possesses its own riches, so it's important to scout out the entire area before deciding how to use your villagers.

The western side boasts the more plentiful food and gold resources: Goats surround your Town Center, and berry bushes can be found just to the south and to the northwest. A search of the southern corner will reveal two separate gold mines and exploring the northwestern corner reveals another. Use villagers to begin foraging the bushes (research Husbandry to quicken the fattening rate of your domesticated animals). Produce additional villagers on this side to quicken food collection, which in turn will fund more villagers for gold mining. The eastern side boasts the more plentiful wood resource—search the southwestern corner of the area for a large forest. Build a Storehouse near the forest and begin wood collection. Gather these resources and advance to the Heroic Age within 10 minutes if possible (make sure you construct the Armory). The sooner the better, because better units and upgrades become available when you advance.

You have a difficult choice—to worship Dionysus or Apollo—when you advance to the Heroic Age. Dionysus' Bronze god power can be saved until the final attack. Further, the Hydra can attack multiple enemy units at once. However, Apollo's Underground Passage can be used (in conjunction with a Pegasus scout) to circumvent enemy gates.

The two sides differ not only in resources, but also in their needs for specific defenses. On the western side, the enemy periodically attacks with Hoplites, a Hero, and siege weapons. Defend this side by first building—and upgrading as resources become available—defensive Towers facing the enemy gate. Secondly, produce Hypaspists at the Military Academy and mythological units (such as the Minotaur) at the Temple. The Hypaspists counter the enemy's infantry, and the mythological units should assist. Research improvements, such as Athena's Aegis Shield, line and Armory upgrades. Make sure you order some units to destroy incoming siege weapons before they can inflict significant damage.

On the eastern side, the enemy periodically throws Toxotes and siege weapons into the fray. As in the west, defend the gate entrance with upgraded defensive Towers. Build a stable and produce Hippikon to counter the enemy archers. Use at least one Hippikon to intercept any incoming siege weapon before it can begin bombardment of your defensive Towers.

Continue to produce these fighting units for their respective sides even as your divided armies advance toward the mine fortresses.

To simplify the assault, it's easier to advance first on one side, then the other. Attempting to advance both sides at the same time could become difficult to handle. Just make sure you have established Towers and ample defensive units on one side while you advance toward the mine fortresses on the other. Advancing on either side becomes easier with the assistance of siege weaponry. Make sure both sides contain a Fortress to produce siege weapons; build three to five to assist each advance. For the sake of this walkthrough, let's advance the western side first.

On the western side, destroy the gate north of your base with siege weapons, then send your Hippikon through. Level the Towers and military structures just outside your base with siege weapons. An enemy Fortress stands on a hill just to the north. You can assault with Petroboli or send your western forces up the hill to topple the structure. You can also assault other units from this hill; for instance, leave Petroboli there or send Toxotes or Peltasts to stand ground on the edge. Look for other opportunities to do this throughout the mission as you weave units back and forth through the map's central paths.

Don't forget to build a Market and continue heavy resource gathering so you can eventually advance to the Mythic Age. Choosing to worship Hera after you advance adds the powerful Lightning Storm god power to your arsenal. Save Lightning Storm for the final push against the mine fortresses.

Continue northeast and use your siege weaponry to eliminate another military structure and more walls and gates. Continue east and Arkantos spots an enemy Fortress and an opportunity. Level the Fortress and you can link up your forces. Topple the Fortress with Petroboli.

Search the western side of the map for a hill containing a hidden relic. Garrison the relic in your Temple using a Hero.

On the eastern side, use siege weapons to eliminate the gate north of your camp. Follow the path around to the northwest and level the two military structures and discover you're just south of the Fortress. Start pummeling a gate and Towers east of your position until you've leveled the enemy Fortress and the wall blocking access to both sides.

Continue east and level more military structures. Protect your siege weaponry well! Don't forget that since Gargarensis is worshipping Poseidon, militia will appear at destroyed buildings. Topple the two Towers nearby and head north along the eastern side of the map. You've now spotted two unclaimed settlements nearby. Consider advancing a few villagers to build Town Centers here. There are food sources near (pig and deer), and you can regroup and rebuild your army here before pressing onward to the mine fortresses.

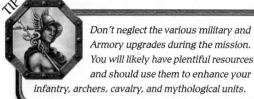

Don't neglect the various military and Armory upgrades during the mission. You will likely have plentiful resources and should use them to enhance your infantry, archers, cavalry, and mythological units.

With your combined forces, level the enemy's structures south of the mine fortresses. Protect your siege weaponry carefully, using your cavalry and infantry troops. Use your god powers—including Athena's healing Restoration—during this final stretch. Order the siege weapons against the mine fortresses. Once both collapse, your mission ends in success.

Missions 9-16 Walkthrough

Arkantos breaches the Underworld by defeating the villains who defend the mine leading under the Earth. The Underworld offers new mysteries and new allies, the haunting Shades. Soon, after carving a path out of the Underworld, Arkantos and his fellow warriors find themselves lost in the desert—but with a new acquaintance, Amanra. You and Arkantos must assist Amanra, an Egyptian Hero, in her battles with Kemsyt to gain an ally against the greater evils lurking in the land.

This chapter covers mission walkthroughs for single-player missions nine through 16 of the Age of Mythology. Beginning with mission 10, Arkantos finds himself allied with Egyptian gods and Heroes. You will no longer use Greek units and technologies or worship Greek gods. Instead, study up on the Egyptians, (see Chapter 4 of this strategy guide) and use their assets to defend yourself against the nefarious Kemsyt and Gargarensis.

Revelation

Initial Objective

◈ Destroy the ram before it breaks down the gate.

Map Highlights

You begin on the western side of the map. Your three Heroes—Arkantos, Ajax, and Chiron—overlook the giant siege ram, which is positioned in the valley below, on the north-western side of the map. Friendly reinforcements arrive from the southwestern corner of the map, while the enemy is being reinforced through three separate tunnels on the eastern side of the map. It's possible to restrict the enemy's passage through one of these tunnels.

Battle Plans

Immediately select your three Heroes—Arkantos, Ajax, and Chiron—on the western edge of the map. Move them south to rendezvous with the first batch of friendly reinforcements, a group of Hoplites and Centaurs. Advance the entire group south with the Heroes in the lead. You'll face Cyclops and Manticores on the way down to the ram. Attack with the Heroes in first; let these warriors absorb the damage because they're tougher against mythological beasts and can regenerate their strength even if they're killed.

Split your troops into two groups: send your three Heroes to the siege ram to battle the Manticores, Chimera, and Ballistae guarding the ram. Invoke Bolt on one of the enemy units should your Heroes struggle, but certainly save the god power if at all possible. Send your second battle group, the Hoplites and Centaurs, to the closest tunnel on the eastern side of the map (the southern-most tunnel of the three). A large boulder rests against the wall at the tunnel's mouth. Assault the boulder with your units; destroying the boulder causes it to fall and block the tunnel. Clear out any any units before attacking the boulder.

> **TIP**
>
> You are given four god powers at the mission's start: Bolt, Restoration, Bronze, and Lightning Storm. Save them as long as possible! Use Lightning Storm against large groups of human warriors. Invoke Bronze to protect your own mortal soldiers in a tough battle. Monitor the health of your units and cast Restoration when many are on the brink of death. Invoke Bolt to terminate a tough enemy unit, such as a Cyclops or Chimera.

After knocking down the boulder, send the Hoplites and Centaurs to the next tunnel just north of your position and repeat the task. There's a second boulder here that can block the central tunnel. Clear out enemy units first then assault the boulder. Use your next group of reinforcements to aid this group in finishing off the boulder. New enemies will arrive from the top tunnel, which can't be blocked. Instead of intercepting these new enemies, remain at the siege ram and fight the enemy arrivals only when they appear in your line of sight near the great door (see Figure 7.1). Continually monitor the western side of the map for new reinforcement arrivals. Once both boulders are blocking the two tunnels, send all new reinforcements immediately to the ram.

It's important to select your own newly arrived reinforcements—an assortment including Ballistae, Hippikon, Toxotes, Hoplites, and Centaurs—as quickly as possible, and to order them to move to and attack the siege ram. By moving your troops to the area and intercepting enemies only when they reach the siege ram, you can eliminate enemy reinforcements and then quickly get back to attacking the siege ram.

Another threat arrives during the mission: Enemy villagers appear and start repairing the siege ram. You can attack the villagers as they approach, or wait until they surround and begin repairing the ram, then invoke Lightning Storm to obliterate the entire group. Don't wait too long, however: A large group of villagers can fix the ram very quickly. Wipe them out before too much repairing can be done. Don't hesitate to use remaining god powers, particularly Restoration and Bronze, as the enemy's attacks become greater. If the ram breaks down the door, the mission immediately ends in failure. Destroy the ram to complete the mission in victory.

Figure 7.1 *Maintain an aggressive attack on the siege ram. Wait until enemy reinforcements arrive at the ram before you disengage and intercept.*

Strangers

Initial Objective

◈ Seek the Shades.

> *Careful exploration of the map reveals several ally units, which will fight for your cause. You'll find a Nemean Lion at the end of a narrow path north of the southern tunnel and three Medusae stand at the end of a path just south of the northern tunnel.*

Map Highlights

Your troops start in the far southern corner. At the mission's start, fog of war shrouds the entire map in darkness. The Shades encountered in the mission's introductory cinematic can be found just to the west of your start position. After you find the Shades, three shrines and relics will appear on the eastern side of the map. You must acquire these relics and move them to the temples in the northwestern corner of the map. Additional Shades and god powers can be acquired through painstaking exploration of alcoves and side routes.

Battle Plans

You begin with three Heroes—Arkantos, Ajax, and Chiron—and a group of Hoplites and Toxotes. You also have a single god power at your disposal, Zeus' Bolt. Assign each unit type to a group, keeping a Hero in front of each group to take the brunt of the enemy damage (because Heroes have more hit points and can regenerate their strength). Head west from your start position to locate the Shades.

◈ **New Objective**: Scout forward. Shades are invisible to enemy units and can see farther than your other units.

A new objective appears after locating the first Shade. Select the Shade and scout him forward along the path until the next objective appears.

◈ **New Objective**: Kill the Minotaur. A Shade vanishes when it steals the soul of an enemy unit.

An enemy Minotaur stands near a collection of ruins. Attack the Minotaur with the Shade unit. The Shade can instantly kill a single enemy unit. In doing so, the Shade disappears and that particular Shade can't be used any longer. After the Minotaur expires, two more Shades appear in the ruins and can be added to your groupings. A new objective appears and three locations are revealed on the mini-map.

◈ **New Objective:** Collect the three lost relics of Hades.

WARNING

Each Hero can carry only one relic at a time. With three relics to retrieve, you must keep your Heroes alive in order to complete the mission. Remember, when a Hero dies, simply eliminate all enemy presence around his corpse and occupy that territory with some units. The Hero will return to life with one hit point. Don't leave a Hero behind!

Add the two additional Shades to your attack groups. The Shades offer a unique attack that should be used wisely. First, they have a greater line of sight than your normal units, so it's wise to lead with a Shade to spot enemy units quickly. The enemy units can't see the Shades and won't auto-attack them. This permits safe reconnaissance of the upcoming areas. Secondly, the Shade's attack—although powerful—can be used only once. After the assault, the Shade vanishes permanently.

The Shade is most effective against mythological units and will kill foes in a single attack. Use the Shades sparingly, allowing your Heroes to fight most battles unless you're overwhelmed and need the added firepower. Put your Shades in their own attack group and use them sparingly in battle (see Figure 7.2). When you need a Shade attack, select one at a time and destroy a worthy target.

Continue following the rocky path around to the north. You'll gain a couple more Shades in nearby ruins. Continue north and engage the group of Wadjets. Your Heroes should be able to handle the

Figure 7.2 *Use Shades wisely! Their powerful attack can get you out of a jam in a hurry!*

group easily so save your Shades for now. Break down the iron gate behind the Wadjets and tackle the enemy Manticore waiting on the other side. Keep your Toxotes safely at maximum range should they engage in the battle. Just beyond the gate is the River Styx. You can't use a ferry here so turn east and continue down the path. Lead with a Shade for maximum line of sight.

Just east a group of Medusa Matriarchs are gathered within a fiery circle. You can't attack these enemies at close range but can use Chiron, who possesses a greater range than the Medusae. Scout the area with a Shade, particularly south of the circle where you'll discover another Shade within some ruins. Add the new Shade to your group as Chiron eliminates the remaining Medusae.

The path forks slightly after the Medusae. The northern fork ends with Minotaur guards in front of an iron gate; the southern fork also ends with Minotaur guarding a gate but there are also a couple Shades nearby. Explore the southern fork with a Shade to acquire more of the undead units. Add them to your grouping. Kill the Minotaur with your Heroes and use a Shade if necessary. Bust through either fence and approach the relic just to the east. Grab the relic with any Hero. A new Shade appears in the ruins and grants the god power of Bronze as a reward.

Scout with a Shade east from the relic and discover a Temple of the Gods at the center of a circular pathway. A large group of Cyclops and Cyclops Elders patrol the circular path. Although it's possible to defeat the Cyclops with your Heroes and several Shades, it's best to time your advance to the east when the largest group of Cyclops is furthest away from your position. Wait until the Cyclops round the path toward the north and move your Heroes east. Attack the smaller group of Cyclops, which your Heroes can handle easily. Break down the gate and continue onward. Remember that the Cyclops can't see the Shades!

Search the path southeast from the first relic to uncover another Shade.

Several Mummies guard this path just south of the second relic. Eliminate the Mummies with your Heroes or use Shades to assist. Keep your human units safely away from the Mummies. Explore an alcove south of the Mummies for another Shade. Break down the iron gate to the north. Cross the path over the River Styx to locate the second relic. Grab the second relic to receive a Restoration god power. Beware of Crocodiles of Set emerging from the River Styx! Search west of the relic for another Shade.

Another Shade can be found on the northern side of the Cyclops' circular path.

Continue north along the narrow path until you reach the edge of the River Styx. Charon will ferry you across the river and warns of creatures beneath the waves (a Kraken is revealed on the mini-map). Charon is a Shade that can be added to your party and the ferry has an attack, which can be used against the Kraken.

Board the ferry and proceed south along the river. As you near the Kraken, more ferries appear to help defend your vessel against the Kraken. Retreat your transport away from the Kraken and use the other ferries to eliminate the beasts. After eliminating the Kraken, disembark your troops at the shore marked by the blue flags. Head northwest to locate a pen containing some friendly Centaurs. Destroy the gate enclosing the units. Add the Centaurs to your groupings.

Head west into the smoldering ruins. As you enter, Hades invokes the Plague of Serpents god power. Use your Heroes to eliminate the serpents and the Wadjet just before the fence.

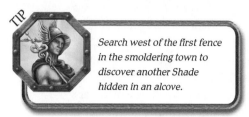

TIP

Search west of the first fence in the smoldering town to discover another Shade hidden in an alcove.

Break down the fence and continue north. Lead with your Heroes and engage remaining serpents and Wadjets. Follow the path through the town around to the north—the final relic is found here inside a circular formation of pillars. Groups of Wadjet and Medusae protect the relic. Eliminate these enemies with the help of Shades. Grab the relic and gain another god power—Zeus grants a Lightning Storm (see Figure 7.3).

◈ **New Objective**: Bring the three relics to the Temple complex.

Scout with a Shade to the west. Follow the narrow path toward the complex. Take the first path to the north to uncover a Minotaur guarding more Shades. Eliminate the Minotaur with a Shade or your Heroes and then add the rescued Shades to your group.

You'll enter a wide clearing with rotted trees, wolves, and ruins scattered throughout. Stay away from the trees—Hades invokes the Forest Fire god power on them. Search alcoves to the northwest, west, and southeast for additional Shades. Use your Heroes to attack the wolves and any present mythological units.

Proceed west through the burning forest. Take the first southern path and battle the series of Minotaur, Cyclops, and Hydra guards with your Heroes and Shades. Don't forget about your god powers! Break down the western fence that encloses the Temple complex. Approach the Temple complex with all three relics to complete the mission in victory.

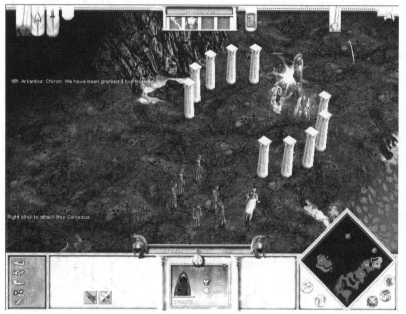

Figure 7.3 *Gain god powers from recovering relics and more Shades by searching alcoves and alternate routes.*

The Lost Relic

Initial Objective

◈ Defend against attacks from the three canyons long enough for your villagers to dig out the artifact.

Map Highlights

Amanra's village occupies the bulk of the map. Your Heroes—Arkantos, Ajax, and Chiron—begin in the center of the map with several Hoplites, Toxotes, and Slingers at their disposal. Three walls, guarding Amanra's village from the followers of Set, lie to the north within three separate valleys. There are several resource areas within the village. Food gathering (Mmmm. Zebras!) can be found to the east; a gold mine lies near the village's center; and wood is being gathered to the west. You are unable to produce more laborers (villagers) during the course of the mission, so they must be put to good use. Locate the mission objective—the excavation—just south of the gold mine.

Battle Plans

Because you can't produce more laborers (Egyptian villagers) during the course of the mission, you must decide wisely how best to utilize the ones you have. You must balance the usual tasks—resource gathering and village defense—with excavating the relic. The mission ends as soon as you excavate the relic. The more laborers you assign to the excavation, the faster the process will go.

This is your first defense-focused mission. You won't need to concentrate heavily on gathering food if you plan to bunker yourself in by building walls (which require gold) and Towers (which require gold and wood) within the three entrances to your base. The enemy's advance will be strong, however. It would be unwise to forgo food gathering completely, because you'll need to produce reinforcement units. Concentrate initially on wood and gold. Then, once defenses have been erected, shift to food so you can create ground troops to counter any enemy attacks that slip through your fortifications.

As the mission progresses, the enemy's attacks become stronger. Therefore, it's important to complete the mission as soon as you possibly

> **TIP**
>
> Instead of simply erecting more Towers, consider adding new layers to your walls. Adding more walls (at the expense of gold) forces the enemy to knock down a segment of each one before they can advance. This slows them down and also alerts you to their presence, enabling you to mount a counterattack. Keep replacing destroyed walls and add multiple layers of walls!

can. To do so, order every available villager to excavate the relic. After setting up a strong defense (as described throughout this mission walkthrough), shift villagers to the dig. Monitor your villagers carefully and send any who are idle to the relic. Use excess food supplies to produce more villagers to excavate the relic.

Immediately divide your Toxotes and Slingers into three groups and position them along the three walls to aid in initial defense. The enemy begins attacking with infantry, which your Slingers and Toxotes can handle easily. After approximately 10 minutes, however, the enemy attacks with Slingers and Catapults, which stand well out of range of your archers. You also can move a laborer up to each wall and erect additional Towers, but those will soon fall to the Catapults, which remain out of range. If you plan on building Towers, keep a few ground units nearby to counter the Catapult. You might also want to use laborers to repair damaged Towers. Should any wall fall, quickly maneuver your Axemen and Slingers to intercept invaders, then bolster their defense.

You begin the mission with two god powers, which you'll almost certainly need to use during the mission to win. Plague of Serpents summons a group of serpents to help defend an area from attack. The serpents won't pursue enemies but will remain until killed. Prosperity

Figure 7.4 *Crowd the valley paths with walls and Towers to slow the enemy advance.*

doubles the rate of gold collection—alas, for a short period of time. Use it at any point during the mission to add additional gold to your coffers. Maximize its effectiveness by sending most of your laborers to mine gold before you invoke the god power. Be sure to research Pick Axe at the Mining Camp to increase gold-gathering rate.

You also could advance into the valleys toward the followers of Set and build walls to throw multiple blocks in their paths. To further complicate their advancement toward Amanra's village (see Figure 7.4), fortify the area with additional Towers.

Should your defenses fail, you're going to need some additional ground units. Shift laborers to food gathering. Build a couple of Barracks and an Armory and upgrade your Axemen and Slingers. (Build more if necessary.) Slingers are generally more useful because they can stay behind the walls. However, you may need some Axemen to attack the siege weapons, especially if the Heroes fall.

You also should build a Temple, which can produce the Egyptian Priest unit used to heal wounded soldiers. This Priest also creates obelisks, each of which enhances line of sight in its area. Use Priests to build obelisks at all three valley entrances to monitor incoming units. You also can build Egyptian monuments, which are used to gain favor with the gods—favor that can be spent on mythological units and upgrades. Anubites are extremely effective mythological units against the attackers.

Amanra's village also contains a Market, which could be used in a pinch to purchase food or wood, or to sell either resource for more gold. For instance, use the Market should you need a quick infusion of gold to fund more walls or Towers.

If it becomes necessary, thorough exploration reveals some additional food sources and gold mines in the area. You'll discover crocodile, crowned crane, and more zebras in the southern corner of the map. Another gold mine can be found to the far west, near another food source—a couple of giraffes.

Select the Egyptian Granary and acquire the Flood of the Nile upgrade. This causes the Nile River to provide free food, which slowly trickles into your coffers.

Once you're comfortable with your defense, move laborers off of resource gathering and put them on excavation duty. Defend the town from attack and excavate the relic to complete the mission.

Even if the enemies breach one of the walls, you can still make a stand near the excavation. Often, you can just finish the excavation even if your town is filled with enemy Spearmen. This scenario also adds quite a bit more troops on the harder levels, including plenty of siege weapons and Scarabs. Some attacks are triggered by time, and others by the percentage complete on the excavation, so just digging as fast as you can doesn't help—you still must deal with those enemy attackers! The mission ends in failure if all laborers die or the excavation is destroyed.

Light Sleeper

Initial Objective

◈ Kill the guards watching over the villagers mining gold.

Map Highlights

You begin in the northern corner of the map, where you lack the military power to tackle Kemsyt's defenses. The Guardian lies southeast of your position but you can't travel directly there. Instead, explore toward the southwest, where a friendly people, the Sepa, have been enslaved by Kemsyt. To receive the assistance you need to escort the Sword Bearer to the Guardian, you must assist the Sepa.

Battle Plans

The mission begins with little hope: You must escort the Sword Bearer to the Guardian, positioned southeast of you. To reach the Guardian, however, you must pass through hostile territory under the thrall of Kemsyt. You'll need help if you are to succeed in your mission. Your Heroes—Arkantos, Ajax, Chiron, and Amanra—begin with Chariot Archers and Slingers.

Amanra states that a nearby oasis village is loyal to Set. Within the settlement, however, are local laborers who were enslaved to mine gold for Kemsyt. Perhaps you can assist the enslaved laborers and hope they repay your generosity with assistance in toppling Kemsyt. Head west to discover the mining operation guarded by many enemy Spearmen, Slingers, and Anubites.

Attack the Spearmen with your Chariot Archers and Slingers. Use your Heroes to assault the enemy Slingers and Anubites. You can position the Chariot Archers and Slingers on top of the eastern hill overlooking the mining operation. This keeps them safe from counterattack but within range to inflict some heavy damage. After defeating the enemies, the Sepa take control of the mining operation and offer you their laborers (see Figure 7.5).

◈ **New Objective:** Bring at least five villagers safely to their Town Center.

Figure 7.5 *Liberate the Sepa and they'll help build an economy and town.*

Proceed south from the mining operation along the path flanked by the obelisks. Lead with your Heroes and follow closely with remaining Chariot Archer and Slingers. Keep the Sepa laborers and the Sword Bearer safely in the rear. You'll enter a winding path through Temples and ruins. A relic lies on the path; grab the relic with one of your Heroes. Keep your human units and Sword Bearer far in the rear— Mummies appear along this path! Defeat them with your Heroes.

Continue to the west and still keep all units other than Heroes out of the path. The god power Plague of Serpents is invoked on the path. Your Heroes will have little trouble combating the serpents but your laborers, Slingers, and Chariot Archers are vulnerable. Retreat any units other than Heroes back out of the path—the serpents won't follow. Eliminate all serpents then continue southwest out of the path. Beware of the crocodiles wading in the shallow water!

Escort the Sepa laborers to the southeast and into the village. Approach the Town Center with the laborers to receive your tribute reward and help from the Sepa people. The village comes under your control and a new objective appears.

◈ **New Objective:** Bring the Sword Bearers to the Guardian before Kemsyt's army reaches it.

This mission does have a time constraint: Kemsyt's army marches along the bottom and left side of the map, destroying Sepa villages in its wake. If you don't get to the Guardian quickly, Kemsyt will make it through all of the Sepa villages and engage your new base. Along with their assistance and Town Center, the Sepa also offer a sizable tribute of food, wood, and gold. The sleeping Guardian is revealed on the mini-map to the east. The defenses are great, however. It would be wise to construct siege weaponry to tackle the Towers while your ground units occupy other enemy units. Time is of the essence! Hurry and assess your base structures and available resources.

Scan your new village and immediately begin collecting resources. Start with the crowned cranes around the Town Center,

> **TIP**
>
> Since you are a faithful worshipper of the Egyptian god Ra, it's possible to produce Priests at the temple and empower other buildings. Produce several Priests and empower other resource centers and your Barracks. Priests also can heal wounded units, so it's wise to keep them near your defensive armies to mend wounds between battles.

then move some laborers on to the farms to the northwest. Other food sources can be found to the far west, including gazelle and giraffe. Locate gold mines to the east and southeast and nearby clumps of trees to the south, where you can begin wood collection. You can also fish the river north of the village.

Use initial food to train additional laborers to and divide them among food and gold to increase your collection rate of resources. You have plenty of wood at the beginning of the mission so concentrate first on food and gold collection. You already have a Temple, so train a couple Priests and use them to empower the resource camps.

The Sepa village also includes the Pharaoh, a unique Egyptian unit that can empower structures and cause them to work faster. For instance, if the Pharaoh empowers a Granary, the surrounding farmers complete their work more quickly. Use the Pharaoh to empower a building, depending on your resource needs. Ra also provides the Archaic Age god power Rain, which increases farm-gathering rates for a short period of time. Once all farms are occupied by farmers, invoke Rain to gain food quickly so you can advance to the Classical Age as fast as possible. You could also save Rain for the Classical Age after you've researched Plow—Rain will have an even greater effect then. At any rate, advance to the Classical Age at the earliest opportunity.

Upon advancement, your worshippers must choose between the Minor Gods Bast and Ptah. Bast offers the Eclipse god power, which boosts mythological speed and attack for a short period of time. Bast also provides several resource-gathering upgrades and the Sphinx mythological unit. Ptah provides the Shifting Sands god power, which can be used to teleport friendly or enemy units to another location—a trick particularly useful in removing some enemy units from a battle. Ptah also offers various military upgrades and the Wadjet mythological unit, a magical cobra that spits venom. In this walkthrough we chose Bast, for the Eclipse power to boost mythological units and the resource improvements.

After advancing, build a Barracks and Armory. Fortify your army with Spearmen and Axemen, and acquire their respective upgrades. Train Sphinx at the Temple if you worshipped Bast. Continue to build Monuments to gain favor even faster. Research Plow then Bast's Sacred Cats at the Egyptian Granary and invoke Rain if you haven't already done so. Research Hunting Dogs before hunting the giraffe and gazelle to the east.

Once an Armory is built (speed its construction with the help of an empowering Pharaoh) and you meet the necessary food and gold requirements, advance to the Heroic Age. You can choose to worship Hathor, who provides the Locust Swarm god power (which destroys enemy farms), a flying transport, upgrades to buildings and mercenaries, and the Petsuchos mythological unit. Or you could choose Sekhmet, who provides the citadel god power (which turns a Town Center into a defensive citadel), the mythological Scarab siege unit, and other upgrades to siege, Chariot Archers, and Slingers. We chose Sekhmet for the Scarab siege unit (see Figure 7.6) and the upgrades to Chariot Archers and siege weapons.

Figure 7.6 *Siege weaponry plays an integral role in the assault on Kemsyt's base. Worship Sekhmet for the Scarab unit.*

Upon reaching the Heroic Age, build a Siege Works (to produce Siege Towers) and a Migdol Stronghold (to produce Chariot Archers, Camelry, and Elephants). Build the Migdol Stronghold facing Kemsyt's terrain so the huge structure can serve as a defensive Tower. Add Towers here to because Kemsyt increases his attacks. Research Irrigation to improve farming and start shifting laborers off of gold and on to wood to fund creation of Chariot Archers and siege weapons. If you plan to advance to the Mythic Age or wish to trade resources, build a Market. Don't forget to upgrade your units at the Barracks and Armory as necessary.

Train a total of five siege units; use Catapults if you advanced to the Mythic Age. You'll need the siege weapons to bust down the gate, Towers, and Migdol Stronghold's protecting Kemsyt's eastern base. Support these units with Chariot Archers and Camelry (upgrade each at the Migdol Stronghold and Armory) and a mixture of mythological units, such as Bast's Sphinx. Advance the siege weapons east toward Kemsyt's gate (assault the lower gate, south of the hill). Guard your siege weapons carefully against counterattack. Topple nearby Towers before advancing toward the Guardian.

WARNING

The followers of Set can convert and control animals! Kemsyt will send converted hippos, hyenas, and other beasts into your base along with other military units! Don't think you were just given extra free food. Defend yourself against these hostile creatures!

A Migdol Stronghold protects the area just west of the Guardian statue. Crumble this structure with your siege weaponry. Counter the enemy's Chariot Archers with your Camelry and its mythological units with your Heroes and own myth units (use Eclipse before entering the base). Kemsyt's other military structures are found north of the Guardian. You can send the siege weapons up there or just intercept any newly trained units near the statue. Make sure your military structures back in the Sepa village are still training units. Set their gather points inside Kemsyt's base so these new units can reinforce your attack quickly.

Attack the gate enclosing the Guardian with your Catapults. Eliminate remaining units around the Guardian before sending in the Sword Bearers. When the Sword Bearers and Guardian meet, a new objective appears and the Guardian comes under your control.

◆ **New Objective:** Use the Guardian to destroy Kemsyt's army.

The Guardian is basically invincible and can easily eliminate Kemsyt's approaching army, which consists mainly of mythological units and War Elephants. You can support the

Guardian with your own remaining military or just let the Guardian hack and slash his way through Kemsyt's inferior forces. Move some Priests close to the Guardian; the Egyptian unit can heal the Guardian once you've sustained damage. The mission ends in victory once Kemsyt's returning army has been destroyed by the Guardian.

TIP

Isis' monuments protect Kemsyt's base from god power attack. Therefore, worship Osiris in the Mythic Age so you can use the Son of Osiris god power on your Pharaoh before venturing east. If you've saved Eclipse until this point, invoke just before entering Kemsyt's base.

Tug of War

Initial Objective

◆ Recover the Osiris piece cart and move it into your city before the enemy gets it to their city.

Map Highlights

Although your army (Heroes and a handful of troops) begins in the map's center, as does the Osiris piece cart, the cart is in enemy hands and your ability to produce more military units lies in the northern corner. A winding valley path separates that corner from the enemy's base in the south. Careful examination of the terrain reveals a shortcut. Ascend the hill dividing the path and hug the western edge of the map to shave time off your sprint to save the Osiris piece cart.

Battle Plans

Upon arrival, you don't have much time to survey the large northern base to discover its wealth of military structures. You have a near-unlimited supply of resources; don't bother concentrating on your gatherers—they'll collect plenty of food, wood, and gold to fund your reinforcements. This mission isn't about managing an economy, it's about cranking out a continuous stream of units and sending them straight to battle.

Three Barracks can be found on the western side of the base, and a couple of Migdol Strongholds rest in the back of the base. You'll discover a Temple, with three adjacent relics, on the eastern side of the base. It's possible to garrison these relics inside the Temple by using a nearby Pharaoh, which definitely should be done after queuing up your military units. Finally, you're carrying three god powers into this mission: Vision, Plague of Serpents, and Ancestors.

Immediately group the infantry standing in front of the northern base and click on the mini-map south of the captured Osiris piece cart. Shift your focus to your ambushed Heroes and invoke the Ancestors god power to assist in the fight (and Plague of Serpents if you wish). After the battle, group the remaining troops and follow the Osiris piece cart toward the enemy base (see Figure 7.7) or start escorting the piece cart toward your own base if your god powers were successful.

Figure 7.7 *Invoke the god power Ancestors as you send the first group of units to intercept the Osiris Part Cart.*

The enemy will send reinforcements—many, many reinforcements—to defend the cart. Expect to face squads of Camelry, Axemen, Spearmen, Slingers, and Chariot Archers. On harder difficulty levels, you're attacked more ferociously at the end, including some Anubite and Roc attacks (the air transport drops off some units).

You need more units quickly. Return your focus to the northern base and cue up a mix of infantry, Slingers, but most importantly Camelry and Chariot Archers, using the Barracks and Migdol Strongholds. Set all of these structures' gather points just south of the northern base so you don't have to escort groups of units from the northern base to the cart. You also could upgrade all of these units, though this would burn valuable build time (it's definitely advisable if you're in control of the cart at the time). Don't forget to select the Armory as well and research its upgrade.

Once you reclaim the cart, begin moving it back toward the northern base. Keep your units grouped just behind the cart to intercept enemies as they arrive. Invoke the Plague of Serpents or Ancestors (if saved from the ambush) god power to further slow and damage enemy attackers.

Periodically focus on the main base in the north and continue to produce military units to aid in the cart's defense. It's a fairly straightforward mission. Continue to produce units and send them to the front lines. You will suffer countless casualties at the hands of the enemy, but the Osiris piece cart is the only important element. Maneuver the piece cart back into the northern base to complete your mission in success.

> **TIP**
> Scouting the western and eastern sides of the map reveals two additional relics. You could retrieve these with a Hero or Pharaoh and return them to the temple, but you mustn't break your concentration on creating military units and sending them to retrieve or guard the Osiris cart.

> **TIP**
> Position your Heroes near the two cliffs flanking the path just south of your base. When the piece cart moves under these cliffs, Kemsyt invokes the Shifting Sands god power to teleport groups of Anubites onto the cliffs. The Anubites jump down with their leap attack and attempt to wrestle the cart from your control. Your Heroes can make quick work of these mythological units.

"Isis, hear My Plea"

Initial Objective

◈ Destroy Gargarensis' Migdol Stronghold.

Map highlights

You begin on the far eastern side of the map. You are without Arkantos, Ajax, and Chiron, who have been imprisoned by the enemy. Search the area west of your start position to discover Gargarensis' Migdol Stronghold revealed on the mini-map. Monuments and structures built by the followers of Isis are scattered throughout the area. You can claim these to help gain favor. You also possess three citadels (fortified Town Centers) and a Town Center. Look on the northern side of town to discover an initial food source, pigs and monkeys, and a gold mine. The southwest corner contains more gold, near a second temple.

Battle Plans

Arkantos, Ajax, and Chiron have been captured and taken to an island prison. Your allies suggest a strong diversionary attack—destroying the Gargarensis' Migdol Stronghold—that will force the enemy army to withdrawl. Amanra must create an alliance with a local village and form a strike team to combat the Migdol Stronghold. You've been provided with a mighty mythological unit army—including Scarabs, Petsuchos, and Scorpion Men—to mount the assault on the Migdol Stronghold. On easy difficulty levels, this army would be enough to topple the defenses around the Migdol Stronghold. However, it's wise to add to this army, particularly with siege weapons to crumble Towers and structures quickly.

Start assigning the laborers to various tasks. There are a couple gold mines to the southeast of your base; food sources, including pigs and baboons, can be found to the north; and a forest is located also to the south near the gold. Send Amanra to the southeast and northwest of the start position and convert all ally Monuments to your side. This will increase your rate of favor gain to fund more mythological units.

> **TIP**
>
> It's possible to ignore the diversionary objective and just try to reach the prison without attacking Gargarensis. You'll face greater opposition, though, then if you had destroyed the Migdol Stronghold and forced Gargarensis' army to retreat.

You begin the mission in the Heroic Age with three god powers: Prosperity, which should be saved for when you've researched mining upgrades and have many laborers on a gold mine; Eclipse, which boosts the speed and attack of mythological units and should be used before the attack on Gargarensis, and Locust Swarm, which destroys enemy farms.

Your Pharaoh appears soon after the mission begins. Order your Pharaoh to empower the Lumber Camp initially. This will quicken the collection of wood deposited to that site (see Figure 7.8). You'll want the wood to fund mythological technology upgrades, including Criosphinx to increase hit points and attack of Sphinxes, and Crocodopolis, to increase the range of the Petsuchos (both of these upgrades require wood and favor). The wood also funds Siege Towers.

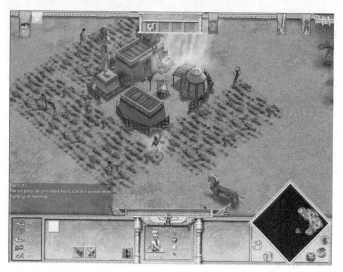

Figure 7.8 *The Pharaoh's empower ability increases a building's efficiency. If you need more laborers, empower the Town Center to train them faster.*

For food sources, use the pigs and baboons north of the start position. Once exhausted, search the northern area of the map for more animals—cranes, crocodiles, giraffe, and water buffalo—or begin farming around a Town Center or Granary.

Train Siege Towers at the Siege Works and bolster your army with additional mythological units (Sphinx and Petsuchos). Gather enough wood to fund both of these units' upgrades, which can be researched at the Temple. Assign the Scarabs and Siege Towers to their own group and use them solely against enemy Towers and structures. Support them with your mythological group army and Amanra.

Assault Gargarensis' base from its eastern entrance. You'll face light opposition around the entrance—nothing your mythological army can't handle. Send in the Siege Towers and Scarabs to topple the Towers and Temple in this first area.

Advance west toward Gargarensis' Migdol Stronghold. Intercept attacking human and mythological units (Gargarensis is following Set so expect converted animals as well). Attack walls, gates, Towers, and buildings with the Scarabs (Isis graciously supplies more during the battle) and Siege Towers. Destroying the Migdol Stronghold forces Gargarensis and Kemsyt to retreat to defensive positions. A new objective appears.

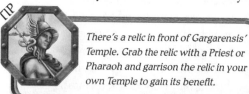

TIP

You can save some gold by sending villagers to the far northern section of the map. A farming community controlled by the followers of Isis can be found here. Erect a Granary and begin plowing unused farms. You'll have another food source, and you'll save the gold you would have paid to build each of those farms.

◈ **New Objective:** Amanra must reach the Transport Ship.

Organize your forces and retreat out of Gargarensis' crumbling base. Head east back to your own base and allow time for your Priests to heal your battle-worn army. When finished, advance north then west along the northern area of the map. You'll encounter scattered enemy units. Defeat them with your mythological unit army. Break down the gate just east of the transport. Send Amanra west toward the ship. Battle a couple of converted animals, then board the transport en route to the prison (see Figure 7.9).

TIP

There's a relic in front of Gargarensis' Temple. Grab the relic with a Priest or Pharaoh and garrison the relic in your own Temple to gain its benefit.

New Objective: Send Amanra to the Abydos harbor to convert a navy.

A new objective appears after Amanra boards the transport. You must venture to the Abydos harbor and gain a navy to assault the defenses around the offsite prison—the harbor's location appears on the mini-map. Maneuver Amanra's transport through the narrow creek and northeast into the Abydos harbor. A new objective appears as you near the docks and ships.

New Objective: Use your navy to break Amanra into the prison.

The Abydos provide Ramming Galleys, War Barges, and a War Turtle

Figure 7.9 *Amanra must use a transport ship to reach the offsite prison.*

to use against the prison defenses. Also, you can train more naval vessels at the Abydos docks (depending on available resources). Add more naval vessels to your group (a mixture of all three). Exhaust all current resources by training these vessels. When ready, advance toward the offsite prison. Keep Amanra's transport behind the fleet and out of harm's way.

Attack prison Tower defenses with the War Barges; counter the enemy archer ships with the Ramming Galleys and War Turtle. Move Amanra's transport to the prison's shore. Unload the transport and attack the prison guards. Enter the prison and attack the stone walls enclosing the other Heroes to complete the mission with success.

Let's Go

Initial Objective

◈ Survive until Setna's transports arrive from the southwest.

Map Highlights

You begin this mission where the last one ended—at the offsite prison. You've rescued your Heroes and a handful of other warriors, and must make your way to the mainland in an effort to locate an Osiris piece cart. A friendly village—the Abydos Resistance—can be found across the bay to the southwest, while enemy-controlled territory lies directly south.

Battle Plans

Gather your troops and position them on the southeastern edge of the island. Note that across the bay several friendly Kebenit, and transports are on their way. You also keep the War Turtle from the previous scenario. As the Kebenit and transports close in on the prison, an enemy transport arrives and drops off a squad of Spearmen. Assault the Spearmen with your Heroes, Avengers, and other troops. When the friendly transports arrive, a new objective appears. By the time you finish off the first Spearmen squad, another may have arrived. Defeat them as necessary.

◈ **New Objective:** Use the transports to move your troops to the flag in the allied purple town to the southwest.

Board the friendly transports and follow the Kebenit and War Turtle escort to the south-western shore to discover a friendly town controlled by the Abydos Resistance. Kamos' pirate ships may follow your fleet; assault any pursuers with the Kebenits and War Turtle. Your units must disembark and approach the Town Center to receive a tribute of resources from the townspeople (see Figure 7.10). The Abydos Resistance offer their support to recover the Osiris piece from Kemsyt, located on an adjacent island to the south.

Figure 7.10 *Approach the Abydos Resistance to receive tribute and a new area to settle, gather resources, and build an army.*

◈ **New Objective:** Capture the Osiris piece cart and move it outside the city's south gate.

There are two enemies on the map: Kamos' pirates are located just north of your new village and attack primarily with a naval fleet and Kemsyt's island stronghold to the south, which sticks with defensive in order to protect the Osiris piece from capture. Kemsyt moves the piece around the city to keep it safe (countdowns appear on the screen).

You begin the mission in the Classical Age and need to begin resource collection, particularly wood, if you are to challenge Kamos' navy. You should deal with Kamos' first to end his naval attacks. To do so, you must destroy the Lighthouse marked on the mini-map near the northern corner.

Only a few laborers are at your disposal. Spend current food resources on training more laborers. Send them to chop wood near the Lumber Camp northwest of the Town Center (empower the Lumber Camp with the Pharaoh). Research Husbandry before processing the numerous goats surrounding the Granary south of town. Once all laborers are trained and chopping wood, check the goats and make sure they've neared their maximum fattening level of 300.

Kemsyt sends small squads of human and mytholog- ical units beginning early in the mission (after about half of those laborers have been trained). Defend the northern edge of your base with your current army;

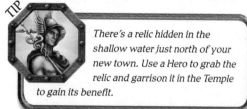

There's a relic hidden in the shallow water just north of your new town. Use a Hero to grab the relic and garrison it in the Temple to gain its benefit.

attack enemy mythological units with your Heroes. Lure the enemies near your defensive Towers and Town Center so these structures can aid in the attack.

Once the laborers have been trained, shift six to seven of them off of wood collection and on to processing the goats at the southern Granary. Process one goat at a time to give extra time for the others to fatten completely. You can also research Flood of the Nile at the Granary, which provides a slow trickle of food for the rest of the mission. Shift another five laborers off of wood collection and start mining gold at the pit east of town. Start researching resource improvements (Isis also provides the Prosperity god power to increase gold gathering rates for a short period of time).

As food becomes available, start constructing Monuments so you can fund mythological units later in the mission. Build an Armory to meet the requirement to advance to the Heroic Age. Advance to the Heroic Age at the earliest opportunity. Consider worshiping Nephthys for the Ancestors god power (an offensive tool or a last-resort defensive measure) and the Scorpion Man mythological unit.

You likely have plenty of wood by this point so shift more laborers to gold mining. Take the Pharaoh off of the Lumber Camp and empower the Mining Camp instead. Build a second dock during the advancement to Heroic Age. Once you advance, start building a naval fleet, including six to eight War Barges. Also construct several Ramming Galleys to defend the siege ships against Kamos' archer ships.

> There's another, very important, food source you should exploit after toppling the Lighthouse: perch schools. Build fishing ships at the dock and assign each ship to its own endless school of perch.

Start building Houses as you need them and train Scorpion Men (the excess wood comes in handy here). Also train Anubites and research the Feet of the Jackal upgrade. When your ships are ready, bombard the Lighthouse on the northern side of the map. When the Lighthouse falls, Kamos' ships won't be able to see the reefs offshore. You no longer have to worry about Kamos' pirate ships.

Now that you're in the Heroic Age, build a Market (for trading resources and as a prerequisite for advancement to the Mythic Age); a Siege Works to produce Siege Towers and, eventually, Catapults in the Mythic Age; and a Migdol Stronghold (see Figure 7.11) to produce Chariot Archers, Camelry, and War Elephants.

Take particular care in placing the Migdol Stronghold. Because the structure also serves as a large defensive Tower, place the building facing the northern entrance of your base. Research Burning Oil at a Tower so the Migdol Stronghold's defenses can inflict close-range damage. The added defense along your northern border helps fend of Kemsyt's attacks while you bolster your mythological unit army and advance to the Mythic Age. When you advance to the Mythic Age, choose to worship Thoth. You'll receive the devastating Meteor god power, which can be used to pummel the Kamos' structures or help weaken the defenses protecting the Osiris piece.

It's worth dealing with Kamos' base because he hordes several relics, which can greatly benefit your attack on the southern island and recovery of the Osiris piece. Train some siege weaponry (Siege Towers or Catapults) to deal with Kamos' Town Center and Barracks. Combat any human or mythological defenders with your own Heroes and army.

Now it's time to recover the Osiris piece, which has probably been moved to the furthest possible place—near the Wonder on the south-eastern side of the map. Upgrade your War Barges to Royal War Barges and research the Naval Oxybeles to increase their range. Reinforce your ground forces with several Catapults (research Draft Horses and Engineers at your Siege Works). Board transport ships with your Heroes, mythological units, and siege weapons. Send the entire fleet just north of the Wonder where an enemy Tower guards a small narrow inlet.

Figure 7.11 *The Migdol Stronghold also serves as an effective defense against incoming enemy units. Don't forget to research Burning Oil!*

Topple walls with the Catapults and War Barges and defend against enemy units with your own army. After crushing the walls, proceed east into the stronghold. Avoid the Migdol Strongholds (though your Catapults can make short work of them). Head south toward the large Wonder—you'll find the Osiris piece cart just in front. Approach the cart to capture it.

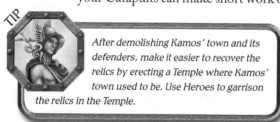

TIP

After demolishing Kamos' town and its defenders, make it easier to recover the relics by erecting a Temple where Kamos' town used to be. Use Heroes to garrison the relics in the Temple.

Select the Catapults and bombard the wall to the west. Danger lurks on the other side so be prepared to defend your siege weapons against attack! Just west beyond the crumbled wall is a collection of defensive structures, including Towers and Migdol Strongholds. If you chose to worship Thoth, unleash Meteor on these buildings and follow up with siege attack. Invoke Eclipse (if you haven't already) to boost your mythological unit attack and eliminate all nearby units.

Guide the Osiris piece cart around to the south. Crumble the gate impeding access to the southern edge of the map. Once the gate is down, move the cart to the marked flag to complete the mission.

Good Advice

Initial Objective

◆ Follow Kastor.

Map Highlights

Your dreamland begins on the western side of the map. Kastor is there and will lead you toward your first tasks. The second stage of the mission begins on the far eastern side of the map. Athena's third task takes you back to the Underworld.

Battle Plans

At the beginning of the mission, you control only Arkantos. Although your Hero sleeps in Amanra's camp, this mission takes place in Arkantos' dream. Kastor, Arkantos' son, heads northeast toward the temple. Follow Kastor. Ignore the relic for now and continue to follow Kastor to the Temple beyond. Speak with Kastor when he stops. A new objective appears.

◆ **New Objective:** Garrison the relic into the Temple and defend the Temple.

Return to the relic you passed a moment ago. To have Arkantos capture the relic, click on the relic with Arkantos selected. Two Cyclops appear on either side of the relic. Defeat them with Arkantos (Zeus will invoke Restoration should Arkantos need healing). Garrison the relic in the Temple.

More Cyclops appear around the temple after Arkantos garrisons the relic. These new Cyclops start pummeling the structure. You'll also spot Gargarensis with the Cyclops! Attack the Cyclops group immediately. Zeus won't abandon you in this time of need—the statues surrounding the Temple animate and fire lightning attacks at the Cyclops (see Figure 7.12). Zeus also invokes Restoration again if Arkantos requires healing. Eliminate all of the Cyclops (allow the lightning to do most of the work).

Figure 7.12 *Have faith that Zeus will help you defend the Temple.*

◆ **New Objective:** Defeat the guardians of the Shrine just ahead.

Continue northeast, to the shrine beyond the temple. Five Chimeras guard the shrine. Assault them. When you do, Arkantos' friends, the other Heroes (Chiron, Amanra, and Ajax) appear out of thin air to assist in the battle. Eliminate the Chimeras and approach the shrine. Athena appears, with another task for you to complete.

◈ **New Objective:** Destroy the large boulder to escape the Underworld.

Athena transports both you and Kastor to the Underworld (you are still in Arkantos' dream) and sets you to another task: Escape the Underworld by destroying the landslide to the north. Fortunately, a large, friendly army of infantry, archers, cavalry, Priests, and siege weaponry can assist you. You also have the use of Shades of Hades, which can kill enemy mythological units in a single blow. Use the Shades sparingly!

Send Arkantos and Kastor toward the boulder wall. Organize the friendly army into various attack groups. Set the siege weapons to their own grouping so you can use them to attack the boulder wall while your ground troops attack the wall's defenders. Hydra and Avengers guard the wall. You'll also encounter the Anubite Theris at the wall. He's the Anubite Arkantos killed in a dream in Age of Mythology's introductory cinematic.

Assault the various mythological creatures. Spread out your attacks; if you concentrate all your army on one creature, many might not be able to get into the battle because your units may be too closely packed together. Advance the siege weapons and begin pummeling the landslide.

Don't let your guard down after eliminating this batch of enemies. More will appear, including Scorpion Men and more Hydra. Use remaining Shades of Hades against the second wave of mythological units. Zeus sends his aid once again by invoking a Lightning Storm god power. Defend your siege weaponry from the mythological units, and keep the siege attack focused on the landslide. Once the boulders crumble and the passage opens, escort Arkantos through to begin the next stage of the mission.

◈ **New Objective:** Safely transport Arkantos and Kastor to the beach marked with white flags.

Kastor and Arkantos begin in the southern part of the map, ashore of several transports and Triremes. Your destination lies just to the north, at the white flags. Upon reaching town, search the area west and northwest of town for additional food, wood, and gold sources. The enemy, and their Wonder, can be found to the northeast, where they cover that side of the map, well protected by guard Towers.

You should immediately notice a "twist" in this dream sequence. For starters, Arkantos is wearing red clothing instead of his traditional blue. Careful examination reveals that you're red (usually reserved for the enemy's color) on the mini-map as well. Check out the transports and note that Gargarensis and Kamos are among the passengers. And Black Sail ships are escorting your transports! Something strange is afoot!

Maneuver Arkantos and Kastor toward the transports and board the vessels. (The others contain mythological units such as Hydra, Manticores, Cyclops, and Avengers. One transport houses villagers.) Group your pirate ships and transports separately.

Advance your pirate ships toward the northern beach first—a large enemy fleet guards the shoreline. Just when it looks like you won't survive, Kraken appear from the western waters and sink the enemy ships. Send your transports to the shore and order all units to disembark. After you reach the white flags, a new objective appears.

◈ **New Objective:** Train an army and destroy the enemy wonder.

You're under attack immediately—a trio of enemy Siege Towers bombards your new Town Center. Send your mythological units and Arkantos to intercept the threat. Eliminate all three Siege Towers. After the battle, position your mythological units and Arkantos north of your Town Center to protect against new attacks (see Figure 7.13). Start food collection, using the goats west of your Town Center. Use the incoming food to continually produce villagers, and order them to collect food as well.

Build a Temple so you can deposit the relics found around the map. You're already in Classical Age. Build a Granary and research Husbandry to quicken the fattening rate of your herd of goats. Start mining the gold just

Figure 7.13 *Prepare to intercept enemy attacks with your large group of mythological units.*

northwest of town. Place a storehouse nearby to serve as deposits for gold and for the nearby wood. Queue up 14 villagers at the Town Center. Send eight to mine gold and the rest to chop the nearby wood.

Build a Military Academy, Archery Range, Stable, and Armory. Train Hoplites to counter the enemy's predominant unit, cavalry (though your mythological unit army alone is very formidable). If you wish to explore the sea, wait until the Heroic Age. Although you could mass Triremes, the enemy possesses Juggernaut siege ships and Pentekonter hammer ships, both of which can make short work of a group of Triremes. If you possess enough wood, it's also possible to fish the perch schools near your dock for additional food. Hunt the bears, boars, and deer near your town before processing the

> **TIP**
>
> Scout around your new town to discover more resources. The northwest corner contains an unclaimed settlement surrounded by bear, boar, and deer. There's also a gold mine just east of the settlement. More goats can be found north of your town. Don't forget to hunt for relics!

goats. Research Hunting Dogs after Husbandry to increase hunting gathering rate. Begin farming once all food sources sources are depleted.

Advance to the Heroic Age and choose between Aphrodite and Apollo. Aphrodite benefits villagers and can invoke the Curse god power to turn a group of enemy units into pigs. Apollo offers the Underground Passage, which you can use to transport troops quickly to enemy territory. Apollo also can turn your Temple into a source of healing. If you worship Aphrodite, research Divine Blood to increase villager gathering rates and speed and Golden Apples to increase favor rate.

After Age-advancement, erect a Fortress on the northeast side of your town to further protect against attacks. When the Fortress is finished, produce three to four Petroboli. Once in the Heroic Age, you can add siege and hammer ships to your naval fleet if you wish (see Figure 7.14). You can use your fleet to clear enemy ships and guard Towers near shore, but it's a difficult task—the Towers can rip through your vessels quickly. Build a Market to meet the requirements for advancement to the Mythic Age. Arkantos is worshipping Hades. After reaching the Mythic Age, train all Greek Heroes and Hades' unique archer unit, Gastraphetes, which are effective against infantry and buildings.

Begin advancing northeast, toward the enemy town. Use your Petroboli against the enemy Towers, defending your siege units with mythological units, Greek Heroes, and any other units you've produced. After toppling the Towers, bombard the Fortress just north of the gate. Is that

Figure 7.14 *You can produce a sizable navy to combat the enemy's ships and Towers, but it might not be the wisest use of resources.*

Theocrat there? Attack the gate with siege weapons. The enemy retaliates with a group of cavalry, infantry, and Hero units—Ajax and Chiron? Eliminate the Towers and military structures just beyond the gate.

Push toward the Wonder. Guard the Petroboli with your imposing army. As soon as you're safe from enemy attack, assault the Wonder with all your units and siege weapons. When the Wonder falls, the mission ends in success.

Missions 17–24 Walkthrough

Arkantos, Ajax, Amanra, and Chiron split up in search of three parts of Osiris. Our Heroes must reunite these pieces of the God to stop Gargarensis and Kemsyt from opening a gate into the underworld. Amanra searches for the part within Kemsyt's stronghold; Chiron excavates a part from an ancient Tamarisk tree; and Arkantos and Ajax must contend with Kamos' villains to recover their part.

This chapter covers mission walkthroughs for single-player missions 17 through 24 of the Age of Mythology campaign. Although you begin this set of missions using Egyptian units and structures, Arkantos soon finds Norse allies. At that point, you will begin to use Norse units and technologies and worship Norse gods. Familiarize yourself with the Norse (see Chapters 5 and 14), and attempt to unite their clans against a common enemy!

The Jackal's Stronghold

Initial Objective

◈ Get Amanra to the village.

Map Highlights

You begin in the eastern corner of the map. Kemsyt's island stronghold is situated in the northwest corner of the map, with the position of the Osiris part revealed within it. The floodplain farming village is located along the southern and southwestern area of the map. Locate an unclaimed settlement southwest of your start position. Begin gathering resources to produce the military units you'll need to take the Osiris piece from Kemsyt.

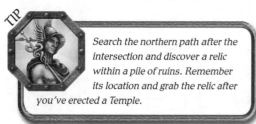

TIP

Search the northern path after the intersection and discover a relic within a pile of ruins. Remember its location and grab the relic after you've erected a Temple.

Battle Plans

Amanra leads six Egyptian Camelry units and a pair of Axemen, on the far eastern side of the map. Amanra announces that there are floodplain farmers in the area and perhaps they will help in your effort to mount an attack against Kemsyt's island stronghold. Head west and discover a couple of rhinoceroses wandering around here. Keep their location in mind; later in the mission you can hunt these animals for food.

An enemy squad stands guard at an intersection splitting the path north and west. Eliminate the enemy units. Micromanage your Camelry and withdraw any unit that's suffered significant damage (see Figure 8.1).

Figure 8.1 *Protect wounded Camelry by withdrawing them from the battle.*

Return to the intersection and head due west until you reach farms and an unclaimed settlement. Approach the settlement with Amanra to greet the floodplain farmers. You gain the laborers surrounding the Town Center.

◈ **New Objective**: Bring Amanra to any additional buildings or Villagers to convert them to your cause.

Send Amanra around the floodplains to convert buildings and villagers. Move Amanra north of the Town Center to convert houses and a Tower, which can protect the harbor while you train a navy. Guide Amanra west to find a Temple (and a relic nearby), more houses, and additional laborers and farms. Continue all the way to the southern corner to uncover three relics near an unclaimed settlement. Build a Temple here to garrison the relics easily.

Use your initial food supply to produce 14 more laborers. You have access to two gold mines—a smaller one closer to the west and larger mines to the southwest. Send nine laborers to mine gold and five to chop wood at any of the forests around your Town Center. Use the Pharaoh to empower the Lumber Camp—you're gonna need the wood to fund a navy and siege weaponry! Starting laborers (and any that you convert) should be farming (research all upgrades, including Bast's Sacred Cats) or hunting the plentiful water buffalo around the floodplains. Start researching resource upgrades, including Bast's Adze of Wepwawet improvement that increases wood gathering rates (though you'll need Monuments to gain favor first).

You begin the mission in the Heroic Age with three god powers: Eclipse, Ancestors, and Prosperity (invoke Prosperity after researching Pick Axe, Shaft Mine, and Quarry). Build a Migdol Stronghold, Siege Works, and Market then advance to the Mythic Age. Worship either Thoth or Osiris. We chose Osiris for the Son of Osiris god power and the Funeral Barge naval benefit. Invoke the Son of Osiris god power on your Pharaoh and use him to empower resource camps before sending him into battle against Kemsyt's forces.

Construct an additional dock and begin researching the naval upgrades (Enclosed Deck and line improvements to archer ships and siege ships). Build a couple transports (or Leviathan) and start training archer and siege ships. You will also need eight to ten upgraded Ramming Galleys to combat Set's War Turtles (extremely important!).

Build houses as you need them until you've maximized the population cap. Erect an Armory and research its upgrades (which will also benefit your ships) and Burning Pitch. Train mythological units (Scorpion Men, Sphinx, Mummies), Migdol Stronghold units (Camelry and War Elephants primarily), and Catapults until you have at least three transports packed to the gunwales. Don't forget Priests to serve as healers!

If you need additional population cap room to train more naval or land units, start building Town Centers on the unclaimed settlements around the floodplains. Since you're worshipping Isis, these new settlements provide even more to your population cap.

Send your naval fleet out of the harbor and encounter Set's fleet of archer ships and War Turtles. Counter the War Turtles with your Heavy Ramming Galleys. Sink the archer ships with your War Barges. Protect your Transports carefully and pull them back toward your town and Towers if necessary. After eliminating the enemy fleet, escort the transports to the southwestern side of Kemsyt's island. Bombard the units and structures along the shore with your War Barges (see Figure 8.2).

Disembark on the southwestern side of the map, and eliminate the defenders. Use your Priests to heal your units before assaulting the gate and wall just east of your position. Attack the gate with Catapults and batter the enemy wall to the

Send the upgraded Pharaoh (research Nephthys' Pharaoh upgrades) in the transports. The Pharaoh is a powerful mythological unit counter. Research Osiris' New Kingdom and use the second Pharaoh to continue empowering resource camps back at your base.

Figure 8.2 *Use your fleet to pound the enemy's shore defenses.*

ground. Start up the hill and use siege weaponry on the gate and any structures within range. Use your plentiful ground troops intercept enemy defenders. Don't forget your god powers! Invoke Eclipse and Ancestors as necessary.

Advance toward the Osiris piece and combat enemy units guarding the way. Sneak Amanra out of the group and send her to the part. If she's attacked, use your other units to come to her aid. To complete the mission, Amanra must simply reach the Osiris piece. Even if the battle is raging, as soon as Amanra stands next to the box containing the piece, the mission ends in success.

A Long Way From Home

Initial Objective

⬥ Seek help from the desert nomad camp to the east.

Map Highlights

You begin in the southern corner of the desert with Chiron, some Axemen, a Priest, and Norse units including Jarl, Raiding Cavalry, and two Ox Carts. The enemy base lies to the north. The Tamarisk Tree, integral to your mission, rests just below and dangerously close to the enemy base. Head east from the start position to locate a nomad camp—start building your base here.

Battle Plans

Chiron's little mixed command lies on the southern edge of the map. You lack laborers, so it's impossible to build a Town Center and begin developing an economy or military army. You must seek assistance from a nearby nomad camp; perhaps they can help you.

Move the troops to the east and make contact with the nomad camp. The nomads offer their help in leading the way to the Tamarisk tree—if you protect their camp from attack. A new objective appears as you automatically accept their offer.

⬥ **New Objective**: Send laborers to cut down the Tamarisk tree and recover the head of Osiris.

Survey the nomad camp and make note of its offerings, which include a Market and Temple. There are plenty of goats around, and a gold mine can be found just east of the camp. To the east is an unclaimed settlement and more food, including an elephant. Search northwest of town to discover another gold mine, and even more goats. Escort the goats to their new home near the Town Center, though wait until they fatten before processing them. Instead, send four laborers northeast of the Town Center and hunt the Zebra there. Drop a Granary (or move an Ox Cart) and research Husbandry. Produce three more laborers to begin collecting more resources.

With resources coming in, begin raising other needed structures, including a Temple, Barracks, Armory, Monuments, and houses. Attacks will arrive from north, northeast, and west of the nomad camp. Erect Towers to protect these areas of your base and prepare your defenses to intercept enemy attackers. Bolster your army with additional Axemen and mythological units, and start spending resources on military improvements at the Barracks and Armory.

You can use the Market to trade resources and advance to the Heroic Age faster. Chose to worship Hathor or Nephthys (we selected Nephthys for the improvements to Pharaohs and Priests and the Scorpion Man mythological unit). Erect a Migdol Stronghold—place the structure to the west, north, or northeast section of your base to add defense—and a Siege Works. Maintain a steadfast defense around your base to hold off Gargarensis' incursions.

Shift to farms after depleting the supply of goats. Start spending

Stopping the Mummy Attacks

Mummies are attacking the nomads! Periodically Mummies appear from the western and eastern sides of your base and assault your structures and turn human units (usually laborers) into minions. Fortunately, the Mummies aren't discriminatory and also attack Gargarensis' units and base. However, it's better rid yourself of the Mummy threat for two reasons: first so you won't have to deal with the problem any longer and secondly because destroying the Mummy tombs provides a large amount of gold into your reserve. Locate the two Mummy tombs southeast of town along the edge of the map and to the far northwest (just west of Gargarensis' base and near a Temple). After destroying the northwest tomb, search just south to find a couple relics.

resources on economic improvements, such as Pick Axe, Plow, and Hand Axe (and more if you can spare the resources). Use the your ample resources to begin training Migdol units, Camelry, Chariot Archers, and War Elephants. Upgrade all of these units at the Migdol Stronghold and the Armory. Assign these units to defend your base against Gargarensis' attacks while you accumulate the resources necessary to advance to the Mythic Age.

Choose to worship Osiris or Thoth at the Mythic Age. We selected Osiris for the Son of Osiris god power. This converts a Pharaoh into the Son of Osiris, who can fire an enormous lightning attack from his staff. Research Osiris's New

A Long Way From Home ✕ 147

Kingdom to provide a secondary Pharaoh to continue empowering resource camps. Don't forget about Nephthys' upgrades to Pharaohs (making them stronger against mythological units). Research them to improve your Pharaohs and Priests.

To complete the mission, you have to successfully escort a large number of laborers (the more the better, but at least 10) to the Tamarisk Tree, and excavate Osiris's head. The nearby enemy town, however, won't hesitate to send large groups of units to stop your workers from completing the task.

Fortunately there's no time limit on the retrieval of the head, so you can spend time building your town defenses, such as walls, Towers (be sure to improve the Towers' capabilities), and the Migdol Stronghold. The stronger the defense, the fewer units you'll lose defending the town. Produce several Priests to heal wounds.

Advance your army toward the Tamarisk Tree. You and Chiron should command a mix of Camelry, Chariot Archers, War Elephants, mythological units, and Priests—and, if you worshipped Osiris, the Son of Osiris. Escort as many laborers as you can spare; you shouldn't need any more resources if you've purchased available improvements, built town defenses, and produced a sizable army.

Maintain position at the tree. You could even use laborers to build Towers, walls, or a Migdol Stronghold to help protect the area. However you do it, keep the laborers at work on the tree and defend them from enemy attacks. Stay around the tree and any defenses you've erected: If you explore too far north, you risk disturbing more enemy units and coming under fire from the enemy's Towers.

Use available god powers (Eclipse and Ancestors) to help defend the area from enemy assaults. If any laborers are attacked and retreat, order them back to the tree to resume their duty. The mission ends successfully when the laborers have completed the excavation of Osiris's head.

Watch That First Step

Initial Objective

⬨ Capture the Black Sail ships to the east, by destroying the forward base that guards them.

Map Highlights

You begin on a southern island just west of the Black Sail ships (revealed on the mini-map). Kamos's stronghold can be found in the far northern corner. After capturing the Black Sail ships, guide them to the northwest to find an unclaimed settlement. You'll stage your battle against Kamos here, but you might need to return to the southern island for resources or additional units.

Battle Plans

Arkantos and Ajax lead a large army of Champion Hoplites, complete with an Egyptian Siege Tower and Catapult, to the east. They hope to capture the Black Sail Transport Ships, in order to evade the local villains and to reach Kamos and the captured Osiris part. Rain and Bronze god powers are available to them for the mission. Save Bronze until you face the tough defenses of Kamos' stronghold; you should be able to eliminate the defenses around the Black Sails easily.

Organize your troops into four groups. Place Arkantos and Ajax in the first group; the Champion Hoplites in the second group; and the Siege Tower and Catapult in the two other groups. Move east and toward the Lighthouse. You'll spot a ramp leading down to the southeast. Keep

all units stationary except your two Heroes; move them down the ramp in the lead. Anubite guardians block the way to a neutral Temple below. Attack the Anubites with your Heroes.

As Arkantos and Ajax dominate the battle against the mythological units, use one Hero to scout a bit east to discover a Migdol Stronghold in production. Maneuver your Catapult forward and bombard the building from long range. A few enemy units—War Elephants, Slingers, and a Colossus—remain in the area, guarding a Dock to the east where the Black Sail ships are found. Use your the Heroes against the Colossus and the Hoplites against the War Elephants and Slingers. Remove wounded Hoplites from the field: You'll soon receive a Priest to heal wounded units.

◈ **New Objective**: Use the Black Sail ships to transport troops across the bay behind Kamos's base (near the blue flag), and claim a settlement.

A new objective appears after you have eliminated all units and structures guarding the Black Sail ships. The neutral villagers who worship at the Temple show their thanks by offering to build Colossi for you. The Colossi appear periodically at this Temple, and you can return in the Black Sail Transports to pick them up. Eventually, after Kamos detects your base, you will have to find another way to retrieve the Colossi (more on this later).

Move all your units, including siege weapons, onto the Transports and guide them to the northwestern corner of the map (the blue flag is revealed on the mini-map). Although the waterway includes many defenses, none will attack. Disembark at the blue flag and head north. You soon will discover a group of Egyptian refugees with no love for Kamos. They offer to help. Three laborers, a Pharaoh, and a Priest are now under your control. Use the three laborers to build a Town Center on the refugees' settlement. To hasten the process, the Pharaoh should empower construction. In the meantime, command the Priest to heal any wounded units.

✦ **New Objective**: Quickly build up a large force and siege Kamos's base. Stay behind the large forest to remain undetected until you are ready to attack.

A counter appears in the upper right corner of the screen. You have 12 minutes before Kamos scouts the area and discovers your presence. Select the Town Center and queue 14 laborers. No other food sources are available so start processing the goats next to the Town Center. Alternatively, you could build a Granary, research Husbandry, and send trained laborers to collect gold from the eastern mine. Switch to food once the goats have fattened. Select a laborer and build an Armory. Start building Houses to support your units and new laborers.

> **TIP**
>
> The friendly Temple worshippers freed earlier will alert you when they've completed a Colossus. Move a Black Sail Transport to the shore and carry the Colossus back to your settlement. After Kamos scouts the area, the enemy defenses in the waterway will start reacting to your Transport. To compensate, worship Hathor at the Heroic Age for the Roc air-transport unit.

Once the goats have fattened, shift 10 laborers onto food and the rest on the gold mine just east of your settlement. You may also need a couple on wood to prepare for Migdol Stronghold Chariot Archer units and siege weapons. Continue to gather food and gold until you meet the requirements to advance to the Heroic Age. Upon advancement, choose to worship Hathor, rather than Nephthys. Hathor's Roc mythological unit becomes vital, both to collect Colossi at the Temple and to retrieve resources from the southern island.

After racing to the Heroic Age, build a Barracks, a Temple, and then a Migdol Stronghold. Place the Migdol Stronghold toward the east—where the minions of Kamos will appear. You've likely run out of goats by now; it's time to switch to farming. Before doing so, research Shaduf to reduce the cost of farms (the improvement requires wood, and you have plenty). Build farms around the Town Center and continue empowering the structure with your Pharaoh.

Build a Market, Monuments, and Towers around the Migdol Stronghold as resources become available. Begin reinforcing your army with Camelry, Chariot Archers, and Spearmen (for use against War Elephants).

When the countdown hits zero, Kamos sends a few Camelry units into your area. From that point on you can't use the Black Sail Transports to retrieve Colossi. Instead, use the Egyptian Temple to create the Roc flying transport unit. Don't move the Roc directly to the Colossi, though: Head directly south and then east to the Colossi (see Figure 8.3), so the Roc won't be shot down by the enemy vessels in the map's center. The Roc also is important when the

Figure 8.3 *After Kamos discovers your incursion, use the Roc flying transport to recover Colossi.*

gold mine expires in your northern base. Move the laborers to the southern island and start mining there.

Eliminate Kamos's Camelry scouts. The enemy will begin walling off the entrance to their base. Crush the wall with your Catapult. Build a Siege Works and add additional Siege Towers to your siege weapon group. Reinforce your army with eight to 10 Camelry units, the same number of Chariot Archers, and 12–15 Spearmen. If you have the favor, add mythological units to your groups. Research unit improvements as resources allow. As soon as you can, advance to the Mythic Age and worship Thoth to invoke Meteor to level the defensive structures on the paths leading up to Kamos's stronghold (Monuments prevent god powers within Kamos's city).

The remainder of the mission requires a slow push to the east. The path will divide. Follow the southern path (the northern route lies too close to a Migdol Stronghold). Use Heroes against mythological units and mythological and human units against other enemies. Crush Kamos's structures and towers at long range with Catapults.

Advance slowly, so you don't trigger too many enemies at once. Protect your siege weapons and patiently allow them to batter Kamos's base structures before advancing. Make your way to the northern edge of the map, where most of Kamos's defenses are planted. Counter the War Elephants with Hoplites and Spearmen, and counter enemy mythological units with your Heroes.

◈ **New Objective**: Defeat Kamos. He has been found on the North side of the base.

Kamos is protecting his piece of Osiris on the northern side of his base. Anubites, in turn, guard Kamos. Counter them with your Heroes. Surround Kamos with all of your units to terminate the enemy Minotaur. Defeating Kamos recovers the Osiris part, and completes our Heroes' mission with success.

Where They Belong

Initial Objective

◈ Build up and fight toward the Osiris pyramid. Survive until Arkantos arrives with his Osiris piece.

Map Highlights

You begin on the southern edge of the map in two separate bases. The eastern base contains ample food sources, with goats near the Town Center and berry bushes along the southern edge of the map. Both bases include gold mines. In fact, the eastern base has two. The western base offers more hunting opportunities, however, with goats, hippos, and giraffe to the east of town. A row of trees separates the east and west towns. The stronghold of Gargarensis and Kemsyt—where they're trying to dig an entrance into the Underworld— waits in the northern corner of the map.

Battle Plans

At the start of the mission, your forces are separated in the southern corner of the map. Chiron's army sets up camp in the western base, where the primary structures are a Temple, a Town Center, and defensive Towers. Amanra commands the troops to the east. The eastern base contains a Market, Barracks, and defensive Towers.

Figure 8.4 *Scout the area carefully to discover possible resources and bonuses such as relics.*

Survey the area to find the available resources (see Figure 8.4). The western base features three primary food options: slaughtering goats; hunting rhinos, giraffe, and hyena northeast of town; and fishing in the small lake east of town. A single gold mine lies in the western camp. The main woodland separates the western and eastern bases. The eastern base has two food sources: goats, and berry bushes south of town. Two gold mines—one west and one east—can be found near town. Both bases house Osiris piece carts.

Start collecting resources with available laborers. Use available food to train laborers and assign them to gold and wood initially (around 80% on gold). Build a Granary and research Husbandry before slaughtering the goats. Collect the wood from the line of trees dividing the western and eastern bases. The sooner you can cut a hole through the trees, the sooner you can combine forces for added defense and, eventually, offense. Use the Market in the eastern base to trade resources as needed, and command the Pharaoh to empower a structure depending on your resource need. A new objective appears moments into the mission— Arkantos has less than 30 minutes to arrive with his Osiris piece cart!

TIP

Use Chiron to scout northeast from the western base. Several types of animals wander here, and can be hunted for food. However, the real prize is a relic near the unclaimed settlement. Have Chiron grab the relic, and garrison it within your temple to receive its bonus.

◈ **New Objective**: Kemsyt will have the passage to the Underworld open in 30 minutes.

A counter appears on the right side of the screen, indicating time remaining until the gate opens. If the counter runs to zero, the mission ends in failure. Time is important in this mission. By the time Arkantos finally arrives, you need to have produced a powerful army capable of advancing into Gargarensis and Kemsyt's stronghold. Build missing structures as soon as possible, including an Armory, a Migdol Stronghold, and Siege Works. Don't venture too far to the north of your towns. Enemy Towers are very close and will disrupt your building. Use the Catapult in the east to topple the eastern Tower. Begin shifting laborers off of gold and wood as needed. Start hunting in the west and foraging in the east until your goats have fattened completely.

Construct a Barracks in the western base to provide additional defensive units, and build a Temple in the eastern base so you can produce Priests to heal your units. You also will need Egyptian Monuments, to gain favor to produce mythological units, and Houses to increase the population cap.

You begin with three god powers: Rain, Plague of Serpents, and Ancestors. Don't hesitate to use either Plague of Serpents or Ancestors for defensive purposes should the need arise. After your food sources run dry and you've begun farming, invoke Rain to increase production for a short time.

Gargarensis sends infantry, Sphinxes, Chariot Archers, and Siege Towers periodically against both of your bases. Build extra Towers to provide extra defense, and position your Migdol Stronghold strategically to help defend the base. Spend resources on Barracks, Migdol Stronghold, and Armory improvements to upgrade your units' capabilities. Keep your military focused to maximize your resources. There isn't time to upgrade everything. For example, a sound army for this mission would include Champion Chariot Archers, Anubite Guardians, Champion Spearmen, Priests and (upon reaching Mythic Age) the Son of Osiris. If you advance to the Mythic Age, use the Siege Works to add Catapults to your groups.

Building a strong army is the most important use of resources, although it's still possible to win if you spend the resources required to advance to the Mythic Age. At advancement, choose to worship Osiris, rather than Horus. The Monuments of Isis protect Gargarensis's stronghold from god powers, so Horus' Tornado can't help you there. Instead, select Osiris, and invoke the Son of Osiris god power on your Pharaoh.

After erecting adequate defenses, begin advancing on both sides and use Catapults or Siege Towers to topple the Tower defenses between your southern bases and Gargarensis' stronghold up north. Continue up the eastern side and discover a relic resting near an enemy Temple. Demolish the Temple and claim the relic for your own. Clear out these defenses north of either base before Arkantos arrives so you won't have to deal with these structures when time is dwindling down.

> **TIP**
>
> Don't save your god powers until the end of the mission! Gargarensis's base has Monuments that block god powers, rendering them useless. Use those god powers before attacking his base!

◈ **New Objective**: Arkantos has arrived from the east with the last Osiris piece! Bring all three pieces to the Obelisk near Osiris's pyramid.

With about 10 minutes remaining, Arkantos and Ajax arrive on the far eastern side of the map. Fortunately, along with his Osiris piece cart, he commands Champion War Elephants, a group of Catapults, and an Avenger. That's excellent firepower, and the cue for you to begin your final advance toward the enemy base.

You are also provided with two laborers in the east, and can build a Town Center on the nearby settlement if you wish. Send Arkantos and his army north and follow with one laborer, for reasons you'll discover in a moment.

Intercept any incoming enemies, but don't fret if your southern towns are attacked. You need to continue pressing north toward Gargarensis. Topple Towers with siege weaponry, and press north. Make sure your Osiris piece carts follow your army! They're integral to completing the mission!

Advance an army just south of Gargarensis' base and discover a small lake protected by an enemy Tower. Explore the area and discover a neutral village, including Houses, a Dock, and fishing boats. It's possible to rescue these slaves to Gargarensis and convert them to your cause. Simply demolish the Tower adjacent to the Dock and the thankful village repays the debt by continuing to fish the lake and sending the food into your reserves.

Keep moving Arkantos north, and you'll discover another relic. If you wish to gain its benefit, use the laborer you've advanced, and build a Temple. When it's finished, send Arkantos to garrison the relic. Rendezvous your armies on the southern side of Gargarensis's base. Crush any towers and structures with siege weaponry.

You need to move all three Osiris piece carts to the obelisk west of the pyramid, and dig into the Underworld. You won't be able to cast god powers here because of the high concentration of Isis Monuments. Keep enemy troops to the west occupied with your ample forces, while maneuvering the piece carts into position. The mission ends successfully when all three Osiris piece carts arrive at the obelisk.

Old Friends

Initial Objective

◈ Collect and protect as many pigs as you can.

Map Highlights

Arkantos and Ajax begin as boars on the southern edge of the map. Enemy villagers can be found just north of your start position. Nearby towns contain more pigs. You'll eventually locate the Temple of Zeus to the far northwest, where you will convert your group of pigs back into soldiers. Circe's enemy Citadel covers the eastern side of the map.

Battle Plans

Although this mission begins with humor (you and your Atlantean army have been converted to pigs!), the mission ends with climatic battles against the evil sorceress Circe. As you land on the southern shore, both Arkantos and Ajax are transformed into boar Heroes. The two boars will be your only method of attack until you can convert Arkantos, Ajax, and the rest of the army back into their former selves. Four other pigs, also former warriors, are nearby. Group the two boars for attack, and place the four pigs in a secondary grouping. Use the boars to attack the approaching enemy villager. Maneuver the pigs away from the villager to keep them safe.

Start moving to the north, keeping the vulnerable herd of pigs in the rear. You'll soon spot a village—and it contains more pigs! Send your Hero boars to break the wooden fence enclosing the pen (see Figure 8.5), and group the pigs with the ones you already have. An

TIP

As they do in human form, Arkantos and Ajax in boar form regenerate health over time. If either becomes seriously injured, wait a minute or two before advancing further.

enemy villager arrives, happy to slaughter a couple of boars. Retaliate with your boar Heroes. He'll realize he's overmatched and retreat to a nearby tower. Don't engage; instead, follow the path toward the northeast.

Two wolves emerge from the woods, hoping for an easy meal. Focus the attack of both boars on a single wolf. Eliminate both wolves and press eastward, into a new village. Two villagers approach. Attack them with the boars—they wise up and retreat to the nearby tower. Don't follow; instead break apart the wooden fence on the southwestern side. Free the pigs, add them to your group, and receive a new objective.

Figure 8.5 *Explore the enemy villages to rescue the pigs!*

◈ **New Objective**: Find a way through the gates to the Temple of Zeus.

You must herd your porcine army to the Temple of Zeus, in the northwest corner of the map. Once the animals arrive, the Temple will automatically convert them back into their human form. In the meantime, however, there are more pigs to collect. Start moving to the east and discover another pigpen. Break the fence, and add the pigs to your group. A final village can be found just to the north. Move the boars here and collect a final group of pigs from their pen taking care to attack the villager before moving to the pigs.

Move both groups to the northwest through the opening in the enemy wall. As you proceed northwest, enemy Hoplites appear—they stand guard in front of Circe's Citadel, in the northeast, and a small village to the southwest. Assault or avoid the Hoplites; if you do attack, focus the attack of both boars on a single enemy at a time. Keep the pigs moving to the northwest; don't stop them unless an enemy targets them. You don't want to dawdle at this intersection, because additional Hoplites will emerge from the gate. A couple more Hoplites stand guard at the wall just before the Temple. Occupy them with your boars while the pigs approach the Temple. Should a boar be wounded severely, pull it back and allow the other boar to continue the attack.

◈ **New Objective**: Build up and defeat Circe by destroying the Fortress at the heart of the Citadel.

A new objective appears after the approach to the Temple. It's time to build a base and amass an army large enough to topple Circe and her Fortress. There's an unclaimed settlement just to the east. Eliminate the enemy villagers here with your new Hypaspists and Peltasts. Use the villagers that were converted from pigs to build a Town Center on the settlement. You're in the Classical Age, and need military structures quickly. Circe won't leave you alone for long!

Use your food supply to queue up more villagers. Assign villagers in equal groups to the gathering of food, gold, and wood. Eventually, you'll need to shift some to gaining favor by worshipping at Zeus' Temple. Build an Armory, Military Academy, Archery Range, and Stable. Build the Armory first to advance to Heroic Age as quickly as possible. Use available wood to fund defensive Towers (spend resources to upgrade them as well). Place them inside the wall southeast of your town. Consider completing that wall, to delay enemy attacks even further.

Circe's forces attack frequently from the opening south of your town. Use Towers and additional walls to hinder their advance. Build a mixture of infantry, ranged units, cavalry, and Minotaurs (your first available mythological unit), after gaining some favor. Since the enemy sends their own mixture of units, it's important to counter each of them with the specific unit type that is best against that unit. As soon as the resources become available, advance to the Heroic Age.

> **TIP**
>
> There are a couple of enemy resource operations near your town: Gold and lumber are being collected to the northeast, and another enemy gold mine is operating to the northwest. Eliminate these villagers as soon as possible, but be alert! Destroying the enemy storehouses produces Militia.

You can choose to worship either Dionysus or Apollo. Although Dionysus provides the Bronze god power, which would be effective during the assault against Circe, consider Apollo for his Temple of Healing improvement. This turns the Temple of Zeus into a healing source, which you can use between Circe's attacks to mend your units' wounds.

There's a significant lack of food in the immediate area, so begin farming after you've collected ample wood and erected several Towers. Build a Granary and research Plow and Irrigation as soon as possible to increase farming rate. Build walls to hold off the enemy's advance (line the walls in front of the enemy gates south of your town) and allow your Tower (and Fortress after reaching Heroic Age) to weaken approaching attackers.

Figure 8.6 *Circe aggressively attacks the southern side of your base. Protect the area with a Fortress.*

After advancing to the Heroic Age, erect a Fortress near the southern wall to further guard the town from attack (see Figure 8.6). Consider upgrading your Towers, if the resources become available. Build a minimum of four Catapults to besiege Circe's bases. Construct a Market if you wish to advance to the Mythic Age—which we definitely recommend, because you can make good use of Hera's Lightning Storm god power. Improve all units at their respective military structures and the Armory.

Circe, a powerful sorceress, is ensconced in two bases. Your primary objective should be the Fortress to the east. You can pound the smaller western village (situated approximately south of your town) fairly easily with your Catapults. Protect your siege weaponry diligently, using your ground forces.

Advance to the east, up the hill toward the Fortress, bombarding the Towers first. Intercept any attackers with your ground forces and withdraw your Catapults if necessary. Save Bronze or Lightning Storm (if you received them) until the enemy attacks in numbers that are difficult to defeat easily.

Clear out all enemy Towers and other structures before bombarding the Fortress. There will be a final confrontation, so either make sure all your units are healed at the Temple (if you selected Apollo), or produce new units to increase the size of your army (set your military structures' gathering point to Circe's stronghold). You could even move up villagers and erect Towers at this point, for added firepower.

Assault the Fortress with Catapults only. Circe and two Nemean Lions appear after the Fortress sustains heavy damage. Circe possesses an impressive lightning attack. Defeat Circe and the lions, then resume pummeling the Fortress. When it topples, your mission is a success.

North

Initial Objective

◈ The avalanche has split your forces. Reunite them and claim a settlement.

Map Highlights

An avalanche has left your forces scattered across the map. Arkantos, accompanied by a Norse Hersir and two Throwing Axemen, begins in the north. Other forces—including Amanra, Norse gatherers and Dwarves, and more Hersir—are scattered east and south of Arkantos. You need to locate an unclaimed settlement. You'll find one just northeast, and another just southwest, of the map's center. Finally, prepare to contend with three enemies in this mission: one in the northern corner, one in the southern corner, and another spanning the northeast and eastern corners.

Battle Plans

First focus on the northern group, with Arkantos. Move them southeast and rendezvous with the Norse gatherer, the Dwarf, and the Ox Cart. You're now in the Norse culture, worshipping the God Thor. You'll find the nearest

> **TIP**
>
> You begin with one god power for the mission: Dwarven Mine. Invoke Dwarven Mine to place a gold mine anywhere on the map. There are gold mines near each settlement, but it might be to your advantage to place one closer to your Town Center (sending an Ox Cart to gather food or wood). Better yet, save the god power in case any current gold mine is exhausted. The amount of gold in the Dwarven Mine depends on the Age in which it's used: The more advanced the Age, the more gold.

unclaimed settlement just northeast of your position (though another can be found to the southwest). Select the three Hersir near the settlement and add them to your assembled army.

Move all remaining scattered troops to the unclaimed settlement. The Norse differ from the other cultures in many ways, including construction techniques. Dwarves and gatherers concentrate on collecting resources, while military units build structures. Use your military to construct a Town Center on the unclaimed settlement. Prepare for an attack north of the construction: A group of lurking wolves attacks your group. A new objective reveals your mission for the area.

◈ **New Objective**: To escape the pass, defeat Gargarensis' forces by destroying enemy Temples.

Scout the area for resources. You'll discover a gold mine just east of your new Town Center, and there's ample wood surrounding you. Your main food source should be hunting. It literally pays to hunt, because the Norse gain favor by hunting, as well as through combat.

Use the Dwarves to mine the gold to the east, and gatherers to hunt and collect wood. Position Ox Carts carefully between at least two resources, if possible, to minimize the walking distance for all resource collectors. Use your initial food supply to produce more gatherers, and order them to assist in the hunt or in wood-collection, as your needs dictate. Switch to farming in the Classical Age or search for new areas to hunt. Research Hunting Dogs and Thor's Pig Sticker if you plan to concentrate mostly on hunting.

You need a Temple to advance to the Classical Age, and Houses to increase your population cap. Use the military to build them as necessary. Because you worship Thor, you also can build Thor's Special Armory, which improves the weapons and armor of infantry and cavalry, in the Archaic Age.

Upon reaching the Classical Age, worship either Forseti or Freyja. Forseti offers the Healing Spring god power, creating a spring that will heal nearby units; the Troll mythological unit, which is a slow but potent archer; and improvements in speed and hit points to the Hersir. Freyja provides the Forest Fire god power, which burns a targeted forest to the ground; the Valkyrie mythological unit, which can heal your units and those of allies; and improvements to cavalry speed and hit points.

Consider Forseti, as the enemy doesn't possess a significant wood operation, making Forest Fire a less useful god power than Healing Spring. Also, although the Valkyries can serve as healers, they also cost valuable resources—the Healing Spring doesn't! Research Forseti's Hall of Thanes improvement to Hersir units, and create more at the Norse Temple!

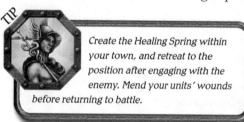

TIP

Create the Healing Spring within your town, and retreat to the position after engaging with the enemy. Mend your units' wounds before returning to battle.

In the Classical Age, build the Norse Longhouse, which is akin to the Egyptian Barracks and produces Ulfsark infantry units, Throwing Axeman ranged units, and Raiding Cavalry units. Like the Temple, it also produces Hersir, the Norse Heroes. Build an Armory as well, if you hadn't in the Archaic Age, and begin saving resources for the advance to Heroic Age, when you can build Portable Rams, the Norse siege unit you'll need to topple the enemy defenses and Temples.

After advancing to the Heroic Age, worship either Skadi or Bragi. Skadi offers the god power Frost, which freezes a group of enemy units for a short period of time; the Frost Giant, which also possesses a recharging freeze attack; and improvements to farmers and the attack of Throwing Axemen. Bragi provides the Flaming Weapons god power, which causes the weapons of your human soldiers to burst into empowering flame; the Battle Boar mythological unit; and improvements to Ulfsarks and to the speed of mythological units.

Consider Skadi for the Frost god power and Frost Giant unit. You'll face an onslaught of enemies in the eastern base, and Frost provides an added weapon against their attack. When you reach the Heroic Age, construct the Hill Fort, which can produce Portable Ram siege weapons and Jarl cavalry units. Produce at least five Portable Rams, and support them with a combination of Hersir, Jarl, and Throwing Axemen.

Enemy attacks will arrive from the north, east, and south of your town. Protect these areas with upgraded Towers and careful placement of your Hill Fort. The northern enemy sends Mountain Giants; the eastern enemy sends Ulfsarks; and the southern enemy sends Einherjar.

Assault the southern enemy first. (Don't forget to first use your resources to improve units at their respective military structures and the Armory.) Einherjar mythological units guard the southern town. Use your grouped Portable Rams against gates, walls, Towers, and other structures (see Figure 8.7). When enemy troops arrive, move the Portable Rams safely behind your army. Level the Temple with your Portable Rams. Search the area for a relic before returning to your town. Heal your wounded at the Healing Spring as necessary, and advance north to discover a second enemy.

Follow the same procedure in the north: Use the Portable Rams against gates, walls, Towers, and structures, and support them with your ground forces. Mountain Giants units defend the northern base. Defeat them, level the Hill Fort and Temple, and return to your base.

The final enemy base covers the northeastern area of the map. Advance east from your base and you'll encounter a gate protecting the entrance to the final base. Assault the gate with your Portable Rams and keep other units out of range of the nearby Hill Fort and Town Center. You could

Figure 8.7 *Pummel enemy gates with Portable Rams, but keep support units nearby to counter the irritated enemy defenders.*

even build some defensive structures to aid in the fight. Do so before attacking the gate and triggering the foes. Invoke the Frost god power when enemy numbers become high. You can freeze the units providing extra time to topple the structures before the enemy units can resume their attack.

You're currently just west of their Temple. From the Hill Fort and Town Center head directly east. Protect your siege weaponry well, and invoke Frost (if available) as needed. Topple the final enemy Temple to successfully complete the mission.

The Dwarven Forge

Initial Objective

◈ Find a settlement and build a Town Center.

Map Highlights

There's an unclaimed settlement on a hill south of your base. A Giant protects the area, however. Send your Heroes to investigate and eliminate the Mountain Giant.

You begin on the southern edge of the map.

The nearest unclaimed settlement can be found just north of your start position, and twisting cavern paths are found just north of the settlement. Search the far northeast corner for the Giants' Temples. After you complete your settlement, the Dwarven Forge appears on your mini-map, in the northern center of the map.

Battle Plans

Arkantos, Ajax, Chiron, and Amanra team up with two Dwarven Heroes, Brokk and Eitri, and agree to help them recover the Dwarven Forge from enemy Giants. In exchange, the Dwarves will provide passage to Midgard. Usher your six Heroes, Ulfsarks, and gatherers due north. Lead with the Heroes to counter the Mountain Giant and Troll defending the unclaimed settlement. Support your Heroes with Throwing Axemen.

After terminating the guards, use the Ulfsarks to construct a Town Center on the settlement. Scout the area west and east of the settlement with your Heroes. A group of elk, bear, a waterway with fish, and a gold mine are found to the west. To the east are two sets of berry bushes, more elk, and another gold mine.

◈ **New Objective**: Kill the Giants and Trolls near the Dwarven Forge to recapture it.

You're over the population limit. Build two Houses with the Ulfsarks, then produce an Ox Cart at the Town Center. Send the Ox Cart west, toward the herd of elk (research Hunting Dogs). Use your gatherers to start hunting these elk, then the bear. You receive two Dwarves from the Town Center. To produce more, you'll need another House (if you haven't already built one). Queue a total of five Dwarves and send them to the western gold mine adjacent to the forest. Position the second Ox Cart at the edge of the gold mine and adjacent forest. Queue up five more gatherers and start chopping wood near the new Ox Cart (and near the Town Center).

Use the Ulfsarks to build an Armory when the wood becomes available. Continue to collect resources and research gathering improvements as quickly as possible. When you meet the requirement, advance to the Heroic Age. Begin worshipping Bragi, for the Flaming Weapons god power (which will assist your human units against the mighty Giants). During the time it takes to advance in Age, use the Ulfsarks to build more Houses.

Your six Heroes should be able to fend off enemy attacks, all by mythological units. Monitor the passageways east, north, and west of your base for intruders. After exhausting the game animals in the west, move your gatherers and Ox Cart east. Hunt the elk and forage for berries there.

Use the Ulfsarks to place a Hill Fort (after reaching the Heroic Age) and Temple on the eastern side of town, near the food gatherers. At the Temple, start producing Hersir; at the Hill Fort, start producing Jarl. Both units are effective against mythological units. (Your Ulfsarks will barely dent the Mountain Giants.) You should also produce a couple of Valkyrie at the Temple, but you might need additional favor to do so. Don't produce units too aggressively: You have enough to defend against early attacks, and you still should advance to the Mythic Age.

Construct a Market with the Ulfsarks, and after meeting the resource requirements, advance to the Mythic Age. Worship Baldr, whose Ragnarok god power can prove useful in the mission's final stages. Continue producing Jarl and Hersir until you have 12–15 of each. You also should produce four to six Portable Rams. If you run out of food sources, start farming. When you have plenty of wood, switch most of your wood gatherers to gold or farming. You'll need more wood only to build Portable Rams. Trade any extra wood for gold at the Market.

> **TIP**
>
> You were provided with a Dwarven Mine god power to begin the mission. Even though there's a gold mine to the east, you may want to invoke Dwarven Mine once your dwarves have exhausted the western mine just to save the time required to move the Dwarves and Ox Cart east.

Head into the cavern through the eastern entrance. Continue north, then northwest, to the northern edge of the map. You'll bypass a route to the west that would send you toward the Dwarven Forge. Before you can go there, you must obliterate the Giants' production centers in the north. Beware: There are many defenders. This is a great moment to invoke Flaming Weapons! Use Portable Rams against structures. Counter the Mountain Giants, Fire Giants, and Trolls with your Heroes, Jarl, and Hersir. Send Jarl to intercept the enemy Ballistae. Continue to reinforce your army with new units at your base. Once you have the favor, include some Valkyries, Battle Boars, and Fire Giants.

hidden Relics

Begin moving troops up the eastern passage. You'll enter what appears to be a cavern. A group of enemy Dwarven miners are attempting to break through a wall, just to the north. Attack the wall and the Mummies inside the adjacent room. Clear out all hostile units, then collect the three relics from the treasure room and return them to your Temple.

Level all of the enemy structures and kill all of the enemy units in this northern corner. Then head southwest toward the Dwarven Forge. Additional Mountain Giants and Trolls defend the area (see Figure 8.8). Don't allow your units to split up. Concentrate all attacks on one or two enemy units before moving on to the next target. When you have eliminated the defenders, a new objective appears.

> **TIP**
>
> Depending on difficulty level, Fire Giants may emerge from the Dwarven Forge's own lava pool to attack. Also, the Giants usually invoke a Healing Spring to the west of the Forge. Capturing this valuable area can yield the Healing Spring and a place to build buildings, including a settlement (level the Giants' Town Center with Portable Rams).

Figure 8.8 *Use your Heroes, Jarl, and Hersir against the Mountain Giants and Trolls around the Forge.*

◈ **New Objective**: Defend the Dwarven Forge until the Giants retreat.

You must defend the Forge for eight minutes to complete the mission. Move your Portable Rams south of the Forge and eliminate the Temple and other structures here quickly. Brokk and Eitri suggest another weapon against the Giants. If you click on the three Dwarven Forge structures, you can research three valuable improvements. Giantslaying Blades add bonus damage versus Giants to all of your attacks; Osmium Mail makes human soldiers more resistant to hack attacks; and the Asbestos Shields improvement makes human soldiers more resistant to Fire Giants. Research Giantslaying Blades and Asbestos Shields first.

You can't build structures in the Forge area (though you can build on the bridge to the east). Use the Hersir to drop a Hill Fort or Towers here. Continue to reinforce your army with new Jarl, Hersir, and mythological units. Assault the Giant attackers as you did the defenders—concentrate attacks on one or two Giants. Don't spread yourself too thin. Even though Jarl and Hersir are effective against mythological units, the Giants are still mighty strong. Don't hesitate to invoke Ragnarok if you worshipped Baldr. Move all your gatherers and Dwarves—now Heroes of Ragnarok—to the Dwarven Forge to aid in its defense. Keep the Dwarven Forge intact for the full eight minutes to complete the mission.

WARNING

Be careful around the western river of the Dwarven Forge area. Jormund Brood mythological units patrol the waters to the west, and can strike your units with their ranged steam attack.

Not From Around Here

Initial Objective

⬥ Protect Skult and his flag. Move Arkantos, Skult, and the Folstag Flag-Bearer along the dirt path to the flag.

Map Highlights

The Heroes, Skult, and the Flag-Bearer begin on the southern edge of the map. You can spot the exit at the far northern edge of the map. The Giants' Temples are scattered throughout the western and eastern areas of the map. If you investigate the map's center (and just north of the center), you trigger the second stage, and base-building portion, of the mission. It's wiser to explore the western and eastern edges before maneuvering toward the middle.

Battle Plans

Arkantos, Amanra, Ajax, and Chiron must escort Skult and the Folstag Flag-Bearer through treacherous Giant territory to the exit at the northern edge of the screen. You start the mission with two god powers—Bolt and Healing Spring. Save these god powers for later in the mission. You also possess groups of Heavy Hoplites and Heavy Throwing Axemen to assist in the battles against the Giants.

Begin the mission by separating your troops and assigning attack groups. Place your Heroes in the first battle group, and separate the Hoplites and Axemen into their own groups. Assign the Flag-Bearer his own group so you can easily select and withdraw him as necessary.

Advance to the north. You'll spot Mountain Giants and a Frost Giant. Lead the attack with your Heroes. Support with the ranged Throwing Axemen and send in the Hoplites last. A Giants' Temple can be found just west along the path, and it will continue to produce Mountain Giants until it's destroyed (see Figure 8.9). Send your units to the Temple, defeat the defenders, and obliterate the vile structure. Resume your northward course and battle more Giants. Once again, send in your Heroes first. After the Giants attack the Heroes, bring in the Throwing Axemen and Hoplites.

> **TIP**
>
> The Folstag Flag-Bearer has better line of sight than your Heroes or military units. Lead the advance with the Flag-Bearer so you can spot enemies sooner. However, quickly pull the Flag-Bearer back, to keep him away from the threatening Giants.

You'll reach an intersection. Head east first. (You'll spot an enclosed pen of pigs south of the path. Remember this location for later.) Several Temples can be found in the eastern corner of the map. The first rests in an alcove south of the path. Protect your more vulnerable units from the Giants by attacking the enemies with your Heroes first. Find more Temples along southern and northern paths along this eastern route.

Figure 8.9 *Eliminate the Temples to cut off production of more enemy Giants.*

The eastern edge of the map is a dead end, but does contain several Temples. Explore every nook and cranny and eliminate all Temples. Move slowly so you don't alert too many Giant defenders at a time. After clearing the area, return to the intersection. Place the Healing Spring in the map's center if your units need to mend their wounds.

Proceed west from the intersection. The western edge of the map mirrors the eastern edge; it's an eventual dead end, but does contain several of the Giants' Temples. You'll find many Mountain Giants protecting the western region.

Support your Heroes with the Throwing Axemen and Heavy Hoplites. Assault and destroy all the Temples before returning to the intersection. Now head north, to discover a new problem—the Giants have blocked the path with a boulder wall that can only be destroyed with siege weaponry.

⬦ New Objective: Build up a defensive base near the boulder wall and advance to the Heroic Age.

Select your Throwing Axemen and have them build a Town Center on the unclaimed settlement and an Armory. Produce gatherers and Dwarves at the Town Center and begin collecting resources, particularly wood and gold, which will fund the structures and the Portable Rams required to level the boulder wall. Defend your town from any Giants that attack (if you missed any during your trek through the mountain paths).

Advance to the Heroic Age as soon as possible. You can choose to worship Njord or Bragi. Njord offers the Walking Woods god power, which causes trees to animate and attack nearby enemies. Njord also provides improvements to Jarl and naval units, and offers the Kraken and Mountain Giant mythological units. Select Bragi for the Flaming Weapons god power, the Battle Boar mythological unit, and the improvements to Ulfsarks. (You won't have naval units, so Njord's naval improvements and units are useless.)

> **TIP**
>
> *Don't forget those pigs you discovered earlier in the mission! Move a unit to the enclosed pen and break down the stone wall. Move the pigs to your Town Center, research Husbandry, wait for the pigs to fatten, then use your gatherers to start collecting food.*

◈ **New Objective**: Build siege weapons and break through the boulder wall. Destroy the Giants' Temples to weaken their attacks.

Shift resource-gathering units to wood, unless you have enough to build the Hill Fort and to start producing Portable Rams. Build the Hill Fort when possible, and a Longhouse, if you wish to produce its units. Build a Temple and bolster your army with mythological units and Hersir, and build a couple of Portable Rams at the Hill Fort (You need them to take down the boulder wall.) Research improvements as resources become available.

You will face more Giants after breaking through the wall, so invoke Healing Spring in your town (if you haven't already) and use the god power to heal your units before pushing forward. Make sure to add more units to your army. Start pummeling the boulder wall with your Portable Rams (see Figure 8.10). After you inflict significant damage to the wall, a new twist interrupts the mission. The enemy invokes the Forest Fire god power on the western, eastern, and southern edges of the map. This burns down the forest, paving the way for more Giants to invade the area.

Figure 8.10 *You must construct Portable Ram siege weapons to break down the boulder wall blocking the path to the exit.*

◈ **New Objective**: Escape the Giant army. Move Skult, Arkantos, and the Folstag Flag-Bearer to the north end of the pass.

There's little time to waste. Move the Portable Rams out of the way (you no longer need them) and start advancing beyond the boulder wall. You can lead with the Flag-Bearer to utilize his enhanced line of sight, but be prepared to have him retreat behind your military units. Expect your town to be ravaged by god powers. Ignore that, and continue north toward the exit. Eliminate any lurking Giants with your Heroes and military units.

You'll reach a forest blocking the path. Fortunately the Gods are smiling on you: The Gods invoke Forest Fire to clear the path. After the trees burn, move your Heroes, Skult, and the Flag-Bearer north. The mission ends in victory once Arkantos, Skult, and the Flag-Bearer reached the marked area on the northern edge of the map.

Missions 25-32 Walkthrough

Arkantos seeks the aid of the Norse in Scandinavia for help against the terror of Gargarensis. While you'll find some allies among the Norsemen, others aren't as friendly, and will fight to prevent your incursions. Guide Arkantos and his Hero comrades through dangerous, snow-covered Scandinavian lands to search for new allies who can help foil Gargarensis' plans for domination.

During the first six missions of this chapter, Arkantos must rely on the Norse culture. You will no longer use Greek or Egyptian units and technologies, or worship Greek or Egyptian gods. Instead, learn the tactics of the Norse (see Chapter 5 of this strategy guide) and use them to defend yourself against the forces of Gargarensis and of rival Norsemen. Arkantos will revert to Greek units, technologies, and gods for the campaign's final two missions.

Welcoming Committee

Initial Objective

◈ Protect Skult and the Folstag Flag Bearer.

Map Highlights

As your mission begins, a small battle is raging not far from you. Eventually you'll need to deal with nearby Norse clans in the northwest, northeast, and southeast corners of the map.

Battle Plans

When the mission starts, get Skult and the Folstag Flag-Bearer behind your troops and out of enemy range. Send in your Heroes to battle the attacking Norsemen. Support your Heroes with your military units, which include Hoplites, Toxotes, Throwing Axemen, and Heavy Raiders. A new objective appears once all attacking Norsemen have been eliminated.

◈ **New Objective**: Create an ambush. Built at least five Towers.

Enemy bases are in the northwest, northeast, and southeast areas of the map. More bad news: You won't be able to produce military units for the duration of the mission. You also have the Healing Spring god power, which can be used between attacks to mend the damage to your units. Position the Healing Spring in the center of the map, because you'll be passing through here often to reach other enemy bases.

The hill at the center of the frozen lake makes an optimum ambush point. Construct five Towers around the perimeter of the hill; place the Healing Spring at the center of the hill protected by the Towers. Use the downtime during Tower construction to heal your wounded units by placing them adjacent to the Healing Spring. A new objective appears after building five Towers.

◈ **New Objective**: Use the Folstag Flag Bearer to lure the clan leaders into an ambush. Defeat all three leaders.

The enemy bases are revealed on the mini-map. Move your troops to the outskirts of the northwest base. Scan the mini-map and note the enemy troops inside. The Hersir inside the base is considered the leader. Killing the leader converts the town and its resources to your cause.

Lure the enemy troops out by moving the Folstag Flag-Bearer close to the town. You may be surprised at the ferocity of their assault. Order the Flag-Bearer to retreat behind your Towers placed near the frozen lake, and engage the enemy with your ground troops near these defensive structures. Use your Hoplites against enemy cavalry and your Heroes and ranged troops against infantry. If the Hersir attempts to flee the town, focus all attack on him. Kill the Hersir, and the town and its remaining military units are converted (see Figure 9.1).

You still can't produce military units; the added resources will fund only Towers and the Crenelations improvement, which causes Towers to attack moving targets more effectively.

Make a pit stop at the Healing Spring and ensure all of your troops are healed. Spend resources gained from eliminating the first Norse clan to build additional Towers near your ambush point. Lure the enemy from the northeastern base out with the Folstag Flag-Bearer, but don't get the Flag-Bearer killed. Retreat to your ambush point. Target the enemy Ulfsark primarily with your Throwing Axemen and Toxotes. Order your Hoplites against the Jarl. Support both squads with your Heroes Target the enemy Hersir once he's lured outside the base to gain further resources to spend on more Towers.

Figure 9.1 *Defeating the town leader provides additional resources for your army.*

You can build walls along with the Towers. Construct walls near the ambush point to create choke points forcing the enemy units toward your concentration of Tower firepower.

Follow the same procedure with the final enemy base, which can be found on the southeastern side of the map. You should have plenty of resources at this point, so bolster your attack with plenty of Towers. Spend all remaining resources on Towers facing the southeastern base. Champion Ulfsarks, Raiding Cavalry, and Ballistas populate the final town. Lure them out with the Folstag Flag-Bearer and battle near your defenses (see Figure 9.2). Counter the Ulfsarks with Throwing Axemen and Toxotes, and counter the Raiding Cavalry with Hoplites.

If you still have Flaming Weapons or Bronze, invoke that god power to assist in this final battle. It's vital to conduct the battle near your Towers. If you spot the Hersir as he is lured from the town, focus all attacks on him. As soon as this third Hersir dies, your mission ends in success.

Figure 9.2 *Use the Flag-Bearer to lure enemy units out of their town and into your ambush.*

Union

Initial Objective

◈ Follow the trail to the first Norse clan.

Map Highlights

You begin on the northern section of the map. The Blackhammer clan can be found just south of your start position. Explore the western edge of the map to discover the Lothbrok clan. Finally, the Forkbeard clan can be found on the southern part of the map.

Battle Plans

Arkantos, Ajax, Amanra, and Chiron begin with new allies: The Valkyrie Reginlief and Shieldmaidens join a group of Huskarls in assisting your Heroes. You must locate three proud and independent Norse clans and somehow convince them to band together in the battle against the nefarious Gargarensis.

Trolls are attacking the Blackhammer clan, just south of your start position. Quickly move your units south and eliminate the attackers. When you have defeated the Trolls and moved south into the Blackhammer base, the Blackhammer clan offers your group the use of their buildings and units and a new objective. Fulfill the objective and the Blackhammer clan will be convinced to join your cause.

◈ **New Objective**: Defeat the Trolls in the mines to the north.

You're provided with gatherers and Dwarves to begin resource collection. Position your Heroes on the southern edge of the base—the next wave of Trolls will arrive from that direction to assault the Blackhammer structures. Scout the southwestern area of the base to discover goats, farms, and a Dwarven gold mine.

> **WARNING**
>
> In early Ages, the Dwarven gold mine doesn't last as long as a typical gold mine. However, the Trolls guard several rich gold mines. Use available gold to strengthen your army. If you run out of gold, it's time to mount the attack against the Trolls and their underground passage.

Send the Norse gatherers to farm (wait until the goats fatten before processing them) and the Dwarves to mine gold. There are a couple gatherers near a forest; start collecting wood with these units. You are provided with the Dwarven Mine god power to begin the mission. You can invoke this power should you run out of gold before defeating the Trolls.

Your Heroes should be able to handle the trolls, though you can use Blackhammer's military structures to produce additional units. New Trolls will arrive periodically through an underground passage. Don't attack the passage first, though; concentrate your attacks on the Trolls. Eliminate all the Trolls and then start attacking the underground passage. As you attack, more Trolls emerge from the passage. Shift attack off of the passage and onto the Trolls. Defeat all Trolls and the underground passage to complete the objective and win over the Blackhammer clan to your cause.

New Objective: Exit the mines and find the second Norse clan.

The Blackhammer base becomes yours. Scan the town and make sure any new gatherers are active and collecting resources. Scan the area near the former underground passage to discover a new group of Dwarven miners and an Ox Cart. Free them by destroying the stone enclosure. Start mining the plentiful gold in the area.

Technically, you don't have to build the Towers on the actual flag sites. To accomplish the objective, just build the five Towers near the flagged sites around the Lothbrok base.

Once again it's possible to remain steady inside the Blackhammer base and concentrate on resource gathering before heading west toward the next Norse clan. Concentrate on wood gathering to fund your upcoming objective.

Figure 9.3 *Use Norse military units to construct five Towers near the marked locations.*

Advance to the Heroic Age before pressing onward. After Age-advancement you can choose to worship Skadi or Bragi; both offer useful god powers and mythological units. Spend the resources necessary to improve your military. Then it's time to proceed through the south passage and across the frozen river to find the Lothbrok clan's base.

New Objective: Build five Towers near the flagged sites around this Norse village.

To convince the Lothbrok clan to join your cause, simply assist them in defense by constructing four Towers at their designated areas (see Figure 9.3). Move in Norse military units and begin construction of the Towers on the flagged sites. Move other units to the southern edge of the Lothbrok base—an assortment of enemy Giants is approaching from the south to attack the clan base. Eliminate the Giants and continue to build. A new objective appears once all four Towers are in place.

New Objective: Cross the river to the east to find the third clan.

You'll find the Forkbeard clan just east of Lothbrok territory. Before heading their way, however, you should continue to gather the resources you'll

The Source of the Giants

Before heading east to locate the third Norse clan, locate the path south from Lothbrok's base—it's along the western side of the map. Advance south with your Heroes in the lead (plus any Hersir or Jarl you've created, which are also effective against mythological units). Several Mountain and Frost Giants attempt to impede your attack. Defeat them with your counter mythological units. Destroy the Temple to stop the Giants' production. Resume course east from Lothbrok's base to locate the third Norse clan.

need to advance to the Mythic Age. You must choose to worship either Baldr or Tyr upon advancement. Baldr offers the Ragnarok god power, which turns your gatherers and Dwarves into mighty warriors. Baldr also provides the Fire Giant mythological unit; Tyr offers bonuses to Ulfsarks and provides the Fimbulwinter god power. Select Baldr for the powerful Fire Giant mythological unit and the potential to use Ragnarok should you need the added fire-power against the final enemy Giants.

Move your military units east from the Lothbrok base to find Forkbeard's clan, and discover how you can help him. Fulfill his objective and he will band with the other two clans and join you against Gargarensis.

◈ **New Objective**: Destroy the Watch Tower to free the third clan leader's daughter.

A new location appears on your mini-map: the far southern corner of the map, where Forkbeard's daughter is being held. You'll face an assortment of Giants on the way to the southern corner, including Frost, Fire, and Mountain Giants. Use resources to acquire improvements at military structures such as the Armory. Add more Hersir—effective against mythological units—and Portable Rams—effective against Towers, walls, and buildings—to your groups.

Advance south into the Giants' base. Move slowly to trigger the fewest enemies possible. Lead the attack with your Heroes, and support them with Hersir and other military units. Topple the Temples to cut off Giant production. Continue pushing south and eliminate the defenses around the location of Forkbeard's daughter.

One final task remains: destroy the Tower in the southern corner of the map to free Forkbeard's daughter. Surround the Tower with your units, and topple it. When this is done, you'll have gained Forkbeard's allegiance and united all three clans, completing your mission in success.

The Well of Urd

Initial Objective

◈ Build an army and destroy the gate to the Well of Urd.

Map Highlights

The five Heroes start in the southern area of the map. The gate protecting the Well of Urd is revealed on the mini-map and can be found near the northern edge of the map. Gargarensis' base protecting the gate is massive and covers most of the upper half of the map. A small enemy outpost can be found to the west. You'll construct your town on the entire south-eastern corner of the map.

Battle Plans

Arkantos, Ajax, Chiron, Amanra, and Reginleif command an army of Jarl, Huskarls, and Raiding Cavalry in the southern area of the map. Scan the mini-map to discover the location of the Well of Urd. Although your town won't face much aggression (occasional attacks from the west and northwest), the enemy has a very stiff defense. You'll have to punch through it in order to reach the gate. You'll need a substantial army to defeat the mighty defenders protecting the gate to the well.

Begin by using the Huskarls to build a Temple your start position. As soon as the Temple has been completed, advance to the Classical Age. It would be wise to worship Heimdall: This Minor God's Undermine god power can crumble enemy walls and Towers, giving your invaders the edge. Upon advancing, you also should build a Longhouse and Armory.

You're worshipping Odin for the mission, which means a Temple provides two free Raven scouts when you reach the Classical Age. Should a Raven die, it will reappear at the Temple. Use the Ravens first to scout the area around your base for additional resources, then to scout the Well of Urd to gauge enemy defenses.

Figure 9.4 *After reaching the Classical Age, send Odin's Raven scouts to explore the area around your base for new sources of food and gold.*

Scout the area for resources with Odin's two Raven scouts (see Figure 9.4). You'll discover two gold mines on the hill west of town. (Enemies will disturb your resource collectors here.) Berry bushes and roaming caribou (use Odin's Great Hunt to increase their numbers) provide early food sources. More berry bushes can be found to the far east of town.

For additional food, scout the far eastern corner of the map for hunting grounds. (It's wise to exhaust hunting options: Among the Norse, hunting gains favor.) There's also a relic there, which one of your Heroes should grab and garrison in your Temple.

Finally, protect your gold mines and Dwarves with a couple of Towers. The enemy will send the occasional cavalry or ranged unit to disrupt your resource gathering.

Advance to the Heroic Age after building the Armory. Choose to worship Skadi or Njord. (Skadi's Frost Giant is a valuable mythological unit.) Also construct a Hill Fort and Market after Age-advancement. If you wish, build a couple of portable rams and level the enemy's western outpost, with support from your Heroes and troops.

Both attacking quickly and building up are double-edged swords. If you attack quickly, you won't have

There's a secondary enemy outpost to the west of your base. It houses a Town Center and gold mining operation. It's possible to level it with your current troops, so it might be wiser to wait until the Heroic Age, when you can produce portable rams. There's also a relic near this outpost.

the most powerful troops the Norse have to offer but Gargarensis' defenses will be weaker. If you wait to attack, your army will be stronger but so will Gargarensis. You should definitely be patient about your mission until you've reached the Mythic Age. You need the most powerful units and improvements available before attempting an assault on the mighty defenders guarding the well. Build the necessary Houses to support a large army. Use the Market to trade resources in order to advance to the Mythic Age as quickly as possible. Once you do, you can worship either Baldr or Tyr, but consider Baldr for the Ragnarok god power—you can turn all your gatherers and Dwarves into Heroes, adding great power to your assault.

> **TIP**
> Before approaching the outskirts of the well gate, consider using your military units to construct Towers and Hill Forts to aid in the assault. These structures provide an added attack, and could distract enemy forces facing your own units. Acquire all Tower improvements.

Start acquiring military improvements at the Armory and other military structures. Train Hersir and Jarl, the units most effective against mythological units. Construct three to five portable rams to level Towers, gates, and other enemy structures quickly. You also should complement your army with Frost Giants or Fire Giants, if you chose to worship Skadi or Baldr, respectively.

There are a couple of avenues for your assault. The enemy's base covers much of the northern area of the map. You can head directly north from your base, or head west and beyond the enemy's outpost, and proceed north from there. It might be best to take the quicker route, straight to the north. Gates, walls, and Towers protect enemy territory from your invasion. You should advance slowly and take care to eliminate all Towers and defensive buildings you encounter. The enemy will reinforce its massive defensive army. Destroy military structures (primarily situated south from the Well of Urd) to prevent more enemies from entering the action (see Figure 9.5).

Lure the enemy to your units. Don't rush haphazardly into the area around the gate, or you will find yourself overwhelmed. Target myth units with your Heroes, Jarl, and Hersir;

Figure 9.5 *The enemy offers a mighty defense. Eliminate their military structures to avoid facing reinforcements.*

counter Norse human units with your appropriate troops and mythological units. It's possible that you will fail in the first assault. Make sure you eliminate as many enemy structures as possible before conducting the battle, so the enemy can't reinforce its defense. If you are beaten back, continue gathering resources and use the Market to trade resources as needed. Keep producing a mixed group of units to gear up for another assault.

There's no time limit for the mission, so don't hesitate to build up a dramatic amount of resources to fund all Armory improvements and multiple armies. Switch to farming, once you've exhausted all the berries and hunting options.

- ⬦ **New Objective**: Defeat all of the myth units defending the Well of Urd.

Remove all enemy mythological units from the area (Fire Giants emerge from the Well of Urd). When the gate falls and all enemy myth units have been defeated, the mission ends in victory.

Save Skadi's Frost god power for the assault near the gate. You can invoke the power to temporarily freeze enemy units in the area. This can buy you extra time to eliminate nearby Towers or to focus attacks on any unfrozen enemy units. After the enemy thaws, attack!

Beneath the Surface

Initial Objective

- ⬦ Kill the Fire Giants that guard the Gate Ram before the Tartarus Gate opens.

The key to this mission is not to get too tangled up with the Norse fort above ground. They are more dangerous than those below ground. An early assault might cripple the aboveground forces, but if this fails, it is better to get underground quickly and just try to hold off the attacks above rather than eliminating the enemies one at a time.

Map Highlights

Your forces are separated at the beginning of the mission. Arkantos, Ajax, Amanra, Chiron, and Reginlief start in the Underworld, near the map's center. Your base, which includes a Town Center, Temple, and Longhouse, can be found on the western side of the map. The Giant Ram lies in the far eastern area of the map.

Battle Plans

Your Heroes have entered the Underworld and find a Giant Ram attempting to break down the Erebus Gate. You must prevent the Ram from breaking down the gate by defeating the Guardians around the Ram, a group of Fire Giants. Although your Heroes are near the map's center, the bulk of your base lies out of the Underworld, on the western side of the map.

You don't have a whole lot of time to waste. You can monitor your remaining time by clicking on the Erebus Gate to learn how many hit points remain or the "Percent Damage to Tartarus Gate" indicator in the upper right corner of the screen. To be safe, you should begin your attack on the Ram before the gate's hit points drop below 10,000. In order to meet this timetable, and to fund plenty of units and many, if not all, military improvements, you'll need a strong economy. You're provided with Dwarven Mine, Healing Spring, and Frost god powers. You can't build structures in the Underworld, however, so Healing Spring can't be used to assist your armies once they've moved through the underground passage.

Select your Town Center immediately, and queue up 10 more gatherers. Concentrate initially on food gathering (your Ulfsarks can scout to locate more goats north and northwest from your Town Center). Food sources can be found around the Town Center, including berry

Scout the area in the Underworld near the Well of Urd. Send your Heroes to do it (but avoid the northeast). You will uncover more gold mines and several relics. Have your Heroes snatch the relics and head back through the underground passage to your base above ground. Garrison the relics in your Temple to gain their benefits.

bushes to the west and animals to hunt to the east and south. Exhaust these options before processing the goats (they need to fatten) and starting to farm (see Figure 9.6). Research Husbandry to speed up the domestic animals fattening rate.

After the gatherers are finished, produce an Ox Cart and a few Dwarves and send them into the Underworld to mine the gold southwest of the Heroes' start position. You will want six to seven Dwarves mining gold. Once you've exhausted the gold, scout further southwest for another mine, or go through a passage to the north for another mine. The Dwarven mines in the Underworld don't last long so continually monitor your collectors.

Figure 9.6 *You're on a fast timetable for this mission. Gather resources quickly, to fund the military campaign necessary to topple the enemy's Ram.*

Once you have produced the Dwarves, build four or five gatherers and send them east of the Town Center to start collecting wood. (Position an Ox Cart nearby—particularly if your food gatherers are there hunting.) You need wood to fund structures and improvements. Use your Ulfsarks to build Houses until you've maximized the population cap.

TIP

If you set a gather point on the Well of Urd and another gather point from the other end of the Well, units will automatically move through them.

Assign your Ulfsarks to construct a Hill Fort and a Market. You could start producing units at this point, but it's more important to reach the Mythic Age in order to get various military improvements. Trade resources in the Market to meet the requirements for the Mythic Age as soon as possible.

Advance to the Mythic Age when possible and worship Baldr over Tyr. Baldr's Fire Giant mythological unit offers excellent power (although he'll have to be added to the fight after it's started, since you likely won't be able to afford the favor requirement at first). Plus, Baldr's Ragnarok god power can turn gatherers and Dwarves into Heroes, providing additional might.

Start producing Hersir and Jarl. You can produce Hersir at both the Longhouse and the Temple; create Jarl using the Hill Fort. If you can afford it, start upgrading your cavalry units

TIP

Invoke Dwarven Mine in the Mythic Age in the Underworld. This mine will have 6,000 available gold. You won't have to worry about repositioning your Dwarves for awhile.

at the Longhouse or Hill Fort, and your weapons and armor at the Armory. You need to keep producing until you've reached the population cap.

Remember, monitor the hit points remaining to the Erebus Gate. You must attack when at least 10,000 hit points remain.

Advance northeast across the lava bridge. Lead with your Heroes so they can take the brunt of the attack from the Fire Giants standing guard. Send in your Hersir and Jarl, both effective against myth units, and focus attack on a single Fire Giant. Eliminate the defenders and head south toward the Ram.

The enemy's defense is formidable. You'll face Fire Giants, Trolls, Throwing Axemen, and Jarl. Target the Fire Giants first; they're the most powerful. Eliminate all Fire Giants, then target Trolls and remaining military units. During the battle, shift your attention to your own military structures and replace dead units with new ones. Invoke Skadi's Frost god power during the battle to remove some of the enemies from the battle temporarily. You'll have more success facing fewer enemy units for the duration of the god power.

> After crossing the bridge and defeating the Fire Giants standing guard, allow Reginlief to heal your units or remain idle so any Valkyrie you produced can mend your wounds as well.

Ignore the Ram and concentrate all attacks on the defending enemy units (see Figure 9.7). The mission ends after the Fire Giant defenders around the Ram are eliminated. You may spot a large enemy army approaching from the south—one that's likely too powerful for your remaining units to combat. Thankfully Arkantos orders a retreat to the Well of Urd and the mission concludes in success.

Figure 9.7 *You don't need to defeat the Ram in order to beat the mission. Only attack the defending enemy units to complete the task in victory.*

Unlikely Heroes

Initial Objective

◈ Protect the Dwarves while they cut the haft from the taproot.

Map Highlights

Your forces are split at the beginning of the mission. Your Heroes are on the western side of the map, protecting Dwarves who are mining gold and excavating the taproot. On the northern side of the map, separated from your western army, are a handful of friendly troops and a cart carrying the head of Thor's Hammer. The enemy will attempt to shatter the Hades Gate in the map's center, and you'll encounter other enemies around the eastern side of the map and, eventually, the southern edge of the map.

Battle Plans

Arkantos, Ajax, Amanra, Reginlief, and a Dwarf Hero, Brokk, protect a couple of groups of Dwarves on the western side of the map. You must excavate the haft of Thor's Hammer from the taproot just south of the gold mine. To do so, simply assign Dwarves to the taproot, as if it were a gold mine.

You are provided with plenty of Dwarves, but must decide how to split them up. Keep in mind that you will receive reinforcements throughout the mission, depending on how much gold you manage to mine. The more Dwarves assigned to the root, however, the faster the haft can be cut from the taproot. Consider six Dwarves on gold (protect them with your Heroes) and the rest on the taproot. It's a fair balance, and permits the fast arrival of reinforcements (more reinforcements for every 400 gold collected). The Dwarves warn of a nearby gate where groups of enemy mythological units attempt to break through. Avoid the gate because the enemy units are too strong to fight.

> **WARNING**
>
> *Don't move your western troops too far to the northeast. Depending on the difficulty level, a Norse Nidhogg dragon may lurk nearby. Wait until you have several reinforcement groups (particularly Throwing Axemen) before attempting to take down this beast. Reginlief is the best Nidhogg killer in the game because she has a huge ranged attack with bonus damage against myth units. As long as she can fight the dragon, you should have no trouble.*

- **New Objective**: Finish cutting the haft from the taproot and bring the two pieces of the hammer together.

Eitri arrives at the eastern side of the map with another set of forces—Valkyrie, Hersir, and the second Dwarf hero, Eitri—to the east. Included with the forces are an Ox Cart and a second cart hauling the head of Thor's Hammer. You must reunite the head with the haft to complete the mission. Unfortunately, you can't go directly west; you must take the long way!

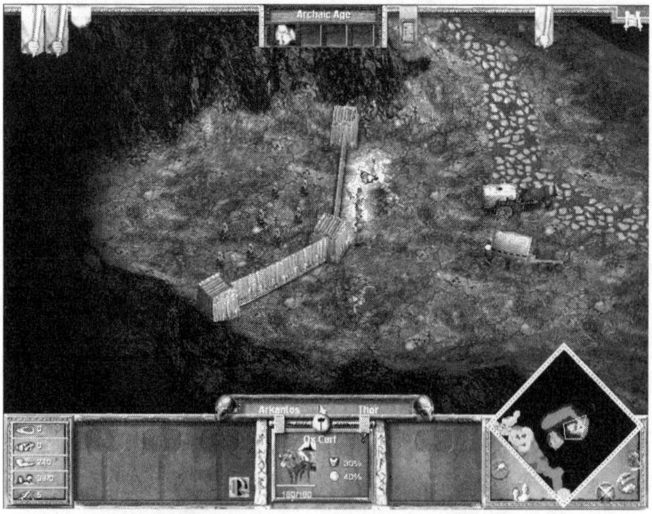

Figure 9.8 *Free these Dwarven miners and use them to mine gold to fund reinforcements.*

Maneuver the eastern group along the path around to the west. You'll discover a couple of enemy Trolls guarding a group of imprisoned Dwarven gold miners (see Figure 9.8). Kill the myth units and destroy the gate to free the Dwarves. Continue east to discover a Dwarven gold mine guarded by more myth units. Position the Ox Cart near the mine and assign all of these Dwarves to gather gold. Beware of a nearby Chimera. Counter it with your Valkyrie and Hersir. Don't let the Valkyrie be killed, however. She can heal your units.

You've likely received your first batch of reinforcements by now. Select them in the southern corner of the map and send them north to rendezvous with your Heroes. Maintain position there and fight any enemies that arrive. The second reinforcement group contains Dwarves. Escort them to the taproot and assign them to help excavate the haft.

Shift back to your eastern group. Scout northwest of the gold mine to discover three Trolls protecting another Dwarven gold mine. Defeat the Trolls. Move to this new mine once the first has been depleted. You also possess the Dwarven Mine god power, which can be used to create another mine.

Your eventual goal is to reunite your western and eastern troops by meeting somewhere in the middle. Your eastern troops aren't very strong and never will be, but your western Heroes continue to be reinforced (at least until all the gold has been used). Defend your positions until you receive several reinforcement groups, then begin to advance. The enemy eventually breaks through the rockfall at the bridge, which will cause enemy attacks to come from south of the taproot. These enemy myth units are very strong and you will need to migrate your forces, including the taproot once its excavated, toward the northeast.

You'll do most of your battling using your western troops. Start moving east across the northern edge of the map. Defeat the Nidhogg with your ranged units, and face several groups of enemy Trolls. You should have little trouble plowing through the Trolls, given your huge numbers of reinforcements. For even more units, search the

Figure 9.9 *Rescue these Hersir and add them to your attack groups.*

northern corner of the map to find a group of imprisoned Hersir (see Figure 9.9). Free them by attacking the gate enclosing them. Add them to your group and head south to meet your western troops and the cart carrying the other piece of Thor's Hammer.

◈ **New Objective**: Bring the two pieces of Thor's Hammer together.

After you uproot the haft of Thor's Hammer in the western area of the map, this new objective appears. Move your larger forces around to the eastern side of the map to meet the smaller band guarding the cart that carries the head of Thor's Hammer. You'll face more Trolls and Fire Giants along the way. After uniting your forces, start heading back with the hammer's head along the northern edge of the map and to the west. When the two pieces of the hammer are near each other, the mission ends in success.

All Is Not Lost

Initial Objective

◈ Find the abandoned mining town and build a Town Center there.

Map Highlights

You begin on the eastern side of the map. The nearest unclaimed settlement can be found just south of your start position. Gargarensis' forces cover the northern and far eastern sides of the map. Odysseus' reinforcements eventually arrive from the west.

Battle Plans

A small squad of Ulfsarks, a group of six gatherers, and an Ox Cart join your Heroes on the eastern side of the map. You possess two god powers to start the mission—Dwarven Mine and Healing Spring—that can be used during the mission. Move your units south to locate the nearest unclaimed settlement.

Order your Ulfsarks to construct a Town Center on the settlement. There are several gold mines, wolves, and bears near the settlement. Position the Ox Cart near the animals, and use the gatherers to hunt the animals and gather food. A new objective appears after completing the Town Center.

◈ **New Objective**: You have 10 minutes to build your defenses before Gargarensis attacks.

You must work quickly to build a viable defense against Gargarensis' threatening force. Scan the area around your Town Center for food sources. You'll discover caribou west of town, wolves southwest of town, and boars along the southern edge of the map. Hunt these animals before resorting to farming.

TIP

Search the area directly west of your settlement to discover a relic in the corner of the map. Garrison the relic in your Temple to gain its benefit.

As you gain food, produce eight more gatherers and assign four each to gold and wood gathering. Once you have the resources, produce Dwarves, and use them to mine more gold; shift the gatherers off gold and onto wood. You want a large amount of wood as quickly as possible, to fund Towers.

There are three entrances to your base. Some walls and Towers are already in place, but you'll need more for your defense. Move a couple of military units into each of the three entrances. Complete the outer wall in each entrance. South of each outer wall, build a couple of Towers. South of the Towers, build another wall to block the entrance. South of that wall, construct another Tower. Repeat until you've built three to five Towers in each entrance and clogged the area with walls (see Figure 9.10).

By the time you've begun wall construction, build an Armory to prepare to advance to the Heroic Age. Use your military units to construct a Longhouse and Hill Fort. Produce some Hersir, Ulfsarks, and Throwing Axemen to further protect your town from Gargarensis' attacks should any enemy units sneak through. Use excess wood for more Towers near your walls. Improve units, weapons, armor, and Towers to bolster defense.

An adequate network of walls and Towers should hold off most of Gargarensis' forces. Be sure to upgrade your wooden walls to stone walls upon reaching the Heroic Age. Also, research Masons and Architects at the Town Center to increase Tower hit points. Position other units to intercept any enemies that get through. Should enemy units breach the first or second walls, build additional Towers at the southern end of the entrances to further weaken incoming enemies.

Figure 9.10 *Barricade the three entrances to your base with a network of walls and Towers.*

◈ **New Objective**: Fight your way to Gargarensis, located near the yellow flags.

After 20 minutes, Odysseus arrives in your town with a large force of Myrmidon, Hetairoi, and Centaurs. It's time to counterattack against Gargarensis. Spend all you have on unit improvements, either at your military structures or at the Armory. Build gates in the walls blocking one of your base entrances. Escort Odysseus, his army, and your other Heroes and units out of your base, and advance north, toward the white flags.

You will face many unit types, including Trolls and Mountain and Frost Giants as you approach Gargarensis. Counter these enemy mythological units with your Heroes, Jarl, and Hersir. Counter Norse human units with your Myrmidon. After clearing out his protectors, approach Gargarensis at the marked position. The mission ends as you engage in battle.

> *TIP*
>
> Leave a small group of Jarl and Hersir in your base to repel any counterattacks, particularly those that appear in the southern edge of your base.

Welcome Back

Initial Objective

◈ Land your troops on Atlantis' shores. Begin construction of a base by claiming a Settlement.

Map Highlights

You begin the mission in boats (and with Pegasi scouts) on the western side of the map. Scout the land just east of your fleet to discover three possible unclaimed settlements. Captured Atlantean Prisoners can be found in various prisons across the eastern area of the map. Priests also found in the prisons can be used to fight Gargarensis formidable myth unit army or to heal your forces.

Battle Plans

Pegasi scouts guide your fleet to its destination. Triremes, siege ships, and hammer ships escort your six transport ships to the east. Before moving your fleet, select the Pegasi and search the shoreline to locate a viable landing zone. Be careful: There are several enemy structures along the shore, including Towers and Fortresses. As you near the shore, Gargarensis' welcomes you with a Meteor god power. Keep your units off land until the god power ceases.

Gargarensis is following Poseidon! Beware of militia that appears at destroyed enemy buildings.

You'll discover two unclaimed settlements nearby—one north and one south. Choose the settlement to the south, because it provides quick access to other resources north and south along the shore and is directly west of the gate the enemy arrives from.

Keep away from Towers as you unload your transport ships, and don't advance any units immediately except your siege weaponry. You need to eliminate the Towers and Fortresses before advancing other units. Topple these structures with your siege weaponry. Now you can use your other units to intercept the militia that appear from the destroyed buildings. Move your villagers to the settlement and begin construction of a Town Center.

◈ **New Objective**: Rescue 15 Atlantean Prisoners. Transport them to the flagged island to the west.

Search the shoreline north and south of your base to find more goats. Move them back to your town and use them as a source of food. Enemy naval vessels patrol the shores, so don't move your scout too close to the water! Use your own ships to eliminate these enemies if necessary.

A new objective appears after you complete the Town Center. You must rescue 15 captured Atlantean Prisoners to complete the task. New locations appear on your mini-map. These are the various prisons where the prisoners (and some Priests) are being held.

You must topple each prison in a different way. For instance, to free the prisoners, you might need to either demolish the Fortress protecting the prison or eliminate the nearby mythological units. Scan each prison position to discover exactly what you must do. There's no rush to rescue the prisoners. Concentrate primarily on base defense before heading east into enemy territory. It's also possible to take advantage of the canals that penetrate the island. Use transport ships (protected by siege ships to use against enemy Towers) to raid the area around the prisons. Rescue the prisoners quickly then return to your defended base with the prisoners and your army on board the transports.

Start producing villagers once you've increased the population cap. Scout north of your settlement to discover a second settlement, with nearby pigs and goats. Move these animals to your initial Town Center. Farm first until these animals fatten (research Husbandry at a Granary to speed up the process). Shift to these animals once they've fattened. Prioritize food collection and gold mining first, in order to quickly advance to the next Age. Assign a couple of villagers to food gathering to fund housing and structures, primarily a Temple and Armory.

Figure 9.11 *Protect the entrance to your base with a Fortress and many Towers.*

Advance to the Heroic Age, where you can choose to worship either Dionysus or Apollo. After advancing, shift villagers to heavy wood gathering (taking several villagers from both food and gold). Start farming, if your food sources have been exhausted. You might also produce four or five more villagers, and send them to the Temple to worship. You will need to fund mythological and Hero units eventually.

Use your wood reserves to start mounting a strong defense (see Figure 9.11). The enemy attacks solely from the narrow passage and gate east of your town. Build a Fortress near the gate.

Complement the Fortress with six to eight Towers, and purchase Tower improvements including Burning Oil. Garrison units in the Towers to increase their power, and after each attack repair the damage to your Towers and Fortress. Research Masons at the Town Center to increase the hit points of your Towers and buildings and research Olympic Parentage to boost your Heroes hit points.

Instead of advancing to the Mythic Age quickly, use your resources on mythological units such as Minotaur and Hydra, with a supporting mix of human units (build two to three Petroboli at the

> **TIP**
>
> A substantial defense at the gate is key to this mission for two reasons: First, the defense will protect your base and units from attack when you're actually in the base. And when you're outside your base to the east, you can retreat to your defensive structures to aid in the counterattack against pursuing enemies.

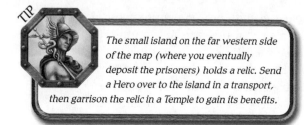

TIP

The small island on the far western side of the map (where you eventually deposit the prisoners) holds a relic. Send a Hero over to the island in a transport, then garrison the relic in a Temple to gain its benefits.

Fortress, too) and all available Greek Heroes. Spend resources on improvements to the units at their respective military structures, and on improvements to weapons and armor at the Armory. Build a Market to trade resources to fund these improvements, as well as your defensive structures. After amassing a large network of Towers protecting the gate and a large army filled with mythological units, consider the advance to the Mythic Age. Worship Hera for the Lightning Storm god power, which you will use shortly.

Use the Petroboli to demolish the enemy gate east of your town. Eliminate any nearby enemy Towers before moving your units east. A second enemy gate lies further to the east at the end of the narrow passage. Destroy the second gate with your Petroboli. If the enemy counters with fighting units, retreat to your network of Towers before attacking them. After the second enemy gate falls, Gargarensis uses an Earthquake god power to level an Atlantean town.

The closest prison is due east from the gates. A mighty Citadel protects it. You'll have to destroy the Citadel to free the prisoners and Priests. Use the Petroboli to assault the Citadel from long range. Keep your support units close by; when the Citadel falls, the prisoners and Priests immediately come under your control and could be attacked by the militia in the area and near the destroyed building. Quickly move the prisoners and Priests to your support units. Losing one won't be a problem, but losing all could mean trouble for the mission.

WARNING

Since you're outside the safety of your base and in enemy territory, large enemy counterattacks are likely. If you've advanced to the Mythic Age, consider using Hera's Lightning Storm on the first large enemy army you encounter.

To prevent enemy reinforcements, destroy every enemy military structure you find. Consider constructing a new network of defensive structures (Towers, Fortress) near the second gate east of your base. This will make retreat easier since it's closer to enemy territory and not beyond the cramped passage. Position rescued Priests within the passage, where they can heal your wounded units! Retreat to them as needed.

If you have the resources, build new Town Centers on the unclaimed settlements north of your town (and any you find in enemy territory) to increase your population cap over its maximum. Build more units and add them to your mobile army.

Approach the Priest prison south of the demolished Citadel. A Fortress protects the prison from attack. Destroy it, and escort the freed prisoners back to your base. Add the Priests to your army groupings and heal your units as necessary.

Avoid the prison that's furthest east for now. You must destroy the Temple to free the Priests there. Sounds easy enough, but it's protected by an enormous number of units, including a powerful Cyclops Hero named Polyphemus. You will have to deal with these foes eventually, however, when the next objective appears. For now, move to the prison to the east that is protected by four Towers. Demolish the Towers with your siege weaponry and rescue the prisoners and Priests (see Figure 9.12). Then move to the northern prisons and rescue the prisoners and Priests within them (eliminating the mythological units). Don't forget to topple any military structures you encounter. Once you've rescued 15 prisoners, a new objective appears.

◈ **New Objective**: Transport 15 Atlantean Prisoners to the flagged island to the west.

Escort the remaining prisoners to your base in the west. Hold off any further enemy attacks with your army. Retreat to your network of Towers and Fortress for added defense against their attacks. Maneuver the prisoners to the western shore. Board at least 15 prisoners on one of your transport ships. Send the transport ship across the bay and west to the island marked with the blue flag. Disembark the transport and move the prisoners to the flag to complete the mission in victory.

Figure 9.12 *Free the Atlantean prisoners and Priests by demolishing the buildings or Towers guarding them.*

A Place in My Dreams

Initial Objective

◈ Advance to the Mythic age and construct a Wonder. Zeus will reward you with his blessing.

Map Highlights

You begin in the southeast section of the map. The mini-map reveals the location of four Plenty vaults, scattered across the northern and eastern sides of the map. The Living Poseidon Statue and Gargarensis guard the Hades Gate to the far northeast.

Battle Plans

Your primary goal is to build a Wonder, which means you must advance to the Mythic Age. You begin the map in the Classical Age, so resources will be your first priority. Use your current food stores to produce eight villagers immediately, and order them all to collect food from nearby animals and berry bushes. As you gather more food, produce an additional four villagers.

You will need Houses to support these new units; assign one villager to build several. Build a Temple, once you're near the food requirement for Age-advancement (and produce a trio of villagers to worship at the Temple for favor). Start assigning your villagers to the collection of gold and wood, leaving six villagers on food. Search the area north of the Norse base to discover more berry bushes.

During the mission, the neighboring Norse and Egyptian villagers will send units to your aid (see Figure 9.13). The Norse village sends Mountain and Frost Giants; the Egyptians send Anubites (and a Son of Osiris Hero). These villages will periodically offer units until the villagers are eventually destroyed by Gargarensis

Construct an Armory and whatever military structures you desire (Military Academy, Archery Range, Stable). Enemy attacks arrive from the north side of your town, so line

Figure 9.13 *Your Norse and Egyptian neighbors periodically send reinforcements to aid in your defense.*

Towers up in that area. Produce three to four more villagers and order them to collect wood to fund these defensive structures. Add mythological units and Greek Heroes to your army.

Ideally, you should reach the Heroic Age before attempting to capture a Plenty vault. It's wise to have siege weaponry to topple any enemy structures you encounter, especially those protecting the vaults. Advance to the Heroic Age and select to worship Dionysus or Apollo. (We chose Dionysus for the Bronze god power, which aids in both offense and defense.)

Build a Fortress near your line of Towers to further protect your base. Construct a couple of Petroboli and advance your units and siege weaponry to the Plenty vault lying second from the western edge.

It's protected by a Colossus, Town Center, groups of Hypaspists and Peltasts, and a Fortress. Counter the Colossus with Greek Heroes, the Hypaspists and Peltasts with mythological units, and the Fortress with your siege weaponry. To capture the Plenty vault, simply select one of your units and move adjacent to the vault. Bombard any nearby enemy military struc-

tures. Your Norse and Egyptian allies are attacked by Gargarensis' Meteor god powers as you gain Plenty vaults. There is no way to save them from destruction.

There's another Plenty vault just to the east, guarded by a squad of enemy mythological units and a Temple. Demolish the Temple and eliminate the units, then capture the vault.

Each time you destroy a Temple, Zeus grants you a Meteor god power (see Figure 9.14). Use Meteor against Gargarensis' structures, either defending vaults or Temples, or those tough Fortresses flanking the entrances into his northern base. Protect your Plenty vaults from capture by building a couple of Towers near each. If an unclaimed settlement lies near a vault, built a Town Center as well.

You should have resources pouring in at this point, and should begin switching all your villagers off their resource-gathering duties and onto worshipping at the Temple. This will dramatically increase the rate at which you gain favor to fund improvements and mythological units. Build a Market if you haven't already; advance to the Mythic Age; and worship Hera or Hephaestus. Selecting Hera provides the Lightning Storm god power, which should be used when defending your Wonder against Gargarensis' attack groups of Polyphemus, Helepoli, and Champion human soldiers. Select Hephaestus if you desire another Plenty vault to further fund your military campaign.

Figure 9.14 *Crush an enemy Temple and Zeus rewards you with a Meteor god power.*

TIP

At your Temple, research the Olympic Parentage improvement to increase the hit points of all Hero units. Research the Monstrous Rage improvement to increase the attack-damage of your mythological units.

After advancing to the Mythic Age, monitor your resources carefully and start construction of the Greek Wonder as soon as possible. Send as many villagers as you can spare (all of them, if possible) and order them to assist in the construction of the Wonder (see Figure 9.15). Your captured vaults should fund any reinforcements you need to finish combing the map for enemy stragglers. Avoid Gargarensis to the north until the Wonder has been completed.

During construction, continue to roam the map with your military units. Capture remaining vaults and, if you wish, destroy remaining Temples. Search the southeastern corner of the map to discover enemy Houses and another Temple. Search east of your town to discover an enemy Town Center and Temple, guarded by Colossi.

TIP

It is a good idea to keep Arkantos close to your base as the Wonder nears completion. The final objective involves the story's Hero and you don't want to have to go rescue him in order to finish the scenario.

New Objective: Use the Blessing of Zeus power on Arkantos and destroy the Statue of Poseidon.

A new objective appears after you finish building the Wonder: Zeus grants you a special power, the Blessing of Zeus. Before using the god power, invoke remaining Meteors on the Fortresses at the southern side of Gargarensis' base (use a Pegasi to spot for the power). After exhausting the Meteors, invoke the Blessing of Zeus on Arkantos to turn your Hero into a nearly invincible warrior. Send your villagers back to the Temple and worship for favor (to fund more mythological

Figure 9.15 *Use all villagers to construct the Wonder, which completes the mission's first objective.*

units or improvements). The Living Statue of Poseidon can be found near the Hades Gate to the north. Beware: Many champion enemy units, as well as Hero units, protect the area.

The Blessing of Zeus has transformed Arkantos into a killing machine—he should have no trouble defeating every unit and building on the map. He's not entirely invincible, though; Arkantos' hit points are very high but it is possible to lose him if you aren't careful. Pull him out of battles and give him time to regenerate before using him again. Head north with Arkantos, Greek Heroes, Petroboli, and a mixture of your favorite available mythological units. If desired, you can even move up forward villagers and use available resources to build Towers and a Fortress at the base of the entrance into Gargarnesis' base. Lure enemy units here for added attack.

Clear out any remaining enemy Fortresses with your siege weaponry. Lead attacks against units with Arkantos; follow with your Greek Heroes and mythological units. Lure the Statue of Poseidon toward your forces. Attack him with Arktantos—the Statue of Poseidon won't be able to withstand the combined power of Arktantos and Zeus.

During the battle with the Statue of Poseidon, enemy mythological units arrive in hordes through the Hades gate. Ignore them and continue pounding on the statue. The mission ends in victory as soon as the Statue of Poseidon crumbles to the ground—ignore those other units! Gargarensis cries out in desperation as the statue falls. There's no one left to help him. With the aid of Zeus, Arkantos has defeated Gargarensis and reclaimed his homeland of Atlantis. Congratulations! You've completed *Age of Mythology*'s challenging single-player campaign!

Advanced Economy

Hopefully by now you've read through the whole book and have a pretty good understanding of how the game plays. You can beat all of the scenarios, and when you play against your kid sister, who just bought the game, you beat her easily. However, every time you try to play multiplayer on Ensemble Studios Online, you find yourself losing far more than you're winning.

Well, fear not. We can help the average player become much, much better. These next five chapters will deal with specific expert aspects of the game, incorporating some of the tricks and tips that the Ensemble Studios multiplayer test team has accumulated through months of playing Age of Mythology and years of playing real-time strategy games. What is a "rush"? Why are the hotkeys important? What food should I eat first, and when should I start farming? How the heck do you play those Norse guys? These questions and more will be answered. We'll start with a look at what you can do to really get your economy rolling.

The Resources

Integral to any real-time strategy game is the economy. While the first thing one may think of in games like these are the huge armies fighting it out on the battlefield, none of that is possible without a strong economic backbone. Building an army and telling them to attack something is easy—understanding and fine-tuning your economy is a work of art. And with a thriving economy, creating an overwhelming army is a piece of cake.

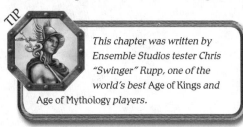

This chapter was written by Ensemble Studios tester Chris "Swinger" Rupp, one of the world's best Age of Kings *and* Age of Mythology *players.*

"The economy" can be defined as all things pertaining to the gathering of resources—how you collect them and what you do with them afterwards. Do you funnel all of your money into the economic improvements, or do you instead get that infantry improvement? How does my opponent always have twice as many resources as I do by the end of the game?

To begin with, knowledge of just what exactly you are collecting is vitally important. *Age of Mythology* incorporates five different resources: food, wood, gold, favor, and population. The most important resource in the early game is food. Here's why.

The most valuable unit in the entire game is the villager. The villager is the one who chops the trees, harvests the food, builds your buildings (usually), and mines your gold. Without villagers, you obviously don't have an economy. And in order to build villagers, you need food. Maintaining an early food supply is incredibly important, as what happens early on can have a ripple effect on the rest of the game. Your primary concern at the start of the game is finding a food source (see Figure 10.1).

The second resource that you need is wood. Collecting wood allows you to build all of the buildings that you are going to need for the rest of the game (with the noted exception of the Egyptians). After food, your next concern is to find a good place to chop wood.

Gold becomes more and more valuable the further into the game you get. Gold is the only resource that is limited (relatively speaking), in that there is a finite amount of it. While food and wood can virtually last forever, gold can run out quickly, leaving you

Figure 10.1 *Seek out food sources through scouting. Search for wild animal herds and try to steal your opponent's herdable animals.*

stranded high and dry if you're not prepared. All of your military units and many of your technologies will cost gold.

Favor is the trickiest of them all to judge. The amount of favor you collect is really just dependent on the style of game you wish to play. Favor can be used to research myth technologies and to build mythological units—neither of which are essential to win the game, but they add a very strong dynamic to your game should you choose to use them.

For more tips on favor, check Chapters 12, 13, and 14 for advanced info on how each culture generates favor from its Gods.

TIP

The fifth and final resource is population. While at first glance you may think that population isn't an economic resource, in reality, population is *Age of Mythology*'s most valuable resource. Assuming all players max out their population room at 160, losing a settlement can make or break a game, as you just lost almost 15% of your population room for military and villagers. (And it's twice as bad if your enemy then builds on your settlement!) Every myth unit you build has to be balanced in your mind as being worth the four or five pop slots that they cost. Especially in the later game, the battles are based less on the economy and more on settlement population control.

Food

There are three ways to gather food in *Age of Mythology*—by foraging for berries, eating animals (those you hunt and those you herd), or planting farms. Eventually during the course of the game you are going to have to plant farms once the wildlife and berries run out—the biggest question is when to start. Before you get to farming though, you need to use up the majority, if not all, of your other available food sources: herdables, huntables, aggressive huntables, and wild crops.

Foraging, Hunting, and Fishing

The first thing you usually want to eat is your wild crops. These are almost always found near your starting settlement and offer some steady early food while you search around for some other food sources. I usually eat these until I find a pack of huntables nearby, and then switch over, leaving a portion of the wild crops in case I need a safe food source later on. Just remember that not all random maps (or scenarios) will provide the same type of food. Watering Hole, for example, has no wild crops, while Erebus has no food at all except for Boar.

The huntables include the passive animals: deer, zebras, giraffes, etc. It's a very good idea to eat these as soon as you can. Before you get there though, make sure to research the Hunting Dogs technology, as that will increase your hunting rate by almost 30%! This makes huntables the fastest early food source by far—and the faster you can get the food in, the faster you can get your economy going.

ES TIP

When hunting a pack of aggressive animals like Walruses on Midgard, your hunters will not auto attack the next animal for fear of the animal attacking. In these situations, use the "Shift + Click" ability to cue commands, and instruct your group of hunters to attack one, then the next, then the next. With this command, your villagers won't become idle after finishing each beast but will move onto the next without your micromanagement.

—Justin "GX_Bear" Rouse

The aggressive huntables are such animals as boars, walruses, and rhinos. They provide a lot of food in one spot and are something you need to always get, but you need to be very careful to make sure you have enough villagers before you attempt to hunt them—you obviously don't want to have any villagers killed in pursuit of food. Usually six or seven is safe for the weaker ones, and nine to 10 is generally enough for elephants and tougher beasts. Again, make sure that you have researched Hunting Dogs before you go out to hunt these animals, otherwise it's not worth your time.

The herdables include pigs, sheep, and goats. As you've read earlier in the strategy guide, the longer these animals are left alive, the more food they provide, as they "fatten." Generally, eating these animals right at the start is a bad idea. Before you get the Husbandry technology, they gather and fatten slowly, meaning it is very inefficient to eat them right away. What I've found to be the best strategy with herdable food is to eat all of my other available sources first. Once they start to run out, get Husbandry researched, so that by the time it's done, you're ready to move on to your herdables. By putting all of your herdables around your Town Center, you'll have a safe food source later on in the Classical Age, when you are usually too busy fighting to have time to move your food gatherers around from various other sources.

Water maps have a slightly different approach than land maps because they add a new element to your food strategy: fishing. The number one advantage to fishing is that it can give you almost the equivalent of a second settlement in that you can build two economic units at a time in the first and second Ages. So while your non-fishing opponent can create economic units (villagers) just at his settlement, you're building two units (villagers and fishing boats) simultaneously. In a short amount of time, you'll be way ahead of your opponent economically. Unless you are planning on attacking very quickly and thus cannot afford the wood, you should fish as soon you can in the Archaic Age.

In many of my games on water maps, I will send one of my starting villagers immediately to the shore to start building a Dock. The sooner you start fishing (as long as you can maintain steady villager production), the sooner it pays off. When fishing, always get your fishing improvements immediately upon reaching the next Age; they make a huge difference to your food production. While slightly difficult, it's not uncommon to have fishing be your entire food source: You can completely eschew farming for the entire game.

Farming

OK, so you've finished off all of your wildlife and berries—now what do you do? At this point it's time to start building farms. Building farms is a very tricky matter of balance in *Age of Mythology:* Once you build a farm, it is an infinite supply of food. They cost 75 wood, though (except for the Egyptians, who must use gold to build farms), which is a lot, and are also easily destroyed. So how do you know when to start building them?

The answer to that question depends on how much preparation you've done before you want to start building farms. If you've run a balanced economy up to that point, but suddenly you've got 12 hunters and only 200 wood, you're in trouble. The best way to address this is to start building farms gradually, and to start stockpiling wood prior to starting them.

Take stock of how many food sources you have left. If you're starting to run out, you're going to want to start assigning all new villagers to wood, stockpiling the resources. Take a few of your hunters and start building some farms with them. This way, once you finish hunting, you only will have a few villagers left to move to farms, and it won't disrupt your economy greatly once you run out of wildlife. Once you start farming, get the first farming improvement as well. Farming without any improvements is just too slow to be viable. For example, farming doesn't get more efficient than hunting until you research the Mythic Age farming improvement!

Going with farms is eventually the best way to run your food production (see Figure 10.2). Farms are much safer for your villagers than having them exposed outside your town, hunting wildlife. The earlier you do it though, the harder-hit your economy is going to be in the beginning. Having to spend that much wood is going to hurt if you're doing it in the first or early second Age.

Figure 10.2 *Although it's a slow means of gathering food, farming does keep your villagers together and often near your town defenses.*

Along those lines, if you are planning on attacking early, in the second or even first Age, you definitely don't want to be farming. A "rush" requires that every available resource is being put into your military—there is no way that you can afford to build farms at the same time. In this situation, you're going to want to be using as much "free" food (wildlife and crops) as you can, before being forced to plant farms.

Wood

Wood is collected from the various tree types, which vary depending on which map you're playing. There are several straggler trees located around your Town Center, which you will generally want to start chopping first. After those are exhausted, you'll need to build a Lumber Camp, Storehouse, or Ox Cart, depending on your culture (we'll refer to these as "drop sites" because that's where villagers drop resources), next to a forest to chop the wood there.

While one may think that chopping wood is easy, there is actually a little more to it than just hacking away. There are two concepts to think about when chopping wood: the tactic of "repitting" and multiple drop sites. The concepts behind both are very similar: distance and congestion.

The way that wood is collected, the villager chops as much as he can carry, at which point he'll carry the wood over to the drop site, deposit the wood, then return to work. The amount of time that he's carrying is "dead" time. During that time, no actual work is being done—he's just carrying wood or returning to work. So the less time he spends carrying, the more time he'll spend chopping, and more work will actually get done.

The way to reduce that carrying time:

◈ Make the distance that he has to travel shorter, by rebuilding the drop site at the edge of the forest—called repitting.

◈ Make it less crowded around him, or use multiple camps, so he doesn't have to bump into all of his fellow villagers.

Repitting involves building a new drop site every five tiles or so, as your villagers chop through the forest. As the wood gets chopped away from the original site, the villagers are walking farther and farther to drop off their resources. By repitting, you reduce their walking time, resulting in more productivity, which more than pays for the cost of the additional drop site. The Norse have a huge bonus in this regard, as they can just move their Ox Cart whenever they want, keeping relative to the edge of the forest.

The second concept is using multiple drop sites. While this may seem obvious, very few people actually do this. Instead of just building one drop site and having 10 guys around it chopping wood, you can build two lumber camps with five villagers depositing wood to each. This will greatly reduce the amount of time villagers spend bumping into each other, allowing them to be more productive. Again, this will quickly pay for itself. The second advantage is that it doesn't leave all of your eggs in one basket. If one of your deposit sites is attacked, you have a second site to use and will likely not lose too much time and economic production (as long as you hold off the attackers!).

Gold

Gold is probably the simplest resource to acquire—just build a Mining Camp, Storehouse, or Ox Cart (depending on your culture) adjacent to the mine. While not as drastic, the same concepts apply to gold as to wood—put your drop site close so the villagers don't need to walk far. (I would recommend a tile or two off of the gold, so the villagers have room to walk between the gold and the deposit site.) And don't overload one gold mine so that the villagers are bumping into each other constantly.

Guard your gold carefully. Since you can't use a Market in the Classical Age, if you lose your gold mine to the enemy, you're in a lot of trouble. Building an extra Tower or some minor walling to block off your gold can make a huge difference.

At the same time, fighting around your enemy's gold is a very good idea in the Classical Age (assuming he hasn't put up an extra Tower or walled off as well). If the enemy has no gold, he can't build any units, and thus you will eventually win.

Finally, remember that you always have the option of acquiring gold with Trade Carts or Caravans. Since Trade Carts only cost food (something you will generally have plenty of later on in the game) it's easy to build them,

ES TIP

When raiding, focus mostly on disrupting your enemy's gold supplies. The more time he spends running around, the less time he'll spend mining gold.

—Nate "Redline" Jacques

and since you can trade with yourself, you don't have to try to coordinate trading with your teammates. A gold miner will generate more gold than a Trade Cart does, so as long as you have gold mines left, your population slots are best spent on gold miners. Once you run out of mines though, those Trade Carts become your lifeline. If the game ends up lasting late into the Mythic Age, you will definitely need to have as many as 15 to 20 Trade Carts to sustain a gold supply.

Population

Age of Mythology uses a dynamic population cap, meaning that there is no hard limit to what your population will be—you control your own destiny there. There are two ways to gain population room: by building Houses, and by controlling settlements.

Houses can be built anywhere you want them to be. They supply 10 population apiece, but are fairly fragile. The limiting factor to Houses is that you can only build 10 total (see Figure 10.3). You can rebuild the ones that are destroyed, but once you've reached that 10 again, no more House foundations can be laid down. Simply running around and destroying your opponent's Houses can be an effective strategy.

The second way to get population is by claiming settlements. Every Random Map has three settlements per player scattered throughout—you start with one of them under your control. Each settlement, at first, provides 15 population. Settlements are doubly valuable because they can fire arrows at enemies, garrison units, and act as drop sites for every resource.

A Heroic Age technology, Fortify Town Center, can be researched at the settlements, which adds an additional five population room per settlement. This is an expensive improvement, a little more than the cost of a settlement, but one you should always research. It provides more population, and just as importantly makes your settlements

ES TIP

Obtaining settlements is important, but be sure to spend your valuable resources on making an army before you build more settlements. While the settlements give you extra population, that extra pop isn't doing you any good when you don't have the resources to use it.

—Jerry "Gx_Iron" Terry

Figure 10.3 *You can build only 10 Houses before you must expand to settlements to increase your population cap.*

tougher, meaning it will be that much harder for your enemy to kill them and deny your population room.

Before we talk about other tactics for improving your economic production, let's review our discussion so far (see Table 10.1).

RESOURCE	CONCEPT
Food	Most important in the beginning, least important near the end. Hunt first, then switch to farms.
Wood	Constantly repit, and build multiple sites.
Gold	Protect mines carefully. Losing gold loses the game.
Favor	Important for mythological units and technologies, but not absolutely essential.
Population	Least important in the beginning, most important near the end. Build all 10 Houses and grab your settlements in the Heroic Age, eventually upgrading them. Raid enemy Houses!

Table 10.1 Age of Mythology *Advanced Resource Strategies*

Improving Economy

Now that you understand the basics of what the economy is, the next question is, "How do I get it functioning like a well-oiled machine? I do all of what you just said, but 'the Sheriff' still has twice as many resources as I do. What am I doing wrong?" There are two elements to improving economy: Get all of the economic improvements; and always keep your economy moving. The first one isn't too hard; the second takes a lot of practice.

Economic Improvements

For food, wood, and gold, there are improvements that will upgrade the gathering rate, located at that particular resource's drop site. Each culture has a slightly different location for getting all of these, but the actual improvements are the same. The sooner that you can get these technologies, the sooner they will pay off for you, eventually putting you ahead economically of your opponent.

It all comes down to "When do they pay for themselves?" If you're planning on doing a very fast attack, getting those technologies early will hurt you more than they will help you, as they won't pay off for several minutes, when you need to be attacking already. However, if you are planning on doing a more economically heavy strategy, where you plan on out-producing your opponent down the road, then getting them as early as you can is a good idea (see Figure 10.4).

Generally these techs will pay for themselves in around five minutes, after which everything is money in the bank. If you find yourself constantly forgetting to get these improvements, one way to always remember is to just make it a habit to select each drop site and get the available improvement as soon as you reach the next Age. It may not always be the best time to get them, but it's rarely a bad decision, and it's far better than discovering at the end of the game that you only got one wood tech the entire game.

Hotkeys

Whenever someone asks me online, "How can I get better?" I usually answer, "Learn the hotkeys." The hotkeys are keyboard shortcuts that will automatically perform a command for you. For example, hitting the V key while your settlement is selected will cause a villager to train. Hitting Ctrl–G will automatically jump you to your Granary, allowing you to quickly research a technology. With a villager selected, hit T: He'll build a Temple.

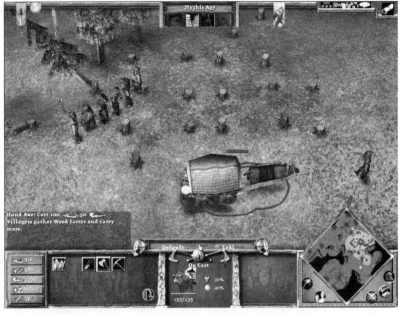

Figure 10.4 *A strong economy includes improvements. Research them upon advancing to the next Age, as they can be easily forgotten!*

The amount of time this can save you is tremendous. Just imagine how much time is spent scrolling the map looking for a building, or constantly moving your mouse over to the villager build icons to build every building you need built. Over the course of a game it adds up—a lot.

It's a fairly difficult transition for a person who has never used the hotkeys to start using them. It may actually make you slower at first. However, very soon you'll begin to notice how much faster you can move around the game, and eventually you won't be able to imagine how to play without the hotkeys. It takes a bit of discipline to force yourself to do it, but in the end it will really pay off.

If the default hotkeys are not intuitive for you or are too scattered across the keyboard, it is easy to remap them. This information is saved with your player profile.

Through the Looking Glass

"I have all of the improvements now. Why am I still behind in economy?" The second portion of running your economy is…well…the actual running of your economy. This is probably the most difficult real-time strategy skill to master. It's what separates the intermediate player from the expert player. There are three major components to this: keeping track of your idle villagers, maintaining villager flow, and balancing your economy.

Idle Villagers

Keeping track of your idle villagers becomes more difficult the later the game goes. If you have 30 villagers, 10 of whom are idle, you're obviously behind the guy who has 24, all of whom are working. Idle villagers crop up often—and not just one or two. It's easy to have over 10 guys standing around doing nothing, after they've, say, exhausted a gold mine or finished building structures. It's also easy to get idles by not updating the waypoint from your settlement. The only way to combat this is to develop habits.

You have to train yourself to look up at the idle villager banner (or hit your idle villager hotkey, default "."), every time you finish a task. Just constructed a building? Go look. Just commanded your army to enter your enemy's town? Go look. Just killed that annoying Chariot Archer in your town? *Definitely* go look. It's hard to do, and in the heat of the game, very hard to remember, but once you start doing it automatically, you'll suddenly notice how many more resources you had than before. The best way is to have someone watch you play, and tell you every time they see the idle villager banner pop up—you'd amazed how often it happens.

Once you start looking at the idle villager banner more often, you also have to get used to quickly assigning those villagers to a task, to clear the banner. When I'm fighting a pretty heavy battle, I can easily end up with a few idle villagers by the battle's end. To combat this, whenever I start returning them to work, I make sure that I get them *all*. If you have 10 idles, and you set one working again, you still have nine idles not doing anything. You don't even have to take the time to have them doing useful things, necessarily. Just get them doing *some-thing*. Even if you take every idle villager and order them to chop at the nearest tree, it's better than nothing. Look to see what resource you need the most of, then grab every idle you find and have them collect that resource. It's tough sometimes to ignore the rest of the game enough to get everyone working, but it's a skill that needs to be developed in order to get the most of your economy (see Figure 10.5).

The easiest way to check for idles is to hit the "." key. That automatically takes you to the latest idle villager. It's far and away the quickest way to cycle through your villagers: Task one, hit the "." key and then task the next one, etc. Also, by holding down Ctrl when you select an idle villager, all of the idle villagers on the screen will be selected. Trust me, it helps.

Villager Flow

The second challenge to running a top-notch economy is maintaining a steady villager flow. There should never be a time through the Classical Age when your Town Center is idle. You need to be always checking back on it to make sure that you are either advancing an Age, researching an improvement, or making another villager. The more villagers you have, the more resources you gather, which means the more you can spend. It's a snowball effect.

Also, remember that once you can start claiming settlements, you can make more than one villager at a time; every settlement can make a villager! There is no magic number for when to stop making villagers, although I would say that you should have between 50 and 55. During the course of a game, I will often make up to 100 villagers, replacing the ones that get killed. Another good habit to get into is cycling between your settlements to make villagers: repeatedly pressing the hotkey H cycles through them, and you can just keep your mouse on the villager button. You can produce a lot of villagers quickly this way.

Balancing your Economy

The third and possibly most difficult aspect of fine-tuning your economy is balance. If you have 2,100 wood, 300 gold, 100 favor, and 50 food, you've got a problem. You want to have a balance between all

Figure 10.5 *A bunch of idle villagers is a huge problem to an economy. While they do nothing, your enemy villagers are collecting bushels of resources.*

of the resources so that you can adjust your economy to whatever you need to counter your opponent, and so that you're maximizing your potential.

If you've been producing Archers and your opponent's countering with cavalry, you need to be able to switch over to infantry. If you do not have the resources to do that, you're in trouble. Likewise, if you have thousands of resources just sitting in your bank not doing anything, you need to be spending it. Get more improvements. Crank out some more units. Do anything you can to take advantage of your resources and keep your economy running as efficiently as possible. Your goal should be to never have more than 100 of any resource.

These three elements are the hardest aspect of the game to learn, and the only easy answer is practice. You have to continue to practice these things so that eventually you don't even have to think about them anymore, you just do them out of habit. Once you start doing that, your economy will be producing like crazy, and you will have the ability to field bigger, better armies and advance in Age much quicker than your opponent can.

ES TIP

Don't be afraid to re-task villagers to different jobs. If you're low on wood and have too much gold, take some of the gold miners and assign them to wood-chopping duty.

—Nate "Redline" Jacques

Check out Table 10.2 for a quick look at the economic tactics we've been discussing.

CONCEPT	EXPLANATION
Economic Improvements	Get these as soon as possible! Research them upon reaching the next Age.
Hotkeys	Difficult at first, but study pays off, with far less wasted time.
Idle Villagers	Check often—then check again!
Villager Production	Maintain villager production; being behind even a few can make or break a game.
Balance	Anything just sitting in your bank is wasted and inefficient. Until you are in the late Mythic Age, strive to be under 100 of every resource. If you're not, start spending.

Table 10.2: Summary of Improving your Economy

Advanced Military Strategies

At this point, you should have a solid understanding of how to manage your economy, creating a ton of resources to turn into an army with which to completely crush your opponents. You can already imagine them quivering in fear of your newfound skills. The problem now, though, is…well…now what? You have this smoking economy, but you don't know how to effectively build up your armies and actually fight. Of course you could just stream masses of units into the enemy town, but that's not the most subtle, or effective, of approaches.

This section of the guide will help you hone your military strategies by explaining in-depth tricks and tactics including scouting, the three "standard" strategies, combined arms, micromanaging battles, and using control groups.

Scouting

> **TIP**
> *This chapter was written by Ensemble Studios tester Chris "Swinger" Rupp, one of the world's best* Age of Kings *and* Age of Mythology *players.*

The most important and arguably the most difficult thing to do is to scout, and scout well. Scouting involves more than simply running around and removing all of the fog of war, although that's important as well. Knowing what buildings and units your enemy has, and where his army is and where it's headed, is absolutely vital. Greeks have the easiest time with this, given their starting cavalry scout, although the principle holds true for all three cultures (see Figure 11.1).

Figure 11.1 *Scout everything—new resources, the enemy's location, choke points, etc.*

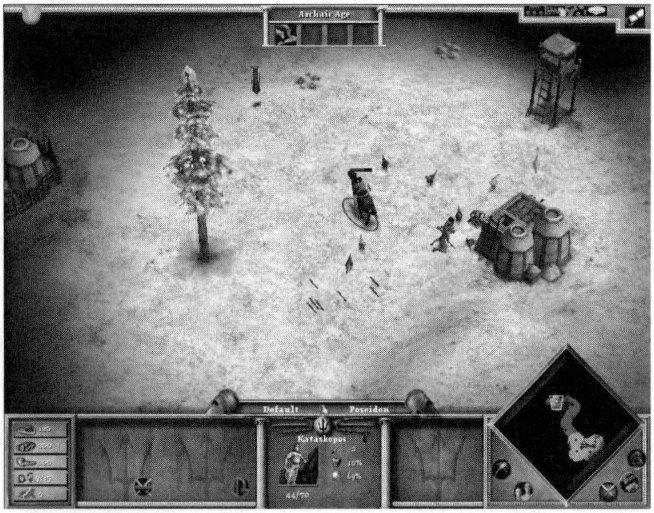

During the course of the game, make sure you always have a unit running around, checking things out. It could be a Pegasus, a Raven, or even a lone Spearman. Finding out where settlements are located or being constructed and where your enemy is planning a surprise attack can make or break the game. Plus, knowing what units your enemy is building tells you exactly what you must produce to counter enemy attacks.

Scouting also helps with one of the most fundamental principles in the game: Don't be afraid to change your strategy! You have to be able to adjust to whatever your opponent is doing; being stubborn will kill you. For example, in one game I played against The_Sheriff_, I was winning the entire game, so I decided to go with all Hippikons and finish him off. He then started to build nothing but Ulfsarks, which of course beat my army. So what did I do to counter that? Why, I was being stubborn, so I threw in *more Hippikons!* He then just built more Ulfsarks, and I ended up losing the game. The moral of the story: Adapt to whatever your opponent is doing. If you see him walling up all over his base, then perhaps your super quick rush isn't the best idea. A delayed and more powerful Classical Age attack to break through his walls in force would be the best decision. Excellent scouting is paramount in knowing what to do.

> **ES TIP**
> *If you see enemy obelisks on the map, destroy them, especially around your town. These structures go down easily. Allowing the enemy to have line-of-sight into your base is a very bad idea.*
>
> —Chris "Swinger" Rupp

> **ES TIP**
> *If you aren't sure what god powers your enemy has, try clicking the Player Status button at the top right. A list of everyone's god powers, used and unused, can be seen here.*
>
> —Matt "Maimin_matty" Scadding

Rush vs. Turtle vs. Boom

In a traditional *Age of Mythology* game, there are basically three approaches you can take: the "rush," the "turtle," and the "boom." This section describes each approach, and covers their advantages and disadvantages.

The Rush

While many new players define a "rush" as whenever someone attacks them before they're ready ("Hey, it's only been 35 minutes! I'm not ready yet."), the true definition of a rush is an attack that occurs as soon as possible, usually as soon as five or six minutes into the game. For someone who's not prepared for it, it can be devastating, but *Age of Mythology* is balanced in such a way that if you can repel the early attacks, you will have a significant advantage and be able to crush even the peskiest rusher. But if a rusher's early attacks work, he can parlay the early setbacks to your economy into a game-winning advantage.

ES TIP

Always keep your military buildings producing units. If you have excessive multiple units queued up in all of your buildings, make more buildings!

—Nate "Redline" Jacques

To rush well, you have to streamline your economy as much as possible in order to attack as fast as possible. This involves not researching any economy improvements, and advancing to the next Age with as few villagers as possible. It's not uncommon for a very fast rusher to advance to the second Age in under five minutes, and possibly under four.

◈ **Advantages**: By attacking before your opponent is ready, you can harass and disrupt your enemy's entire economy without fear of retribution. If you go fast enough, it's even possible to stop the enemy Temple from being built, thus denying your opponent the ability to advance to the Classical Age. Rushing also puts the game in your control: Since you are the aggressor, you are determining where (in his town, not yours) and when (before he's ready) the battles are going to take place. Overall, this strategy is the one most commonly used, and arguably the most effective.

◈ **Disadvantages**: The rush leaves you extremely weak and vulnerable. If your rush is repulsed, you're in a lot of trouble: You have fewer villagers and no economic improvements researched, and thus a much weaker economy. If you have built forward on the enemy—meaning your military buildings are closer to your enemy than to your base, allowing your army to get right into battle instead of having to walk across the map—and your attack is repelled and your forward buildings lost, it's almost time to resign against an equally skilled player.

The Turtle

The "turtle" is the counter to the rush strategy. Turtling involves investing in defenses early, including walls, Towers, and possibly a small military force as well. What the turtle seeks is to protect himself securely while the aggressor bangs his army against walls and Towers to no avail. Thus, all of the resources the enemy spent on the rush are wasted, while you spent fewer resources protecting yourself, and now have the advantage. This also allows the turtler to attack later on outside of his base with impunity, as he doesn't need to fear being attacked while his army is elsewhere.

- ⬥ **Advantages**: The turtle makes your base safe and secure from attack, allowing easier raiding and safer economic development. It also protects you from an early, aggressive rush.

- ⬥ **Disadvantages**: The turtle can be expensive, and if your turtle is "cracked," you're in a *lot* of trouble, as you have no defenses at all inside your base. All of your economy is ripe pickings for the enemy. The approach also limits your expansion somewhat. Protecting yourself inside your base is only good in the short term. Eventually you have to expand outside the safety of your base in order to grab other settlements, or your enemy will take them all, leaving you at a significant population disadvantage. If your enemy doesn't attack and instead "booms" (more on this approach next), then you're behind the enemy economically.

The Boom

The "boom" is the counter to the turtle. The boomer's philosophy is to spend very little on either defense or military, and instead to focus solely on economy. While the enemy is spending resources on military improvements and advancing to the next Age quickly, the boomer is much slower, spending resources on more villagers and improvements to the economy. While the boomer expects to take some losses, they should be easily absorbed, as the boomer economy should be much greater than the opponent's. This permits faster Age-advancement later on, and the ability to research a variety of improvements sooner (see Figure 11.2). Booming is very vulnerable to a rush.

Figure 11.2 *The boomer neglects defense in order to fund villagers and economic improvements.*

- ⬥ **Advantages:** The boomer develops a very strong economy. With slower Age-advancement and more villagers, the economy grows nearly exponentially over that of a non-boomer. If a boomer is left alone and allowed to boom, in the late game he will become unstoppable—try stopping Mythic Age War Elephants and a Meteor God Power with your Classical Age Ulfsarks!

- ⬥ **Disadvantages:** The approach leaves the boomer vulnerable to an early attack—a rush will destroy the boomer's strategy. With no military investment early on, the boomer is an easy target for annihilation.

Quantity vs. Quality

One of the most common questions players have is whether to spend money on a military upgrade or build a few more units instead. Overall, it's more important to first maximize your population before spending money on improvements.

During the course of balancing *Age of Mythology*, the playtest team spent countless hours running combat tests among all of the units to make sure they were balanced. One of the things we found was that adding even one or two units to either side in a test made a *huge* difference in the outcome. For example, Player A has 16 Toxotes, and Player B has 14 Hippikon units (these armies are approximately equivalent in resource cost). The Hippikon side in this battle will win and have around 30% of their hit points left after killing all of the Toxotes. If however, we add just two Toxotes into that battle (now it's 18 vs. 14), the battle would sway drastically, with the Hippikon side only breaking even, or possibly even losing.

The best way to consider military upgrades is to first maximize your population, or get close to it (this applies to all Ages, but is most important in the Classical Age). Then research your improvements, starting with the upgrades at the production centers first (Medium, Heavy, Champion).

When upgrading, make sure you focus on the armor that will protect you from whatever unit type you're primarily fighting. If the enemy is focusing on archers, researching hack armor isn't going to help very much. The attack improvements are always a safe bet, though more expensive than those for armor. However, when fighting ranged units, it's often more important to get the pierce armor (or hack armor, if fighting Throwing Axemen) improvements before the attack improvements, so that your troops will live longer when approaching the ranged units.

ES TIP

When choosing military improvements, go for the Medium/ Heavy/Champion improvements before you choose the copper/ bronze/iron upgrades. The former line will boost both hit points (HP) and attack, while the Armory improve- ments will only boost one statistic for your units. Having Heavy units will give you a significant advantage over Medium units.

—Jerry "Gx_Iron" Terry

How Maps Affect the Approach

Although all three strategies are possible in any game, some are more suited to a specific map type. For example, a turtle approach can be a good idea on the River Nile map because you can prevent the enemy from landing on your side, and perhaps build a Wonder behind your defenses at the same time. A boom is a good idea on maps like Alfheim, as you can protect yourself with a small amount of walling, and then spend other resources on your economy (more villagers, more improvements) to bust out later. On more open maps like Savannah, a rush is advisable, since the nature and size of the map makes it harder to wall in and easier to get to the enemy's base.

Combined Arms

While you may really enjoy making an all-Hoplite army, that army is extremely vulnerable to an anti-infantry army. Using combined arms—producing an army consisting of mixed unit types such as Hoplites and Toxotes, Throwing Axemen and Raiding Cavalry, Chariot Archers and War Elephants, etc.—is the most effective way to fight *by far*. Instead of building that all-Hoplite army, create an army that is two-thirds Hoplites and one-third Toxotes. If an army of anti-infantry units (Throwing Axemen, etc.) came to battle, your Hoplites and Toxotes would destroy it.

Using only one unit type is a very risky, and usually unwise, move that has only a small benefit: You can streamline easier by not having to pay for more unit upgrades and buildings. But overall it's not worth the risk. You always want to have at least two unit types.

Look for combinations that complement each other. For instance, Slingers and Chariot Archers are a bad combination, as they either counter archers (the Slingers) or infantry (the Chariot Archers). Since neither of them counters a unit that is a threat to your army, the combo is wasted. Camelry and Chariot Archers, on the other hand, make a much better combination, because they protect each other. The Camelry can kill any cavalry or counter-Archer units, and the Chariot Archers can kill any infantry that try to go after the Camelry.

Age of Mythology's counter system features two types of units. Mainline, or "natural counters" are the mainstays of an army. These are units like Camelry, Hoplites, and Ulfsarks. When fighting equal-cost numbers of other mainline units, natural counters will win the battle with about 30% of their hit points left over. The second type of counter unit is the "artificial counter." These are units that feature bonus damage vs. one other unit (e.g. Peltasts vs. Toxotes). Other examples are the Throwing Axeman, Slinger, and Hypaspist units. These units will beat equal-cost armies composed of the units they counter, and have 60% of their hit points left—but they will lose horribly to any other mainline unit.

Unit Stances

One of the more subtle expert techniques is taking advantage of the different unit stances in the game. Always leaving your units on Aggressive stance isn't the best way to do things.

For example, if you find your guys constantly being lured away from your buildings and getting slaughtered, put them on Defensive stance, so they'll stay put. Or, if you have a bunch of ranged units covering a gold mine or trying to hide beneath an enemy Tower's fire, place them on Passive stance. They'll continue to shoot, but they won't move anywhere else. The interface can be a bit tricky to use sometimes with stances, so make sure to learn the hotkeys for them.

To Watch or Not to Watch

This is one of the hardest techniques to learn in the entire game—keeping your screen off of the big battle. We all know it's great fun to watch two mighty armies clash—that's likely to be what your opponent is doing. However, if you are watching the battle, then you aren't doing anything else!

During the 15–30 seconds the battle lasts, you could be queuing up villagers, finding and assigning idle villagers, building new military structures, running a secret raiding force behind enemy lines and into his economy, etc., all of which your opponent isn't doing while he is watching the fight. It's very easy to just watch and see how things play out, but while you should check back periodically (by using control groups on the armies that are fighting), you just can't watch the battle and stay competitive at the same time. Unless of course you are already winning so overwhelmingly that it doesn't matter any more!

Micromanaging Battles

Micromanaging, or "microing," a battle involves taking the time to manage the battle instead of letting the computer's artificial intelligence do it for you. Positioning your units to flank the enemy in battle, or tasking them to kill a specific unit (such as that cursed Son of Osiris!), are examples of different sorts of microing you might see in a game.

As we said in the previous section, spending all of your time watching battles is a bad idea. However, spending a few seconds to micro your army can be crucial, so don't feel guilty if you're giving commands to your units while they're fighting. (But do feel guilty if you aren't giving commands, and instead are just watching how the battle plays out.)

Here are some tips and tactics to keep an eye out for when fighting:

🛡 Make sure your guys aren't directly battling their counter units (see Figure 11.3). If your Slingers are shooting the enemy Raiding Cavalry instead of the Throwing Axemen, retask them immediately!

🛡 Avoid letting your fast units get caught up in the middle of a fight. For example, don't let your Raiding Cavalry get bogged down by enemy Spearmen. Instead, swing them around the outside of the battle and go after the Slingers in the rear.

Figure 11.3 *Avoid fighting your counter units! Micromanage the battle.*

◈ Focus your fire, and kill the weak enemy units. This is especially valuable in naval battles, but is true on land as well. While you're fighting, discover which of the enemy's units are almost dead and focus your army's attacks on those units. As I said earlier, numbers are very important, and if you can quickly kill off the weak units in a group, the numbers can easily tilt in your favor. Likewise, if you have a weak Trireme, move the ship to the back of your group. The Trireme can still shoot, but no longer can be targeted and killed easily.

◈ If you see that the enemy is focusing on a particular unit, run that unit away! This will cause the enemy units to follow that one unit. (If they are following instead of fighting, while you continue to fight, then those are all free shots for you!)

Using Control Groups

Control groups are essential for the expert player, almost as much so as hotkeys. Using control groups permits easy access to important areas on the map without having to waste time searching or scrolling. Also, using control groups allows you to give commands to units and buildings without having to move your screen or leave wherever you are currently fighting.

For example, during the middle of a big battle, if you have all Longhouses grouped as "Control Group 4," you can just hit 4 and then the hotkey T to build a new wave of Throwing Axemen. You can also set the gather point to right where you are fighting, all without moving the screen away from the battle. Having a constant wave of reinforcements coming in can easily sway the battle in your favor.

Here is a sample control-group setup to get you started. (Note: All the players I've talked to have their own methods of setting control groups. This is just a suggestion. Feel free to adapt it to whatever works best for you.)

◈ **Ctrl Group 1**: Your scout, in the first part of the game; later, your main army group.

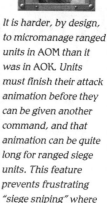

- **Ctrl Group 2**: Any villagers doing special tasks such as walling, away from the main group, that you want to remember to get back to quickly; later, your secondary army group.

- **Ctrl Group 3**: A third army group. (Use three army groups if you have several different raiding parties running around, or three different unit types that you want to keep track of during a battle.)

- **Ctrl Group 4**: Your primary unit buildings. This would be one type of military structure: your Barracks, Longhouses, Archery Ranges, etc.

- **Ctrl Group 5**: Your secondary building set. This could be a different front that you are maintaining (if you had military production areas in two different spots), or a second unit production center, if you are Greek.

- **Ctrl Group 6**: Your Fortress or siege buildings.

Some players like to go even further, using all available numbers, and then numbering individual settlements and even villager resource groups (all of your gold miners, wood gatherers, etc.). It simply comes down to how complicated you want to make it. At some point, you can have so many things grouped that you can't possibly keep track of it all. Getting into a consistent rhythm with control groups is the best way to get good with it, however you decide to implement the tactic.

Walling

Another trick to master is walling, one of the most effective things you can do, although it's one of the most difficult, too. In most games, you should think about putting up a wall at some point (see Figure 11.4).

For example, here is one of Maimin_matty's favorite techniques: Usually around the Heroic Age, he'll just start walling off half of the map with a villager or two while he's engaged in battles. What the wall does for him is contain all of the fighting on the enemy side of the map instead of his. He no longer has to worry about a few Raiding Cavalry flanking his base and destroying villagers. He will always have plenty of warning whenever the enemy mounts an offensive, and if he's lucky, he might even wall off one of the enemy settlements, giving him four instead of three.

Figure 11.4 *Walling serves both as defense and as early-warning system.*

Another of the more subtle, sneaky things to do is to leave a part open, instead of walling completely. The enemy will typically approach at the point you chose. ("Why knock down the wall when there's this nice opening here?") Setting up a choke point using walling can crush an unsuspecting army by leading them right into your Towers or Fortresses. Or, flank the enemy with a secondary army and trap the enemy force within your walling choke points.

ES TIP

You cannot build walls within three meters of unclaimed settlements or gold mines, in order to help prevent the not-so-fun game of trying to wall off enemy resources. Also remember that building foundations are extremely weak in AOM. A wall that is only half-built is useless in preventing an enemy incursion.

—Greg "DeathShrimp" Street

Application

We hope these tips and techniques will help take your military game up a notch. While this section outlines some fundamental techniques, just as we did with the economy in Chapter 10, there's nothing that can replace the number-one way to get better: practice. You need to practice hotkeys, control grouping, micromanaging your armies, etc. These techniques should become second nature so you don't have to think about them anymore. Becoming comfortable with these elements gives you more time to think about the overall strategy of the game.

Don't feel discouraged if these techniques don't come right away. To be honest, I'm still always working to get better at many of these—there's always room to improve. But if you force yourself to do them, and always keep them in the back of your mind, you will find yourself winning more and more games. And as we all know, it's always fun to win!

Advanced Greek Strategies

A player versed in The Age of Kings, or other standard real-time strategy games, will find Age of Mythology's Greeks to be easily understandable and familiar. They're designed to be a transition culture between AOK and AOM. That is not to diminish the Greeks' power, though: They are just as diverse as the Norse or Egypt, and have some extremely potent bonuses

So just what exactly distinguishes the Greeks from the Norse and Egyptians? For one thing, the Greeks start with three villagers, not two. They also have the best scouting. Greeks need just a single deposit site for wood and gold. Greek Heroes are extremely versatile and effective fighters. Greeks also possess the strongest mythological and human units, and have direct control of the rate at which they gain favor from the Gods.

In this chapter, we'll take a look at these benefits, provide an overview of the Greek Major Gods, and outline some sample strategies to get you started mastering this powerful culture.

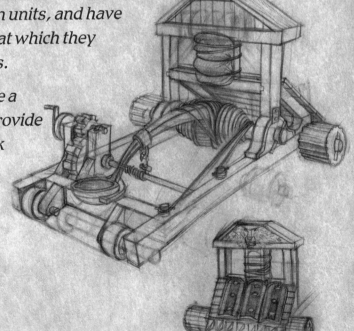

Three-Villager Start

The Greeks start with one more villager than the other two cultures. One more villager; big deal, right? Wrong. Having one extra villager over the course of even 10 minutes can make a huge difference. For example, a villager collecting wood, without any upgrades, will collect about 50 wood every minute. Over 10 minutes, that adds up to 500 more wood than you would have had with only two starting villagers!

Needless to say, that kind of difference can make or break a game between two equally skilled players. In fact, for a long time we were extremely worried about Zeus's Bolt god power being too powerful, because you could immediately run over and invoke Bolt on one of an enemy's early villagers, putting him that much further behind you. We eventually decided it wasn't a game-breaker, and that the other eight first-Age god powers just needed to be good enough to counter that.

TIP

This chapter was written by Ensemble Studios tester Chris "Swinger" Rupp, one of the world's best Age of Kings *and* Age of Mythology *players.*

The Best Scouting

The Greeks have far and away the best scouting in the game: The Kataskopos (a cavalry scout) is without equal in the Egyptian and Norse cultures of the Archaic Age. The Kataskopos is fast, has excellent line-of-sight, and has a fair number of hit points to stand up to settlement fire. This means that right off the bat you need to be running your scout around the entire map, exploring every nook and cranny.

The best way to do this is to "waypoint" your scout, by holding down the Shift key as you right-click in an ever-widening circle around your base. You can do this using the mini-map also, meaning that you don't need to move your main game screen. Doing this is the most efficient way of searching unexplored areas of the map. However, once you set those waypoints up, you can't just leave him alone. Make sure you continually check on your scout (control-grouping the scout to "Group 1" is the best way to do this), to ensure that he isn't getting stuck anywhere and to update his waypoints if he's finished his route. Maybe you can even find and eliminate a near-dead enemy villager (hurt from hunting, for instance) by running around.

While you're scouting, you should be grabbing all of the herdables you can find. In fact, I usually run my scout immediately to my enemy's base area and steal as many of his herdables as I can, before I go back and explore around my own base. Note that map type and the random variation within a map can have a big effect on this strategy. Maps often do not have "medium herdables," and the "close herdables" may be so close to an enemy Town Center that stealing them may be impossible, or even dangerous. Next, it's vital to find all of the settlements—yours and the ones near your

ES TIP

Most maps place one of your two Settlements between you and the enemy and another behind you in a more defensible area. However, losing the safer Settlement to an enemy can be even more devastating.

—Greg "DeathShrimp" Street

opponent—right away. If you can base your attack from one of these settlements, it can be very effective, as he will then have to go through your army and military buildings to get to that settlement. Also, you may be able to wall off his settlements from him. If you're playing as Egypt or the Norse, it's not always easy to find all of the settlements. With the Greeks, you never have to worry about that.

The Greeks also have the Pegasus mythological unit. All three of the Greek cultures can produce the unit, and it's easily the best scout in the game (even better than Odin's Ravens). Since it can fly, walls and water aren't a barrier, and the Pegasus has excellent line-of-sight. Making several Pegasi and leaving them at strategic points on the map to provide line-of-sight on everything your enemy is doing is a very good idea.

ES TIP

The Greeks' single depository for both wood and gold—the storehouse—is a nifty bonus that can save you some early wood, especially in a naval battle where every scrap is vital. Be careful though, as you can end up with all of your eggs in one basket. If you get attacked at your dual-purpose site, you could lose both your wood and gold-mining operations.

—Chris "Swinger" Rupp

Strong Heroes, Mythological Units, and Humans

Every Greek Hero on the board represents the best use of the population slots required. They are excellent counters for mythological units. This is especially true of Mythic Age Heroes—*always* have one in your army. In this fourth Age, the Greek Hero has nearly the hit points and attack strength of a mythological unit, and has no real counter.

Another big advantage for the Greeks is the strength of its human and mythological units. One Greek Hoplite will beat one Norse Ulfsark or one Egyptian Spearman easily. The Hoplite costs a bit more, which does balance them, up to a point—but once everyone is at their population cap, the advantage is definitely to the Greek player. Even if your 40 Hoplites cost significantly more than his 40 Ulfsarks, once you're in the late game and resources are no longer so crucial, your equally "popped-out" army (meaning you are both at your population limit of 160) is always going to win. Greek mythological units are also generally stronger than those of other cultures; they feature more hit points, attack, and armor. Although the Greek units are more powerful, that doesn't mean more is always better. The player with 40 Ulfsarks can probably replace his army much faster than you can replace your expensive Hoplites.

Controlling Favor Rate

The Greeks are the only culture with direct control over favor gain. If you need more favor, just task more villagers on your Temple. If you are gaining too much, task some of those villagers on something else. This advantage is somewhat diminished by the fact that you need to put villagers from your regular economy onto the Temple, which can set you back a bit in the other resources. (It means one or two fewer gold miners, etc.)

Favor also works on a diminishing-returns method. While we were developing *Age of Mythology*, we had problems trying to find the best Greek favor rate. We'd either have it too fast, meaning you saw nothing but armies of mythology units, or too slow, and no one would waste any time praying at all. We eventually worked out a solution whereby the more villagers you have praying, the lower their average efficiency is.

For example, one villager praying will gather about five units of favor per minute. Two villagers praying will get a little over nine, for an average of about four-and-a-half. Three will gather 13, etc. This means you can continue to put more and more guys on favor if you want to, and you will get more and more favor, but your efficiency in doing so eventually makes it a bad idea to keep putting people on the Temples, unless you have nothing better for them to do.

The best way to go is generally two or three villagers worshipping at the Greek Temple. That provides a satisfactory, consistent rate, while still making the best use of all of your villagers. Once you get to six villagers, it really isn't advisable to put more guys on, as the rate has bottomed out and your return is no longer worth it. (Unless you really want that army of Colossi, and don't care if you sacrifice your economy to do it.)

Greek Major Gods

This section includes a brief overview of the Greek Major Gods, with highlights on their civilization bonuses. Use these guidelines to develop your own strategies. For more on the Greek Major and Minor Gods, check out Chapter 3.

Zeus

Zeus's civilization benefits include:

◈ **Better Hoplites.** Since Zeus's Hoplites are faster than others, and do extra damage to buildings, you can use them to raid your opponent's buildings in the early going. Worry less about killing his villagers and instead attack his military buildings and resource deposit sites.

◈ **Starting favor, and faster generation of favor.** Zeus is definitely the best God for creating mythological-unit armies, because he offers increases both in favor-generation and starting favor. With Zeus's starting gift of 15 units of favor, you easily can build an early second-Age mythology unit, such as a Centaur or Minotaur, or research a mythology improvement for your Hoplites.

Poseidon

Poseidon's civilization benefits include:

◈ **Cheaper cavalry and stables.** Obviously cheaper cavalry and stables makes Poseidon *the* cavalry civilization for the Greeks. However, a deceptive strategy when playing Poseidon is to go all Hoplites and Toxotes instead of the cavalry your opponent is expecting to see. For more on Poseidon's cavalry, check out the sample strategies at the end of this chapter.

- ✦ **Free sea scout at the Dock.** Being able to scout the water for free is a very nice bonus. It makes the worship of Poseidon an excellent choice for a naval strategy, in addition to cavalry.

Hades

Hades' civilization benefits include:

- ✦ **Extra damage for Toxotes.** Just as Poseidon benefits a cavalry civilization, Hades is the choice for archer civilizations. For more on Hades' Archers, check out the sample strategies at the end of this chapter.

- ✦ **Free Shades.** This is a very nice bonus. Generally the best way to take advantage of it is to set the gather point for your Temple to wherever you are currently fighting (hotkey the Temple to a control group so you can easily activate it). Any Shades created will move to that gathering point. Having a few extra Shades during your battle can make a big difference!

Greek Sample Strategies

So, now that you know all of that, what should you do with it? This section includes two sample strategies to show you how to take advantage of the Greek bonuses. When designing a strategy to try in a game, there are several factors that you have to think about, before you go into it.

- ✦ What is it you're trying to accomplish?

- ✦ What is the best way to accomplish that goal?

- ✦ How can you take advantage of what the game offers?

- ✦ How do you have to adjust your style of play to reflect your new strategy?

Note that these strategies were written for a pre-release version of the game, and might not work exactly as planned. These are certainly not the only successful strategies for the Greeks, but are intended to get you thinking about how to take advantage of each civilization's bonuses so that you can create your own devastating strategies.

The Poseidon Cavalry Raid

The cavalry rush is designed to be a hard-hitting, fast, raiding type of strategy. While cavalry are very tough units, you don't want to fight your opponent's soldiers or Towers. Your goal is to hit his villagers in unprotected locations and then run away before he can counter. However, cavalry are very expensive units to make. So, those are the goals and the obstacles that we need to overcome. Here is how to go about it.

The first decision is what civilization to do this with. Of the three Greek civilizations, Poseidon is obviously the best, due to 10% cheaper cavalry, 50% cheaper stables, and the Lure god power (which helps keep your food supply going). Cavalry are very food- and gold-heavy, so we'll need to balance our economy accordingly, while still making sure that we get to the Classical Age in around six minutes.

Next will be a detailed description of the start of the game, followed by more general direction as to what to do next. We'll use a "standard" start, but remember that this start can vary greatly depending on what map you are playing on and how many resources are generated for that map, so you have to be able to adapt to the changes.

◈ **First thing:** Queue up three villagers at your Town Center.

◈ **Villagers 1-3.** Task them to build a granary by your chickens and berries. During this time, send your scout in a path around your Town Center, searching the unexplored areas. Find your two starting goats and move them and all subsequent goats close to your settlement.

◈ **Villager 4.** Assign to one of the chickens.

◈ **Villager 5.** Assign to the straggler trees by your Town Center. At this point, you've hopefully scouted enough to find your boars, rhinos, or deer (basically, your huntables) and, if you're lucky, some more goats or pigs. Since you worship Poseidon, you have the Lure god power, which will pull in more of the surrounding animals. Cast it near one of your huntable sources.

◈ **Villager 6.** Have villager 6 go to your huntable area and start building a granary.

◈ **Villager 7.** By now you should have found a spot for your storehouse. Your goal here is to find a place where you can put a storehouse next to both wood *and* gold. Even if you have to go off a ways to find this spot, it's worth doing. Villager 7 will build that storehouse. Make sure he goes to wood afterward. Remember to keep your scout moving. Queue up more waypoints by holding the Shift key and clicking on the map (or the mini-map).

◈ **Villager 8.** Put him on the chickens.

◈ **Villager 9.** Have him build a House, then go to your hunting area. The chickens should be close to being done now, so once villager 9 is ready, send everyone over to the granary. Research Hunting Dogs to boost your hunting rate.

◈ **Villager 10.** Put him on gold by the storehouse.

◈ **Villager 11.** Go to gold.

◈ **Villager 12.** Go to hunting.

◈ **Villager 13.** Go to wood.

◈ **Villager 14.** Build a Temple.

◈ **Villager 15.** Go to hunting (or finish the chickens).

◈ **Villagers 16-20.** At this point you should start to think about advancing to the Classical Age. I recommend worshipping Hermes as your Classical Age Minor God, as he offers mythological improvements to cavalry that will help you later. The Ceasefire god power also can be useful, if you need to hold the enemy off suddenly. Continue to build a few more villagers until you have around 20, and then advance the Age. Distribute the villagers where you need them most: first food, then wood. Once you advance to the Classical Age, get both the wood-chopping and gold-mining upgrades.

Now that you're advancing to the Classical Age, you're going to need wood for your two Stables and a few more Houses. Once you think you're going to have enough wood, start tasking more of your wood villagers onto a gold mine—those Hippikons consume a gold supply pretty fast. Task all new villagers on gold as well. Take two of your wood-gatherers and start building the Stables, followed by the Houses. Start training the Hippikons as soon as you can.

Once you have four Hippikon units, it's time to attack. *Hopefully*, your scout has searched through the entire map by now, so you know where your opponent's base is located. Look for an enemy granary or wood and gold depository, as you will likely find villagers there. Send your four Hippikons to that point.

If your opponent sends units to counter your cavalry, run away. While you can probably fight anything he has, you don't really want to get into a battle yet. Send your army to another spot of his. Remember, you're faster than he is, so you can keep running around!

During this time you should have built three or four more Hippikons—it's incredibly effective to harass at two spots at the same time. By assigning your Hippikon groups to separate control groups, you can continually and easily switch between both armies to maintain a constant attack on two separate enemy resource collection spots.

Continue to raid as long as you can. Eventually the enemy will put counters in key places, At that point, it's time to pull back and stop your raiding. You've probably done enough damage to his economy to give you an advantage. You then have two choices: switch over to archers to slaughter his infantry units, or start switching over to farming and plan to advance to the Heroic Age.

You've knocked your enemy back quite a bit, so it's very unlikely you will be attacked. Instead, expect the enemy to try to boost defenses more. This provides plenty of time to advance. Mix, stir, put it in the oven and you have a very tough strategy to beat!

The Hades Archer Rush

A quick, hard-hitting archer rush can deal a crippling blow to your opponent. Archers are ranged units, meaning they can hit an area and continue to hit while the villagers attempt to run away. Also, the more archers that are gathered, the stronger they become (due to the units on the inside of the group being able to fire to the outside without being counterattacked). The biggest advantage to basing your attack on archers is that they don't cost any food (only wood and gold), leaving food supplies free to build villagers and advance in Age.

The weakness of archers is their low hit points and low armor—archers are killed easily by cavalry and even infantry, if the infantry units can reach the archers. Counter-archer units like Slingers and Peltasts also can make short work of your archer army; be sure to avoid them. If you get into a fight with them, run!

The first decision is what civilization to play. Hades has an archer bonus, making him the best choice. Also, his god path offers the possibility of researching all archer improvements for *every* God, which can make your late-game archers especially lethal.

The start for an archer attack will be the same as a regular start until you advance in Age, where it then plays differently. Since we only need enough food to keep villager production going, our economy will be directed toward wood and gold after advancing.

For the first 15 villagers, use the Poseidon start illustrated earlier.

◈ **Villagers 16-20.** Start preparing to advance to the Classical Age, and as soon as you have enough food, advance. Ares is your God of choice here, as his Pestilence god power is a powerful way to stop your enemy from building counter-archer units. Plus, Ares also has an archer improvement available to research.

Once you're advancing to the Classical Age, research the gold and wood upgrades, and start switching the majority of your economy to gold and wood. You're only going to need about four villagers tasked on food at this point to maintain your villager production. All other villagers should be tasked towards wood and gold to fund your archers (with a slightly higher emphasis on wood, because your Archery Ranges, Houses, and archers are going to take a lot of it).

As soon you reach the Classical Age, place two Archery Ranges and a couple of Houses. Start training the Toxotes! As soon as you can fund an Armory, do so. As you're building your archers, make sure to get the Medium Toxote upgrade, as it also costs only wood and gold.

Once you have four or five archers, it's time to attack. You should have scouted out your enemy's base by now. If he is Egyptian, he will have the automatic Tower upgrade at Classical Age, so you have to be wary. If he is Norse or Greek, check to see if he has upgraded his Towers. If the enemy has Towers up, be careful, because Towers and archers don't mix well. Look outside his camp and see if he has any villagers mining gold, hunting food, or chopping wood outside the radius of his Towers.

If the enemy doesn't have Towers, then move in much closer—you should be able to directly harass his villagers. If the enemy counters with cavalry or slingers, run away. If the enemy sends anything else, at this point you should be able to fight.

Your goal is to disrupt his economy, more than it is to kill villagers. If his villagers are continually retreating from your archers, then they aren't gathering resources, meaning he's falling further and further behind. If he doesn't have a safe place to chop wood or mine gold, then he's *very* limited in what he can do to counter you. This puts you ahead. Continue making archers—the more you train, the stronger they are. Once you have spare wood, build a Stable and/or Barracks and make a few Hippikons if you're facing Egypt, or infantry if you're facing a Greek or Norse civilization. Use these to counter any anti-archer units the enemy sends at you.

Once you have a steady stream of archers training, it's time to switch back to food, so you can get your Armory improvements and start thinking about advancing to the Heroic Age. Research Husbandry, eat the rest of your sheep, and then switch to farming. You should have plenty of wood to use on farms when you need to. Choose to worship Apollo in the Heroic Age if you want to continue the archer trend. You should be miles ahead of your opponent and an easy victory shall be yours.

Advanced Egyptian Strategies

The Egyptians have a completely different game focus from that of the Greeks or the Norse. The powerful Pharaoh completely alters Egyptian play and leaves a myriad of options available to you. Also, the Egyptians don't require any wood for their buildings, which can drastically affect your economy.

This section provides advanced strategies for the Egyptian culture. We discuss Egypt's distinct characteristics—the unique Pharaoh and Priest units; gaining favor from Monuments; the low wood requirement; free Towers; and the ability to train Mercenaries. We include an overview of the Egyptian Major Gods, and provide sample strategies to get you started mastering this unique culture.

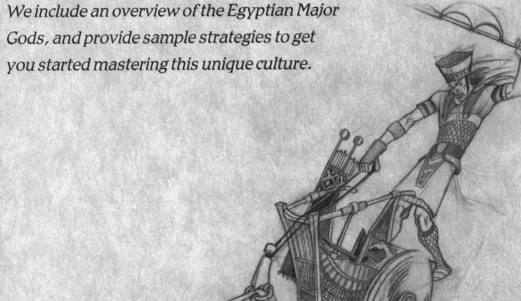

The Pharaoh

The Pharaoh is a truly unique unit in the real-time-strategy genre, and knowing how to use him correctly can make a world of difference.

Here's an overview of the Pharaoh's important abilities:

- **The Ability to Empower.** When a Pharaoh is tasked onto a building, he "empowers" it, causing that building to work faster (training units, researching improvements, etc.) or be built faster. Empowerment even increases the deposit rates to that building: If a laborer normally would drop off 10 units of wood at a lumber camp, he instead drops off 12 when it's empowered. Moving your Pharaoh around your base to balance your economy takes a lot of skill, attention, and planning. Think about where he is going to be most effective. For example, if you have 10 farmers around a granary, yet your Pharaoh is empowering a mining camp with only two laborers, then he's not where he should be. You generally want to have the Pharaoh either at the deposit site with the most laborers working at it, or at the gathering place of whatever resource you need the most. (And then put the most laborers there as well). Also, having the Pharaoh empower building construction can be very important. The Egyptians build structures more slowly than the other two cultures, so using the Pharaoh to help place your first Barracks or Migdol Stronghold to help guard the entrance to your base can be crucial.

  This chapter was written by Ensemble Studios tester Chris "Swinger" Rupp, one of the world's best Age of Kings and Age of Mythology players.

- **The Ability to Heal.** Although the Pharaoh can heal your units, the Egyptian Priests also have this ability. It's generally better to have the Priests healing your army instead of the Pharaoh. The Pharaoh needs to be used for other tasks!

- **Very Strong Counter to Mythological Units.** The Pharaoh is the most effective Hero in the game. By the time he's fully upgraded in the Mythic Age, the damage from his ranged attack is over 20! Combine that with his bonus power against mythological units, and the Pharaoh becomes a very deadly fighter. It isn't usually advisable to move your Pharaoh out of your base to fight mythological units in a forward attack, but if you're being attacked *in or near* your base, always stop empowering and move the Pharaoh into the fight. He will take down all of the enemy mythological units in no time—just make sure to protect him from human units.

- **Doesn't Count Against Population Cap.** One of the more subtle bonuses of Egypt is that the Pharaoh doesn't count against your population cap. When every inch of population room matters, the Pharaoh becomes a much-appreciated bonus unit to your army.

- **Automatically Reborn After Death.** Upon dying, the Pharaoh respawns from your Town Center 90 seconds after death. If he's killed, it isn't the end of the world. (Although that delay can sometimes feel that way when you really need him!)

So what is the best use of the Pharaoh? It really depends on what you're doing at the moment. Having the Pharaoh run out and fight in your army can be very helpful—but is it more helpful than the extra resources you're giving up at home? I recommend keeping him in your base, empowering your economy, until you hit your population cap in the Classical Age. At that point, using that extra fighter in your army is a welcome boost. Plus, after the Age-advancement, the Pharaoh becomes even more effective in battle. For the most part, using the Pharaoh effectively just takes practice to find out what fits your playing style the best.

Priests

Like the Pharaoh, Priests improve upon reaching each new Age. Every time you advance, Priests receive more range, hit points, and attack. They're not powerful enough to be elite fighting units, however. They aren't complete wimps, but they don't perform very well versus human units. Where the Priests shine, though, is in their ability to heal all of your units after every battle.

In every Egyptian army, include one or two Priests. During a battle, they are not very effective fighters or healers, but if you heal all of your units *after* every singe battle, you'll always have more units (and resources) than your enemy. Like all healing in *AOM*, Priests heal idle units much faster than those engaged in combat.

Every unit you heal is one more unit you don't have to replace at full cost of resources and time. Over the course of the game, the saved resources can really add up (especially when you consider the cost of War Elephants). Priests are expensive at 100 gold, but by always building one or two and sending them out with your troops, you're not only protecting yourself against enemy mythological units, but also extending the life of your army, which is more than worth the cost.

Gaining Favor

To gain favor from the Gods, the Egyptians must construct Monuments (there are five total) that gain favor just from their presence. But Monuments require resources and time. Like those of the Greeks and Norse, the Egyptian system of gaining favor has advantages and disadvantages.

On the plus side, the Monuments continue to generate favor as long as they remain standing, providing you with a constant source of favor that doesn't require you to tie up your economy with villagers. It's also very consistent. You can always expect to have a certain amount of favor at a given time, and can plan accordingly.

On the negative side, the cost and "build time" of each subsequent Monument increases. Also, since the favor system is steady and consistent, you don't have the option of quickly getting a few points of favor if you need it. You've also maximized your favor gain once you have all five Monuments built; you can't produce favor any faster. Note that as Ra, you can empower all five Monuments with your Priests. The benefit, however, is only 25% with all five empowered. So unless you really need a lot of favor, 10 population slots and 500 gold isn't worth it.

Build the first Monument within the first few minutes of the game, but not at the very start. (It will make you unable to maintain villager production, so wait until you have a consistent food supply before you build the structure.) Building that first Monument soon should provide 15 to 20 favor at the start of the Classical Age, which is perfect for a mythological unit or improvement.

If you aren't planning a strategy heavy with mythological units, three Monuments is all you need. The structures should provide enough favor for the occasional mythological unit and all of the mythological improvements you desire. Obviously, building four or five will provide more favor, but the greater cost and build time makes the decision unwise unless you plan to build an army of mythological units.

"Free" Buildings

Another key difference for Egypt is that none of their buildings requires wood. They are either free (such as deposit sites) or cost a small amount of gold. This means wood is a resource that Egypt generally needs very little of, allowing the Egyptian player the freedom to focus the economy on food and gold—at least in the early going. As with anything, there are pros and cons to Egypt's free buildings.

The pros:

◈ No wood means your economy can be focused almost solely on gold and food. Obviously, a two-resource economy is easier to manage than a three-resource economy.

◈ Leaving your forest intact helps preserve the natural fortifications around your base. While your enemy chops down all of his forests, leaving his base wide open, your surroundings remain relatively untouched.

◈ Free buildings means you can place multiple foundations at once without having to pay for them all—great for building all of your Houses right away! This also makes relocating deposit sites easier.

The cons:

◈ Egyptian structures are built much more slowly than comparable Greek and Norse buildings. (Perhaps mud bricks take time to bake.) This is the penalty for not having to pay anything for your buildings; the low cost is balanced by the amount of extra villager time you spend building them. Remember that using a Pharaoh to empower construction certainly helps!

◈ With a "no wood" economy, it's very easy to run short of wood for some of the improvements that you need (for instance, improvements to gold mining and farming require wood). You also need wood for Slingers, Chariot Archers, ships, and siege weapons.

Defense: Towers and Mercenaries

Two of the more subtle Egyptian distinguishing factors are the free Tower improvements and the Mercenaries. What exactly are they, and what can they do for you?

Tower Improvements

At the beginning of the Classical Age, Egypt's Towers are improved for free. Instantly! This bonus permits the Egyptian player to play very defensively if he or she desires. With your base naturally protected by Towers immediately, it's very easy to sit back and let the enemy come to you. Also, you could easily build additional Towers all over your base for protection—or at your enemy's base, with a forward attack.

Building an extra Tower over your gold mine is usually a good idea, and putting a Tower over a key choke point or two can help to secure your base. While the Greeks and Norse can upgrade their Towers, too, Egypt's free improvement right at the start of the second Age is a very significant advantage.

Mercenaries

The Egyptian Mercenaries are units that train almost instantly, out of any settlement. However, the Mercenaries last only a short time, and disappear even if not killed. Using Mercenaries effectively is fairly difficult but can have a very positive benefit. On the negative side, Mercenaries last a very short time (45 seconds, 60 if they've been improved). Trying to use them offensively is almost impossible unless you have gained a settlement near a battle. Mercenaries also are very expensive; building a lot can quickly drain your economy.

On the plus side, they are an instantly created army that doesn't require population slots. Mercenaries give you the ability to protect large areas of the map. If you are attacked at a settlement while your main army is off fighting elsewhere, you can quickly make several Mercenaries to ward off the invaders. Mercenary Cavalry are particularly excellent at running out and "killing" siege weapons that are firing at your settlement.

You really have to judge carefully whether a situation is right for Mercenaries. If you are fighting around a settlement you currently hold, it's usually a very good idea to build them there. But if you're fighting on the outskirts of your town, where the Mercenaries would only have time to fight for a few seconds before going away, then you definitely shouldn't build them.

ES TIP

These improved defenses work especially well with another Egyptian quirk: They can build farms in the first Age. While this is rarely a smart strategy when there are abundant resources around, it can be useful if you get pinned down or play a map with low resources nearby.

—Greg "DeathShrimp" Street

Egyptian Major Gods

This section includes a brief overview of the Egyptian Major Gods and highlights their civilization bonuses. Use these guidelines to develop your own strategies with them. For more on the Egyptian Major and Minor Gods, check out Chapter 4.

Ra

Ra's civilization benefits include the following.

- **Monuments are cheaper.** This can save you a lot of resources. A strategy heavy in myth units is easiest to do with Ra, as you can build all five of your Monuments much more cheaply than you can with the other Egyptian civilizations. The Monuments also have more hit points, which can help them survive an attack on your town

- **Ra Priests can empower like the Pharaoh.** Ra's economy is arguably the best in the game. By putting Priests to work at all of your resource drop sites (you can assign only one Priest to each site), you can boost your entire economy. It also helps you build all of your structures faster. However, this bonus is somewhat deceptive: Once you've hit your population limit, you have to be very careful about whether or not to use Priests to empower. They empower at 25%, which means there must be nine laborers working at a deposit site before the Priest is better than just adding two more laborers ($9 \times 1.25 = 11.25$, $9 + 2 = 11$). If you have a Priest empowering a site with only five villagers working there, he's being wasted and the population slot could be better used elsewhere.

- **Chariots and Camelry have more hit points.** This makes going with a heavy Migdol Stronghold strategy quite effective. A successful strategy with Ra is to play defensively and use your Rain god power to shoot you up to the Heroic Age quickly so you can build a Migdol Stronghold or two and start training lots of Camelry. They also move faster.

- **Ra's Pharaoh also empowers gathering at an improved rate (+25%) compared to Set and Isis (+20%).** Combine that bonus with the ability of Ra Priests to empower, and the Ra economy can boom very quickly.

Isis

Isis's civilization benefits include the following.

- **Cheaper improvements.** While cheaper improvements are always nice, the big thing to note here is that Age-advancement is also cheaper, which makes a significant difference in your ability to advance in Age quickly.

- **Priests build obelisks faster and cheaper.** This bonus is far more useful than the average player may realize. Every time I play with or against Isis, I see obelisks all over the map, because the Isis player will usually scout with a Priest by building obelisks everywhere. The structures provide a permanent and extensive line of sight (until destroyed), and although obelisks crumble quickly, usually the enemy won't find them all, leaving you the ability to see in a lot of places. This can be a huge factor; scouting the enemy is crucial.

- **Monuments block enemy god powers.** This is another ability that can really aid in defense. Having Monuments spread around your base, or your ally's base, can make a huge difference when your enemy is looking to fire off that Meteor or Tornado god power in your town. If you're feeling daring, you can forward-build your Monuments near where you're fighting—a useful tactic when you know your enemy has a Lightning Storm or Curse that he's just waiting to use.

Set

Set's civilization benefits include the following.

- **Set's Priests can convert animals.** This is one of the coolest bonuses in the game. Being able to convert all of the wild animals on the map can be a fun advantage for you! Some of the favored tactics amongst playtest team members: Convert a wolf or hyena to scout the map for you; quickly run over and steal one of your enemy's rhinos or boars; or amass an army that's ready to go in the Classical Age by converting all of the lions, tigers, and bears (oh my!) that you can find.

- **Animals are created at your Temple in each Age.** Getting a few free units at the beginning of each Age never hurts; use them for fighting or for eating. You even start with a Hyena as Set, which is a good scout with a decent attack.

- **Pharaoh can summon animals.** This is an often-overlooked feature. Set's Pharaoh has the ability to summon all kinds of animals for either eating or fighting. They train very quickly, but also cost favor, so you have to weigh whether a mythological unit or a crocodile would be more valuable to you at any given time.

- **Slingers and Chariot Archers train faster.** These are the human wood units for Egypt. Training them faster can always be useful, especially in late-game combat. Slingers also have more hit points and better Hack armor, making them more like a mainline unit than Ra or Isis's Slingers.

Egyptian Sample Strategies

So, now that you know all of that, what should you do with it? This section includes a couple of sample strategies that take advantage of the Egyptian bonuses. When designing a strategy to try in a game, there are several factors that you have to think about before you go into it.

- What is it you're trying to do?

- What is the best way to accomplish that goal?

- How can you take advantage of what the game offers?

- How do you have to adjust your style of play to reflect your new strategy?

Note that these strategies were written on a pre-release version of the game and might not work exactly as planned. These are certainly not the only successful strategies for the Egyptians; they're intended to get you thinking about how to take advantage of a civilization's bonuses so that you can create your own devastating strategies.

The Rinx (Also Known as the Ra Sphinx Attack)

This strategy is based around Ra's cheaper Monuments and the Rain god power, which combine to create a huge economy and an army of mythological units that should catch your enemy by surprise. The difficulty inherent in the strategy is that it takes a long time to get going, meaning you have to sit back and play a very defensive game until you have enough resources coming in that you can start building Sphinxes.

- **The Start:** Queue up four laborers (not five) at the Town Center.

- **Laborers 1–3.** Task one laborer to start building your first Monument. (When it's finished, move that unit onto berries.) Task the other two laborers to build a granary (with Priest empowerment) near the berries. Take your two goats and send them on a scout path around your town, eventually ending up back at your Town Center. You're doing this to expand the line of sight outside your town a little bit more. Task the Pharaoh to start scouting around your town, looking for things to hunt—gold, etc. We're using the Pharaoh to scout because he has a much better line of sight than the Priest, and the Ra Priest can empower just as well as the Pharaoh. (This is the opposite of how the other Egyptian "civs" are played.)

- **Laborers 4–8.** Send to berries.

- **Laborer 9.** Place a mining camp. Once the Pharaoh has made one scouting pass around your base, task him to empower the camp.

- **Laborer 10.** Task this laborer to build your second Monument. When it's finished, send him to gold.

- **Laborer 11.** Build a granary by your next food source—hunting or berries (don't research Hunting Dogs—we need the wood for later).

- ◈ **Laborer 12.** Build a House, then help with the Temple (see "Villager 14" below).

- ◈ **Laborer 13.** Second food source.

- ◈ **Laborer 14.** Build a Temple. When it's finished, send Temple builders to gold.

- ◈ **Laborer 15.** Second food source.

- ◈ **Laborer 16.** Food.

- ◈ **Laborer 17.** Gold.

- ◈ **Laborers 18–20.** We need to start getting ready to advance. Keep sending villagers to food until you have the 400, then advance to the Classical Age. Worship Bast for the Sphinxes and Sacred Cats improvement. Once you run out of food, have all of the food laborers start building farms around your Town Center.

When you have 150 food, build your third Monument. As soon as you hit the Classical Age, around six minutes or so into the game, research your two farming improvements immediately—Plow, and Bast's Sacred Cats. The god power Rain will triple your food production, so you'd rather triple the increased rate than the base rate! (For most improvements in the game, the order in which you research them is irrelevant. For some god powers, however, it does matter.)

As soon as both improvements are done and you have built seven to eight farms, have the Priest empower the Town Center and invoke Rain. During this time, you should build your first Sphinx, so that you have something other than Towers to defend yourself with.

That Rain will provide a ton of food, so you won't need to build any more farms for a long time. Instead, continue to build the fourth and fifth Monuments, and train Sphinxes.

Build a second Temple so you can improve the Sphinxes, and at the same time, keep building more of them. When the second Temple is complete, start researching the two Sphinx improvements. Once you have eight or nine Sphinxes, attack. Since the Sphinxes do an area attack with their special power, sending them into a mass of villagers near wood or gold is deadly to the enemy. Be sure to avoid the enemy Heroes, and once you get into your first major battle, invoke Eclipse to boost your mythological units' attack and speed. Unless your enemy has an army of Heroes ready, the Sphinxes should make quick work of it.

The Isis Turtle

While in general rushing straight to the third Age is a risky proposition, Isis has a much better time of it than most. With her myriad benefits and Egypt's natural ability to turtle, it's a viable strategy. The problem with turtling—concentrating on defense, as discussed in Chapter 11—is that it's difficult to decide just how much turtling is needed. Do you build four layers of walls over your entire base, with Towers covering the whole thing, sacrificing your economy to do so? Or do you go with only a light defense, in the hopes that the enemy doesn't attack hard? Isis has less trouble with that question, as she offers two very powerful god powers in the second and third Ages that can get you over the hump, so to speak, and allow you to bust out of your turtle successfully.

These two god powers are Plague of Serpents and Ancestors. Both create instant military units for you, giving you the ability to protect your base without having to commit a large number of resources to turtling up. Used in conjunction right away in the Heroic Age, these two powers can crush any Classical Age army. This allows you to then grab a settlement or two and make a Migdol Stronghold in which to build your elite units and overwhelm your opponent.

A second big advantage with Isis is the 10% reduction in the price of all improvements, including Age-advancement. That bonus makes advancing in Age much easier and faster, as you can afford to click the button that much sooner. And the third advantage is Egypt's natural bonus of free improvements to your Towers—a turtler's dream. Anyway, enough talking: On with the show!

⊕ **Laborers 1–3.** We're not concerned about a Monument right now. We need to be using every scrap of resources for our immediate needs, so send all three to your berries and have your Pharaoh start empowering the granary. Send your Priest on a scouting pattern around your camp. As your Priest gets to the edge of your area, have him build a few obelisks. Not many, but enough that you can expand the line of sight around your base.

⊕ **Laborers 4–6.** Berries

⊕ **Laborers 7–8.** Build a mining camp and start collecting gold.

⊕ **Laborer 9.** Berries

⊕ **Laborer 10.** Find a hunting area and start building a granary. While that's being constructed, research Hunting Dogs.

⊕ **Laborer 11.** Build a House and then go to the hunting area

⊕ **Laborer 12.** Head to hunting as well. At this point your berries should be disappearing, so take the berry-gatherers and the Pharaoh and move them to hunting as well.

⊕ **Laborer 13.** Build a Monument and then go to gold.

⊕ **Laborer 14.** Gold.

⊕ **Laborer 15.** Build a Temple, and then go to gold

⊕ **Laborer 16.** Straggler trees around your settlement.

⊕ **Laborer 17.** More straggler trees.

⊕ **Laborers 18–22.** Allocate to food and gold as you see fit. We don't need any wood in the near future, so ignore it for now. It's time to start advancing in Age, so keep sending villagers to your food sources until you have the 360 that you need, then advance and choose Anubis in the Classical Age. You should reach the Classical Age at a point between five and six minutes into the game.

✦ **Classical Age.** Make sure to continue building villagers once you're in the Classical Age, till you have 28–30, at which point start advancing to the Heroic Age. More details about what to do in this Age are below.

Once you click on the button to advance to Classical Age, have a villager head out and start building walls to cover your base. Make sure that you have at least one gold mine inside your walls (the more the merrier) and make sure that you enclose your entire base. Discovering later that you missed a spot, as the enemy army pours in, is never very much fun. The wall needs to be finished within 30–45 seconds of your opponent's advancing in Age. If you don't think your one villager is going to be able to do that in time, send a few more to help him.

We want to avoid having to farm for as long as possible, so as soon as your first hunting area is done, move to the next one (assuming you have one!). Once that second area is exhausted, it's very unlikely that you are going to have any safe areas left (as your enemy will probably have an army roaming around out there by now), so head back inside your walls.

When it's time to move inside the walls, it's time to start farming—but before we do that, we need to take advantage of our Prosperity god power. Send some of the hunters to gold so that you have around 10 people on the gold mine (more and it just gets too congested), and research the Pick Axe improvement if it's available to you. As soon as that finishes, cast Prosperity, with the Pharaoh empowering the gold mine. This will really boost your gold supplies and give you all the gold you'll need to build your farms and advance in Age. With the extra hunters still left, start building farms around your Town Center. As soon as Prosperity is done, move a few of the gold miners and the Pharaoh to farm production. Remember to also get the Plow improvement for your farms.

During all this, task one of your newly created villagers to build an Armory. The Armory takes a very long time to build, so plan ahead for this. Your enemy may be banging at your walls, so if you have to, improve the walls. But do this *only* if you absolutely have to, as we can't spare the food. Putting up a Tower where they are attacking is the better bet. Worst-case scenario: Use your Plague of Serpents god power to hold them off while you get to the third Age.

Once you have the necessary resources, advance to the Heroic Age and pick Nephthys to get the Ancestors god power. You should be able to make it to this Age in around 10 minutes. As soon as you hit the Heroic Age, take the Pharaoh and a fair number of villagers (five or six from food, or gold if you have a lot extra) and head outside the walls to your closest settlement. With the Pharaoh empowering the construction, the settlement should be created pretty quickly—with luck, before the enemy has time to react. If he does see you there, protect yourself with Serpents first, and then Ancestors if you have to. You need to get this settlement up. Once it's up, his army will have to pull back, at which point you can take those villagers and the Pharaoh and build a Migdol Stronghold right next to your new settlement.

With a settlement and a Migdol Stronghold there, it's going to be nearly impossible for a Heroic Age army to take that area out, so you can start to boom out of both settlements now. Take note of the units he has been attacking you with, and build the appropriate counter units out of your Migdol Stronghold. Start getting your Blacksmith upgrades. Once you feel safe, head over and take your third settlement and continue your boom. You will need a second

Migdol Stronghold when you can afford it, so that you can build your army twice as fast. Eventually you can switch to War Elephants, and just start plowing through the enemy base.

Your enemy at this point should be panicking, seeing you in the Heroic Age already, and he will try very hard to advance to the third Age as well. While he's advancing though, you are expanding your economy, so that by the time he gets to Heroic, you are already way ahead of him, and it's too late. As long as your turtle "shell" stays intact in the early going and you can get your first settlement up, this strategy should allow rushing to the Heroic Age to pay off quickly. You'll leave your enemy choking on your dust.

Advanced Norse Strategies

Take the traditional real-time-strategy formula, add some sugar, spice, and everything mean and nasty, then toss it up into the air a few times and what you're left with is the Norse. Drastically different from the Greeks, Egyptians, The Age of Kings, or anything else out there, the Norse are the most difficult culture to play in Age of Mythology by far. Their entire economic and military makeup is profoundly radical.

This section provides advanced strategy for the Norse culture. We discuss the characteristics that make the Norse different— starting units, Dwarves, mobile deposit sites, infantry construction crews, and gaining favor through combat. An overview of the Norse Major Gods is also included, as well as some sample strategies to get you started mastering this interesting culture.

Two-Villager, Ox Cart, Ulfsark Start

The Norse starting units are very different from those in the other cultures. You don't have to use your villagers (called gatherers) to build anything (more on this later), meaning that all of their time is spent collecting resources. Also, having the Ox Cart right off the bat means that you don't have to build any deposit sites, saving wood and time. (Again, more on this later.)

Since your starting Ulfsark is both your scout and your builder, be careful not to scout too close to the enemy's base unless you are monitoring the Ulfsark closely. Running too close to the enemy settlement and getting killed is definitely not the best way to start the game. Also, be careful and don't build anything too close to your enemy, like a House or Temple, because if he sees you, he could harass your builder and cause you to waste a ton of time and resources. It's always safer to build near your town.

Dwarven Miners

Dwarves are resource gatherers that cost 70 gold (though Thor's Dwarves are cheaper). They're weaker than human gatherers at collecting food and wood (except Thor's Dwarves), but better at gold mining. Having Dwarves is an extremely nice benefit to the Norse culture—you should always build several to do all of your gold mining for you. Also, since they don't cost any food, whenever you're food-starved you can build Dwarves instead, helping to keep your Town Center always working.

In a lot of the games I've played as Norse, I would start saving all of my food around the time I wanted to advance in Age, while still building Dwarves, providing a faster Age-advancement time. I recommend building at least four or five Dwarves, and quite possibly more during the course of the game.

One option that you have at the start is to spend your first 150 gold on two Dwarves. They will pay for themselves fairly quickly, so it's generally a good idea. The only possible hiccup is if you want to research Hunting Dogs right away to enhance hunting, which will leave you with only 50 gold, so you'll have to mine some more before building your first dwarf.

No True Archer

The Throwing Axeman is the closest thing to an archer the Norse have. While this means the Norse player doesn't have to worry about improvements for a third unit type (instead focusing on just cavalry and infantry), it also allows the opponent to ignore defenses against archers.

The Throwing Axeman loses to both of the other cultures' ranged units, leaving the Norse at a distinct disadvantage in ranged combat. You can turn this into an advantage, however, with a sneaky strategy: Use a surprise army of Norse Ballistas in the Mythic Age. Since the Ballistas do pierce damage, and your enemy probably doesn't have any pierce armor improvements, this can be very deadly.

Norse Infantry Build

Norse gatherers can build only farms. This is far and away the most substantial difference in the Norse economy, and drastically changes their entire gameplay. When playing Norse, you always have to be cognizant that you need a military unit or two around to build your Houses, Temples, Longhouses, etc. On the plus side, this fact makes Norse the most aggressive at taking over territory.

For example, as soon as your Norse destroy an enemy settlement, you should immediately drop your own settlement on top, and start building, even if it's in your enemy's base! Since you usually will have 20–30 soldiers at the time, the settlement will go up very quickly, giving you a strong foothold.

On the negative side, Norse buildings are fairly weak. Once you start losing them, they go down like a house of cards. Since you must produce units at your military production centers in order to rebuild, you're in serious trouble if the enemy is destroying these structures.

Thus, building forward is very dangerous for the Norse player. It's generally safer to build your first military base very close to your own base before expanding. As the game progresses, get the building hit-point improvements in the Town Center to strengthen the weak Norse buildings. You're then less vulnerable to building raids, and to the Earthquake god power.

While it's very tempting to just drop Houses wherever your Ulfsark happens to be at the time, this is a bad idea. Because the Houses are weaker, the enemy can easily destroy all of your straggler Houses, leaving you short on population room at a critical time. As we said, the closer your Houses and other buildings are to your base, the safer they are.

Mobile Deposit Site

The Norse can't build traditional deposit sites and must rely on their Ox Carts for everything from dropping off resources to researching economic improvements. This gives the Norse a very nomadic flavor; it's always very easy to transfer your wood-chopping or gold operations. Being mobile allows you to move the Ox Cart as necessary, whether you're escaping a raid, following your wood choppers, or starting a new gold mine. This helps in balancing, and relocating, your economy whenever you need it.

The Ox Cart does have some negatives: It moves very slowly, making it difficult to send across the map to that other gold mine you need. Its lack of speed makes it a vulnerable raiding target, as well. And finally, it builds out of the Town Center, meaning that while you're building one, your Town Center is neither advancing in Age nor building more gatherers or Dwarves for you, which can have a negative effect on your economy.

I wait to build a second Ox Cart until I absolutely have to by gathering two resources from one spot and a third resource at the Town Center. For example, wood and gold with the Ox Cart, and goats at my settlement; or gold and deer with the cart while chopping my straggler trees. Usually I find that I can get by with one cart just fine until I'm ready to advance in Age, at which point I will build the second cart right before advancing.

One temptation that I recommend against is to make a group of farms around a lone Ox Cart. These "Ox Cart farms" generally are badly protected. All your enemy has to do is take out your Ox Cart and all the farms are worthless until you can build a new cart and get it over there. The best way to expand your farming is to do it all around your Town Center, and to branch out an "Ox Cart farm" right next to your existing farming setup. This is safer and more effective in the long run.

Favor Through Fighting

Depending on how you look at it, the Norse have either the best or the worst way of gaining favor. The Norse method of gaining favor, going along nicely with their thirst for blood, is by doing something violent. Favor is generated every time a Norse unit (including gatherers but excluding myth units) does damage. Whether the unit kills an enemy, slaughters a goat, or throws a rock at a building, favor is generated. (Technically, you don't need to get a kill. If a unit provides two favor on death, knocking away 50% of its hit points will net one Favor.) As with everything, there are pros and cons.

The pros:

◈ Favor is virtually free. You don't have to spend any resources or gatherer time to pay for it.

◈ Once you are fighting, Norse favor can easily come in faster than you can spend it.

◈ You will always have favor as the Norse. While it's easy to forget to maintain production when you're playing as a Greek or an Egyptian, with the Norse it's never a problem.

◈ Hersir Hero units can generate a trickle of favor just by being on the map—and generate extra favor when fighting.

◈ Killing oh-so-ferocious goats and deer can even provide favor.

◈ Early Norse mythological units tend to cost less favor than Greek or Egyptian myth units.

The cons:

◈ If you're losing, favor is really hard to come by. Guys who get killed before they can do any damage don't get much favor at all.

◈ If you need just one more point of favor for that Mountain Giant, it can be hard to get it, as fighting isn't always the best option at any given time.

◈ Early-game favor is difficult, as you are rarely in combat in the Archaic Age.

Using your Hersir is the best way to gain favor when you're playing Norse. Hersir units gather twice the favor of regular units while fighting, and they also slowly give you favor just for being there. Norse Longboats and Ragnarok Heroes also receive a bonus to favor gain.

In those situations where you find yourself needing just a bit more favor, you should look around your army and see if there is any wildlife nearby. Killing a rhino or even some zebra will usually get you what you need.

Gatherer Conversion to Ulfsarks

This subtle bonus is one of the more difficult ones to employ. For the price of training an Ulfsark, you can convert a Norse gatherer *into* an Ulfsark. Now, at first glance, you might say, "That's terrible: I just spent 50 food for a gatherer and now I have to spend an additional 50 food and 30 gold to turn him into an Ulfsark? Why would I ever want to do that?"

Well, here are just a few situations where this bonus can come in very, very handy.

◈ Your enemy sends four Raiding Cavalry units against your wood choppers. You have no military there, and your gatherers are going to get chopped to bits trying to run away. By converting even just three of your gatherers into Ulfsarks, you allow the rest of your gatherers to keep working instead of having to run. You shouldn't lose any more gatherers than those three you converted, and you now have three extra Ulfsarks.

◈ You've just lost all of your infantry units and, at the same time, your enemy destroyed a few of your Houses. You suddenly realize that you're at your population cap and can no longer build any military, and thus you can't build any more Houses either. You *can*, however, grab a gatherer or two, convert them into Ulfsarks, and build your Houses. Also, you can use them to quickly build a Tower or a wall to protect your gatherers and town.

◈ Gatherers are immediately converted into Ulfsarks, so if you need something right now, you don't have to wait the sixteen seconds or so an Ulfsark takes to be created!

◈ You could attempt the "Poor Man's Ragnarok." (It should probably be called the "Rich Man's Ragnarok," given the resources required.) While this isn't something I would recommend doing very often, you can create your own Ragnarok of sorts (a variation on Baldr's god power), by creating a lot of gatherers and then converting them all. Since gatherers count as one pop slot while Ulfsarks count as two, you can convert well over your population cap. (Convert 100 gatherers and you suddenly find yourself with over 200 population.) This, however, is *extremely* expensive, so I wouldn't ever do this unless I had a lot of extra resources.

Norse Major Gods

This section includes a brief overview of the Norse Major Gods, highlighting their civilization bonuses. Use these guidelines to develop your own strategies with them. For more on the Norse Major and Minor Gods, check out Chapter 5.

Odin

Odin's civilization benefits include:

◈ **Regenerating human units.** Odin's benefit of human-unit regeneration is huge. The units need to be idle to regenerate quickly, though, so every time you finish a battle of any sort, make sure to have your army stop and rest along the way to regain their hit points. This benefit is better than having a few Egyptian Priests healing you.

- ◈ **The two Ravens.** Using the two Ravens to scout makes Odin's civilization arguably the best among the Norse. Be careful: Don't let them be killed by Tower and Town Center fire, as they take a long time to respawn. You don't want to put one of them directly over your enemy's military operations. If the enemy has any ranged units, they will auto-kill the Raven. And if you are that obvious, the enemy will make an *effort* to build something to kill those Ravens. Your best tactic, after exploring the entire map, is to put the Ravens just off to the side, perhaps over a grove of trees, in order to see everything the enemy is doing without being too conspicuous.

- ◈ **Hunting bonus.** Since Odin provides a natural hunting bonus, you definitely should make huntables your top priority as a food source.

Thor

Thor's civilization benefits include:

- ◈ **Cheaper, better Dwarves.** The ability to build Dwarves that cost less and do more can really affect the way you play Thor. During a typical game as Thor, I will build easily more than half of my economy with Dwarves, using them primarily on gold but also on the other resources if I need to. Being able to build Thor's cheaper, better Dwarves can save you some crucial food down the line.

- ◈ **A Dwarven Armory in any Age.** This was one of the last major bonuses we put into the game, and it really made Thor fun to play. Since you can build the Armory right away, in the Archaic Age (and it costs less than a regular Armory), you can have the structure ready to go during the Classical Age, improving your units. And since improvements are cheaper for Thor, you can easily have the most elite fighting force on the field every time. A good idea for Thor is to sit back and play defensively until you have gotten your Heroic Age Armory improvements (which you can get even though you're still in the Classical Age). Then it's time to fight! Being two levels above your opponent (an attack and an armor upgrade) can swing the battles by over 20% (meaning, if you and your opponent have similar units on the battlefield at approximately the same cost, you'll have 20%of your hit points remaining after the fight). With two similarly sized armies, that is huge. The Armory also makes Thor very powerful in the late game because you can get additional Mythic Age improvements on your attack and armor. Their benefit can be tough to afford and isn't as much of a leap over Iron as Iron is over Bronze, but the ability to have even a small advantage over fully upgraded enemy units can really turn the tide of battle.

Loki

Loki's civilization benefits include the following:

- ◈ **Longhouse units train faster.** While this is a subtle difference, faster training is actually a substantial advantage at high levels of play.

- **Cheaper, faster Ox Carts.** Since Loki's Ox Carts are much faster, I often will use my starting Ox Cart to help scout my base in the beginning, while sending a scout toward the enemy base. An Ox Cart's line of sight isn't that great, but I'm generally not doing anything else with it right away, so it's a good use for it. Also, since Loki's Ox Carts are cheaper, you can build one sooner than you would a regular one, and then its payoff will come sooner, as well.

- **Hersir can summon free Myth units.** This is one of the coolest bonuses in the game. Playing as Loki and using a heavy Hersir strategy is quite possible, and it's certainly a lot of fun (see the sample strategies at the end of this chapter). Having a Battle Boar or an Einherjar pop up in the middle of your battle is just cool. Loki also grants his followers the benefit of reduced favor requirements for mythological units!

- **Faster Hersir.** It's much easier to use these faster Hersir effectively, as slow speed is one of the Hersir weaknesses. This also makes summoning free myth units that much easier.

Norse Sample Strategies

So what can you do with all this information? This section includes two sample strategies that take advantage of the Norse bonuses. When designing a strategy to try in a game, there are several things to consider:

- What is it you're trying to accomplish?

- What is the best way to do that?

- How can you take advantage of what the game offers?

- How must you adjust your style of play to reflect your new strategy?

Note that these strategies were written on a pre-release version of the game and might not work exactly as planned. These are certainly not the only successful strategies for the Norse; they're intended to get you thinking about how to take advantage of a civilization's bonuses so that you can create your own devastating strategies.

The Loki Myth Unit, Hersir Rush

This strategy takes advantage of Loki's inherent mythological benefits. First, Loki's mythological units cost less, making it much easier to train them. Second, your Heroes will summon mythological units on their own while fighting. Since you're going to be building Heroes already, in order to gain more favor, this works out pretty well! On the negative side, the Hersir aren't at their best against human units, so we need to train our mythological units fast, to support them.

- **The Start.** Queue up gatherers at the Town Center.

- **Gatherers 1 and 2.** Send your two starting gatherers to the berry bushes, with your Ox Cart. Your Ulfsark should start scouting in circles around your camp.

- ⬥ **Gatherer 3.** Berries.

- ⬥ **Gatherer 4.** To berries, I say!

- ⬥ **Gatherer 5.** Berries…. Yeah, you get the picture.

- ⬥ **Gatherer 6.** Hmm. Let's go berries, for something different.

- ⬥ **Gatherer 7.** Send him to the straggler trees around your Town Center. At about the same time, start researching the Hunting Dogs improvement. While the improvement is in progress, reassign all of your food gatherers to hunting.

- ⬥ **Dwarf 1.** Gatherer 8. Send him to gold.

- ⬥ **Ox Cart.** Build an Ox Cart and send it to the gold mine, as well.

- ⬥ **Dwarf 1.** Dwarf to gold. Build a House with your Ulfsark now.

- ⬥ **Gatherer 9.** Straggler trees. We need to start gathering wood for another House and our Temple.

- ⬥ **Gatherer 10.** Straggler trees. When the stragglers run out, locate a wood-chopping place next to either your gold mine (preferable), or your hunters, and move your wood operation there.

- ⬥ **Gatherer 11.** Send to food. We should have enough guys on wood now, so we need to start gathering enough food to go up an Age. Continue to move your hunters to different hunting spots as each animal is depleted.

- ⬥ **Gatherer 12.** Send to food. Start building your Temple as soon as you have the 80 wood (your two Dwarves should have gotten you enough gold by now).

- ⬥ **Gatherers/Dwarves 15–20.** A mixture of food and gold assignments, depending on what you need more of. We need to have a large supply of food and gold to build our Hersir. As soon as you've finished the Temple, advance to the Classical Age and then build a Hersir at the Temple.

Upon advancing, the best God to choose with this strategy is Forseti, because his Healing Spring god power is going to help heal your expensive Hersir units after every battle—a power you'll need. Plus, Forseti offers the Hall of Thanes technology to improve your Hersir. Finally, Trolls are cheap and easy to build, and you will need them to counter the human infantry that probably will be sent to counter your Hersir Heroes. As you are advancing to the Classical Age (and after getting the improvements to your gold- and wood-gathering), you will need to continue to build Hersir units at your Temple (while also building Houses, as necessary).

As soon as you reach the Classical Age, place your first Longhouse. Since we can train Hersir out of our Temple as well as our Longhouse, we don't need a second Longhouse right away. Once the Longhouse is built and you have five to six Hersir, kill any of the surrounding wildlife, bears, rhinos, giraffes, whatever, so that you get enough favor to build a Troll. (You also will start getting the favor your Heroes will need to summon mythology units later on.) Once you have your Troll and eight or nine Hersir, it's time to attack.

As the battle progresses, continue to train more Trolls and Hersir. Remember to invoke Forseti's Healing Spring. I recommend placing the structure forward of your military buildings, but don't cast it too far forward, because your enemy can take it over and use it for himself!

Keep your Ulfsark in your base to build Houses and eventually a second Longhouse, followed by an Armory. Once you have enough spare wood, remember to get the Hall of Thanes improvement to your Hersir. Unless your enemy has already prepared a large army of counter-infantry units and Heroes, he's going to be in a lot of trouble, especially when your Hersir start summoning free mythology units!

Thor's Throwing Axeman, Dwarf Attack

This is one of my favorite strategies in the game, and possibly the only strategy that I put together in the beginning of the development process that actually is still viable at the end. This strategy takes advantage of Thor's Dwarf and Armory bonuses.

What we are trying to do here is to completely streamline our economy so that we need very little food. To do this, we will build Dwarves (which cost only gold) almost exclusively, and then Throwing Axemen (wood and gold) almost exclusively. Against a Norse player who counters with Raiding Cavalry, this isn't as effective, but against a Greek or Egyptian who counters with a pierce unit, it can work quite well. The reason it works is because we're also going to use Thor's special Armory to research the Heroic Age pierce-armor improvement right away (also requiring only wood and gold), which leaves our units heavily armored against arrows. Also, since Thor's Longhouses are cheaper, it makes them that much easier to build, allowing for more Throwing Axeman.

◈ **The Start.** Queue two Dwarves right away and set your TC's rally point at your gold mine.

◈ **Dwarves 1 and 2.** Send your two starting Dwarves to your gold mine, along with the Ox Cart. Start mining gold immediately! Get the gold-mining improvement as soon as you can, since you'll need a lot of gold!

◈ **Dwarf 3.** To gold.

◈ **Dwarf 4.** To gold.

◈ **Gatherer 1.** Gold. You might not have enough gold yet to maintain your Dwarf production, so build this gatherer and send him to the mine. After this, though, you should be able to go all Dwarves.

◈ **Dwarf 5.** To gold.

◈ **Dwarf 6.** To gold.

◈ **Dwarf 7.** To gold. Once he gets there, take your three gatherers and put one on straggler trees and the other two on chickens.

- ⬥ **Dwarf 8.** To gold. Now, build an Ox Cart and send it to your chickens.

- ⬥ **Dwarf 9.** To hunting. As soon as you have enough wood, research the Hunting Dogs improvement and send all of your gatherers and the Ox Cart to a huntables area. The Dwarf should be done harvesting his first load at about the time the Ox Cart arrives.

- ⬥ **Dwarf 10.** To hunting (or gold, if you're having trouble keeping up Dwarf production). Have your Ulfsark build a House.

- ⬥ **Dwarf 11.** To hunting.

- ⬥ **Dwarf 12.** To wood.

- ⬥ **Dwarf 13.** To hunting.

- ⬥ **Dwarf 14.** To hunting. As soon as you have enough wood, build your Temple.

- ⬥ **Dwarves 15–22.** Keep building Dwarves and assign them to food until you have the 400 you need. Advance to the Classical Age as soon as possible.

Upon advancing to the Classical Age, worship Freyja so that you can train Valkyries, which will be effective at helping to kill enemy archers. As soon as you have the 400 food required to advance, start pulling food-gatherers off their task and move them to wood. You will need 150 food for your Medium Infantry improvement, but after you have that, leave two guys on food and put all of the rest on wood and gold. If you have the wood, use your Ulfsark to build your Armory during the Age-advancement.

In the Classical Age, build a Longhouse and train Throwing Axemen. Once you have an army of around eight Throwing Axemen and have built all of the buildings you need, it's time to attack. Since this strategy doesn't rely heavily on subtlety, feel free to attack head-on. Our goal is to overwhelm the enemy. Focus on taking out any military buildings that they are trying to put up, and remember to take out their Towers. (Eliminating gatherers is always a plus, but get the military buildings first—if he can't build counters to you, then you can't be stopped).

You can continue to build Dwarves instead of gatherers (keep sending them to wood and gold), so your food resources can be saved for improvements to attack and armor. If you ever feel you don't have time to move your Dwarves to a new gold mine, invoke Thor's Dwarven Mine god power to provide you an extra 1,000 gold (in the Classical Age) at the old mine.

Once you have erected a second Longhouse, research the Medium Infantry improvement. During this, build a third Longhouse. Continue training Throwing Axemen from all three Longhouses. Select the Armory and research both the Classical- and Heroic-Age pierce improvements while you're fighting. Once you start to overwhelm your opponent, switch your gold miners over to a farming operation and play the game normally from then on.

Appendix

This section includes all statistics for Greek, Egyptian, and Norse units, mythological units, and improvements. You'll also find the complete list of relics (randomly placed in single-player, random-map, and multiplayer games) and their benefits, at the end of this Appendix. For more information on military units, mythological units, and improvements, check out Chapters 3, 4, and 5 of this strategy guide, which cover the Greek, Egyptian, and Norse cultures, respectively.

Table Entries Explained

These entry explanations apply to all of the tables in this appendix.

- ✥ **Unit, or Improvement** – The name of the unit or improvement.

- ✥ **Cost** – The resources required (food, wood, gold, or favor) to train the unit or research the improvement.

- ✥ **Hit Points** – The base amount of the unit's hit points, with no improvements.

- ✥ **Attack Damage** – The base amount of the unit's attack, with no improvements. "Hack" damage is done at close range (as with a sword), "pierce" refers to ranged attacks (arrows), and "crush" generally refers to siege weapons.

- ✥ **Bonus Damage** – The base amount of the unit's bonus damage.

- ✥ **Hack Armor** – The base amount of the unit's unimproved hack armor, which helps defend the unit against hack damage.

- ✥ **Pierce Armor** – The base amount of the unit's unimproved pierce armor, which helps defend the unit against pierce damage.

- ✥ **Crush Armor** – The base amount of the unit's unimproved crush armor, which helps defend the unit against siege attacks.

- ✥ **Range** – The base range of the unit, with no improvements.

- ✥ **Line of Sight** – The base line of sight of the unit, with no improvements.

- ✥ **Max Speed** – The base maximum speed of the unit, with no improvements.

- ✥ **Special Attacks** – Any special attacks of the unit, including its best use as a counter unit.

- ✥ **Benefits** – The effects of a particular improvement.

> **TIP**
>
> In all of the tables in this appendix, the percentage values in the Benefits column adjust the unit's base value. For example, if the benefit is 10% to attack, and the unit originally had an attack value of 20, the benefit will increase the base attack by 2, for a total of 22. Research order is not important. All improvements are to the original base value. All numerical values, such as +5 to bonus damage, equal an absolute increase to the base value.

Greek Unit Statistics

UNIT	COST	HIT POINTS	ATTACK DAMAGE	BONUS DAMAGE	HACK ARMOR	PIERCE ARMOR	CRUSH ARMOR	RANGE	LINE OF SIGHT	MAX SPEED
Hoplite	60 food, 35 gold	115	8 hack	N/A	35%	15%	99%	N/A	16	4.2
SPECIAL ATTACK: Counters cavalry										
Hypaspist	60 food, 25 gold	85	5 hack	4.25 to infantry, Hersir, and Heroes of Ragnarok	35%	10%	99%	N/A	16	4.3
SPECIAL ATTACK: Counters infantry										
Toxote	55 wood, 35 gold	60	6.5 pierce	.9 to Raiding	15%	15%	99%	15	19	4.0
SPECIAL ATTACK: Counters infantry										
Peltast	60 wood, 20 gold	70	3 pierce	4 to archers; 3 to Throwing Axemen; 1.25 to Hypaspists and Axemen	15%	20%	99%	16	20	4.0
SPECIAL ATTACK: Counters archers										
Hippikon	40 food, 80 gold	150	9 hack	1.25 to archers	10%	25%	99%	N/A	8	5.5
SPECIAL ATTACK: Counters archers										
Prodromos	70 food, 40 gold	120	6 hack	3 to cavalry	20%	10%	99%	N/A	16	6.0
SPECIAL ATTACK: Counters cavalry										
Myrmidon	70 food, 50 gold	110	10 hack	1.5 to Egyptian and Norse units; 1.0 to Axemen and Throwing Axemen	45%	20%	99%	N/A	16	4.0
SPECIAL ATTACK: Counters Egyptian and Norse units; Zeus only										
Hetairoi	60 food, 100 gold	110	8 hack	3.5 to buildings	10%	40%	99%	N/A	16	4.8
SPECIAL ATTACK: Counters buildings; Poseidon only										
Gastraphetes	120 wood, 80 gold	60	8 pierce, 6 crush	N/A	15%	15%	99%	24	16	4.8
SPECIAL ATTACK: Counters buildings; Hades only										
Petrobolos	150 wood, 200 gold	110	11 crush; 5 pierce	2.5 to ships	30%	90%	80%	28 max, 10 min	40	2.4
SPECIAL ATTACK: Counters buildings and ships										
Helepolis	300 wood, 200 gold	700	17 crush; 5 pierce	N/A	20%	96%	50%	10	18	2.9
SPECIAL ATTACK: Counters buildings; transports units										
Trireme	100 wood, 50 gold	290	6 pierce	3 to transport ships	30%	20%	10%	12	24	6.0
SPECIAL ATTACK: Counters hammer ships										
Pentekonter	100 wood, 50 gold	240	20 hack	N/A	30%	20%	75%	2	16	7.0
SPECIAL ATTACK: Counters siege ships										
Juggernaut	100 wood, 100 gold	480	6 crush	.5 to buildings	10%	50%	10%	18	24	4.8
SPECIAL ATTACK: Counters archer ships										
Jason	100 food, 50 gold	250	9 hack	7 to myth units	25%	35%	99%	N/A	16	4.3
SPECIAL ATTACK: Counters myth units; Zeus only										

continued

UNIT	COST	HIT POINTS	ATTACK DAMAGE	BONUS DAMAGE	HACK ARMOR	PIERCE ARMOR	CRUSH ARMOR	RANGE	LINE OF SIGHT	MAX SPEED
Odysseus	200 wood, 2 favor	320	8 pierce	7 to myth units	20%	30%	99%	18	20	4.0
	SPECIAL ATTACK: Counters myth units; Zeus only									
Heracles	350 food, 4 favor	400	10 hack	7 to myth units	25%	40%	99%	N/A	16	4.3
	SPECIAL ATTACK: Counters myth units; Zeus only									
Bellerophon	400 gold, 6 favor	400	20 hack; 100 hack for jump attack	5 to myth units; 7 to myth units for jump attack	20%	40%	99%	14 max, 4 min jump range	16	6.0
	SPECIAL ATTACK: Counters myth units; Jump Attack with area-effect damage; Zeus only									
Theseus	100 food, 50 gold	240	9 hack	7 to myth units	25%	40%	99%	N/A	16	4.3
	SPECIAL ATTACK: Counters myth units; Poseidon only									
Hippolyta	200 wood, 2 favor	240	9 pierce	7 to myth units	20%	30%	99%	18	20	4.3
	SPECIAL ATTACK: Counters myth units; Poseidon only									
Atalanta	350 wood, 4 favor	350	8 hack	7 to myth units	35%	40%	99%	N/A	16	6.0
	SPECIAL ATTACK: Counters myth units; Poseidon only									
Polyphemus	400 gold, 6 favor	540	15 hack; 5 crush; 60 hack for gore	5 to myth units; 7 to myth units with gore attack	40%	40%	99%	N/A	20	2.9
	SPECIAL ATTACK: Counters myth units; Gore Attack; Poseidon attack only									
Argo	250 wood, 8 favor	480	8 pierce	5 to buildings and myth units; 3 to transport	40%	25%	20%	16	24	4.8
	SPECIAL ATTACK: Counters myth units; bonus ships damage vs. buildings; Poseidon only									
Ajax	100 food, 50 gold	240	9 hack	7 to myth units	30%	35%	99%	N/A	16	4.3
	SPECIAL ATTACK: Counters myth units; Hades only									
Chiron	200 wood, 2 favor	300	7 pierce	7 to myth units	20%	20%	99%	14	20	5.3
	SPECIAL ATTACK: Counters myth units; Hades only									
Achilles	350 food, 4 favor	340	9 hack	7 to myth units	40%	45%	99%	N/A	16	5.5
	SPECIAL ATTACK: Counters myth units; Hades only									
Perseus	400 gold, 6 favor	360	7 hack	10 to myth units	20%	40%	99%	5 for Medusa stoning	16	4.3
	SPECIAL ATTACK: Counters myth units; carries Medusa's Head to "stone" units; Hades only									
Kataskopos	N/A	70	2 hack	N/A	10%	70%	99%	N/A	14	5.5
	SPECIAL ATTACK: Scout; free but can't be replaced									

Greek Mythological Unit Statistics

UNIT	GOD	COST	HIT POINTS	ATTACK DAMAGE	BONUS DAMAGE	HACK ARMOR	PIERCE ARMOR	CRUSH ARMOR	RANGE	LINE OF SIGHT	MAX SPEED
Pegasus	All	50 food, 2 favor	140	N/A	N/A	50%	50%	99%	N/A	18	5
		SPECIAL ATTACK: Flying Scout									
Hippocampus	Poseidon	N/A	70	N/A	N/A	10%	70%	99%	N/A	16	6.6
		SPECIAL ATTACK: Naval Scout									
Shade	Hades	N/A	275	6 hack	N/A	20%	20%	99%	N/A	16	4.0
		SPECIAL ATTACK: Hades only									
Cyclops	Ares	250 food, 22 favor	500	15 hack; 12 crush; 30 hack for throw attack	3 to myth units	40%	50%	80%	N/A	16	3.2
		SPECIAL ATTACK: Bonus damage vs. myth units; can throw human units									
Minotaur	Athena	200 food, 16 favor	300	15 hack; 10 crush; 60 hack for gore attack	3 to myth units	60%	50%	80%	N/A	20	4.0
		SPECIAL ATTACK: Bonus damage vs. myth units; Gore Attack against humans									
Centaur	Hermes	150 wood, 12 favor	220	12 pierce; 24 pierce for accuracy attack	3 to myth unit	25%	35%	80%	12	20	5.0
		SPECIAL ATTACK: Bonus damage vs. myth units; recharging accuracy attack: double damage and doesn't miss									
Manticore	Apollo	300 wood, 28 favor	420	11 pierce; 15 pierce for recharged attack	1 to myth units	30%	60%	80%	16	20	4.3
		SPECIAL ATTACK: Bonus damage vs. myth units; recharging attack for more projectiles and increased damage									
Nemean Lion	Aphrodite	250 gold, 25 favor	660	20 hack, 10 crush; 12 hack splash damage from roar attack	3 to myth units	30%	60%	80%	N/A	16	4.8
		SPECIAL ATTACK: Bonus damage vs. myth units; recharging roar attack inflicts splash damage									
Hydra	Dionysus	250 food, 28 favor	800	20 hack, 10 crush	2 to myth units	60%	40%	80%	2.0	16	4.0
		SPECIAL ATTACK: Bonus damage vs. myth units; grows heads after kills to increase attack									
Scylla	Dionysus	200 gold, 15 favor	1,000	25 hack, 12 crush	N/A	40%	70%	99%	N/A	16	5.3
		SPECIAL ATTACK: Grows heads after kills to increase attack									
Chimera	Artemis	200 gold, 30 favor	600	20 hack; 15 hack for fire attack	3 to myth units	60%	60%	80%	8 for fire attack	16	5.3
		SPECIAL ATTACK: Bonus damage vs. myth units; recharging fire-breathing attack inflicts splash damage									
Colossus	Hephaestus	300 gold, 40 favor	1,100	20 hack, 50 crush	3 to myth units	50%	80%	80%	N/A	16	2.4
		SPECIAL ATTACK: Bonus damage vs. myth units; can eat wood and gold to regain health									
Medusa	Hera	250 gold, 40 favor	360	15 pierce, 12.5 crush	N/A	60%	70%	80%	10	18	4.3
		SPECIAL ATTACK: Can "stone" units									
Carcinos	Hera	200 wood, 20 favor	720	20 hack, 12 crush	N/A	70%	60%	80%	N/A	16	4.3
		SPECIAL ATTACK: Boiling blood released upon death									

Greek Improvement Statistics

IMPROVEMENT	GREEK GOD	COST	BENEFITS
Medium Infantry	All	150 food, 150 gold	+10% to attack and hit points, +1 to line of sight
Medium Archers	All	150 wood, 150 gold	+10% to attack and hit points, +1 to line of sight
Medium Cavalry	All	200 food, 100 gold	+10% to attack and hit points, +1 to line of sight
Heavy Infantry	All	300 food, 300 gold	+10% to attack, +15% to hit points, +1 to line of sight
Heavy Archers	All	300 wood, 300 gold	+10% to attack and hit points, +1 to line of sight
Heavy Cavalry	All	400 food, 200 gold	+10% to attack, +15% to hit points, +1 to line of sight
Champion Infantry	All	500 food, 400 gold	+10% to attack, +20% to hit points, +1 to line of sight
Champion Archers	All	500 wood, 400 gold	+10% to attack and hit points, +1 to line of sight
Champion Cavalry	All	700 food, 200 gold	+10% to attack, +20% to hit points, +1 to line of sight
Levy Infantry	All	300 food	-20% to infantry train speed
Levy Archers	All	300 food	-20% to archer train speed
Levy Cavalry	All	300 food	-20% to cavalry train speed
Conscript Infantry	All	500 food	-20% to infantry train speed
Conscript Archers	All	500 food	-20% to archer train speed
Conscript Cavalry	All	500 food	-20% to cavalry train speed
Conscript Sailors	All	500 wood	-20% to ship train speed
Draft Horses	All	300 food, 200 gold	+20% to siege weapon speed
Engineers	All	300 food, 500 gold	+10% bonus damage vs. walls to siege weapons, +2 to range of Petroboli and Catapult, +50% crush damage to siege towers and Portable Rams, +25% pierce and +25% crush to ranged siege weapons.
Masons	All	200 food, 300 wood	+20% to building hit points, +5% to building crush armor
Architects	All	400 food, 500 wood	+20% to building hit points, +5% to building crush armor
Archer Ship Cladding	All	200 wood, 200 gold	+10% to archer ship pierce damage, +4 to archer ship range, +20% to archer ship hit points
Reinforced Ram	All	300 wood, 200 gold	+10% to hammer ship hit points and hack damage
Naval Oxybeles	All	500 wood, 200 gold	+9 to siege ship range, +12 to siege ship line of sight, +10% to siege ship hit points, +2 to bonus damage vs. buildings
Olympic Parentage	Zeus	200 food, 10 favor	+25% to Hero hit points
Lord of Horses	Poseidon	150 food, 10 favor	+4 to cavalry line of sight
Vault of Erebus	Hades	200 food, 10 favor	+0.75 gold per second
Will of Kronos	Ares	200 food, 25 favor	+50% to Cyclops hack attack; +100% to Cyclops crush attack; -25% to train speed
Phobos' Spear of Panic	Ares	200 food, 15 favor	+10% to Hoplite hack damage
Deimos' Sword of Dread	Ares	200 food, 15 favor	+15% to Hypaspist hack damage
Enyo's Bow of Horror	Ares	250 wood, 20 favor	+10% to Toxote pierce damage
Labyrinth of Minos	Athena	250 wood, 20 favor	Reduce Minotaur cost by 25%; +40 to Minotaur hit points
Sarissa	Athena	200 wood, 25 favor	+20% to Hoplite hack armor
Aegis Shield	Athena	300 wood, 25 favor	+10% to infantry pierce armor
Sylvan Lore	Hermes	300 wood, 20 favor	+25% to Centaur hit points; +30% to Centaur speed

continued

IMPROVEMENT	GREEK GOD	COST	BENEFITS
Spirited Charge	Hermes	250 food, 35 favor	+10% to cavalry hack attack and cavalry speed
Winged Messenger	Hermes	50 gold, 10 favor	Reduce Pegasi cost to zero; -50% to train speed; +6 to line of sight
Oracle	Apollo	200 wood, 10 favor	+6 to line of sight of all units and buildings
Temple of Healing	Apollo	150 gold, 20 favor	Idle units near Greek Temple are healed one at a time
Sun Ray	Apollo	200 wood, 40 favor	+10% to archer, Centaur, and Manticore pierce attack
Roar of Orthus	Aphrodite	300 food, 20 favor	+50% to Nemean Lion pierce armor; +20% to Nemean Lion hack armor
Golden Apples	Aphrodite	300 food, 200 gold	+15% to villager worship speed
Divine Blood	Aphrodite	200 food, 35 gold	20% faster villagers; +20% to villager build speed; +10 to carry capacity
Bacchanalia	Dionysus	300 wood, 20 favor	+5% to hit points for all units
Thracian Horses	Dionysus	400 food, 30 favor	+20% to cavalry hit points
Anastrophe	Dionysus	300 food, 20 favor	+20% to Pentekonter hack damage; +10% to velocity; -25% to training speed
Flames of Typhon	Artemis	400 food, 20 favor	+30% to Chimera hack and fire-breathing attack; +20% to Chimera hit points
Shafts of Plague	Artemis	400 gold, 40 favor	+15% to archer pierce damage
Trierarch	Artemis	300 gold, 40 favor	+20% to Trireme crush armor
Hand of Talos	Hephaestus	300 wood, 20 favor	+100 to Colossi hit points
Shoulder of Talos	Hephaestus	300 gold, 20 favor	+200 to Colossi hit points; +20% to Colossi hack armor
Forge of Olympus	Hephaestus	300 food, 60 favor	Reduce Armory improvement costs by 25%
Weapon of the Titans	Hephaestus	400 gold, 20 favor	+10% to Myrmidon, Hetairoi, Gastraphetes attacks
Face of the Gorgon	Hera	400 wood, 30 favor	+33% to Medusa hit points
Athenian Wall	Hera	400 wood, 30 favor	+30% to building hit points; +10% to wall hit points
Monstrous Rage	Hera	250 food, 20 favor	+25% to mythological unit hack, pierce, and crush attacks

Egyptian Unit Statistics

UNIT	COST	HIT POINTS	ATTACK DAMAGE	BONUS DAMAGE	HACK ARMOR	PIERCE ARMOR	CRUSH ARMOR	RANGE	LINE OF SIGHT	MAX SPEED
Axeman	40 food, 30 gold	70	5 hack	4 to infantry, Hersir, and Hero of Ragnarok	40%	5%	99%	N/A	16	4.3
	SPECIAL ATTACK: Counters infantry									
Slinger	60 wood, 24 gold	65	3 pierce	4 to archers; 3 to Throwing Axemen; 1.25 to Hypaspist and Axeman	15%	20%	99%	16	20	4.0
	SPECIAL ATTACK: Counters archers									
Spearman	50 food, 20 gold	70	7 hack	1.2 to cavalry	40%	20%	99%	N/A	16	5.0
	SPECIAL ATTACK: Counters cavalry									
Chariot Archer	100 wood, 40 gold	90	8.5 pierce	N/A	30%	25%	99%	20	24	5.3
	SPECIAL ATTACK: Counters infantry									
Camelry	50 food, 70 gold	125	8 hack	1.75 to cavalry	15%	30%	99%	N/A	16	6.0
	SPECIAL ATTACK: Counters cavalry									
War Elephant	180 food, 70 gold	450	12 hack	3 to buildings	10%	40%	99%	N/A	16	2.9
	SPECIAL ATTACK: Counters buildings									
Pharaoh	N/A	100	12 pierce	5 to myth units	15%	15%	99%	N/A	16	4.0
	SPECIAL ATTACK: Counters myth units; empowers buildings (20% to gather rate, 200% to build rate, 30% to train rate)									
Priest	100 gold	90	3 pierce	7 to myth units	10%	0%	99%	N/A	8	3.6
	SPECIAL ATTACK: Counters myth units; heals units; Ra's Priest empowers buildings (25% to gather rate)									
Mercenary	90 gold	85	8 hack	N/A	45%	30%	99%	N/A	20	4.3
	SPECIAL ATTACK: Counters cavalry; fast training speed; short lifespan									
Mercenary Cavalry	120 gold	190	8 hack	N/A	60%	70%	99%	N/A	22	5.3
	SPECIAL ATTACK: Counters archers; fast training speed; short lifespan									
Siege Tower	200 wood, 100 gold	350	50 crush; 3 pierce	N/A	5%	96%	90%	12 for ranged, 3 for ram	20	2.9
	SPECIAL ATTACK: Counters buildings; transports units									
Catapult	200 wood, 200 gold	115	50 crush; 10 pierce	2.5 to ships	30%	90%	80%	10 min, 28 max	40	2.4
	SPECIAL ATTACK: Counters buildings and ships									
Kebenit	100 wood, 50 gold	290	6 pierce	3 to transport ships	30%	20%	10%	12	24	6.0
	SPECIAL ATTACK: Counters hammer ships									
Ramming Galley	100 wood, 50 gold	240	20 hack	N/A	30%	20%	10%	N/A	16	7.0
	SPECIAL ATTACK: Counters siege ships									
War Barge	100 food, 100 gold	480	6 crush	.5 to buildings	10%	50%	10%	18	24	4.8
	SPECIAL ATTACK: Counters archer ships and buildings									

Egyptian Mythological Unit Statistics

UNIT	GOD	COST	HIT POINTS	ATTACK DAMAGE	BONUS DAMAGE	HACK ARMOR	PIERCE ARMOR	CRUSH ARMOR	RANGE	LINE OF SIGHT	MAX SPEED
Anubite	Anubis	100 food, 15 favor	200	13 hack; 15 hack for jump attack	3 to myth units	60%	65%	80%	4 min, 8 max for jump attack	16	5.3
SPECIAL ATTACK: Bonus damage vs. myth units; Jump Attack with increased damage											
Sphinx	Bast	120 food, 20 favor	300	11.25 hack, 5 crush; 20 hack with whirlwind attack	3 to myth units	45%	60%	80%	N/A	22	5.3
SPECIAL ATTACK: Bonus damage vs. myth units; Whirlwind Attack with increased damage											
Wadjet	Ptah	150 wood, 15 favor	240	16 pierce	N/A	20%	30%	80%	18	20	3.8
SPECIAL ATTACK: N/A											
Petsuchos	Hathor	200 gold, 20 favor	480	20 crush; 50 pierce	N/A	30%	50%	80%	20	24	3.6
SPECIAL ATTACK: N/A											
Roc	Hathor	150 gold, 15 favor	350	N/A	N/A	40%	25%	80%	N/A	20	5.3
SPECIAL ATTACK: Transports units											
Leviathan	Nephthys	200 gold, 20 favor	1020	25 hack	N/A	40%	60%	80%	N/A	22	4.2
SPECIAL ATTACK: Transports units											
Scorpion Man	Nephthys	150 wood, 25 favor	500	25 hack, bonus poison damage	2 to myth units	50%	40%	80%	N/A	16	5.0
SPECIAL ATTACK: Bonus damage vs. myth units; poison damage											
Scarab	Sekhmet	300 food, 20 favor	670	12 crush, 6 hack	5 to buildings	30%	75%	80%	N/A	16	3.2
SPECIAL ATTACK: Bonus damage vs. buildings; toxic blood-splatter when killed											
Avenger	Horus	250 food, 30 favor	600	28 hack; 25 hack splash damage with whirlwind attack	3 to myth units	60%	40%	80%	N/A	18	5.3
SPECIAL ATTACK: Bonus damage vs. myth units; recharging Whirlwind Attack inflicts splash damage											
Mummy	Osiris	200 gold, 35 favor	350	12 pierce	N/A	35%	50%	80%	12	18	4.0
SPECIAL ATTACK: Can convert human units into Minions											
Phoenix	Thoth	200 gold, 30 favor	400	20 hack, 30 crush	N/A	15%	55%	80%	4	20	3.6
SPECIAL ATTACK: N/A											
Sea Turtle	Thoth	300 food, 20 favor	960	25 hack, 20 crush; 100 hack, 30 crush with buck attack	N/A	40%	70%	80%	N/A	22	5.3
SPECIAL ATTACK: Recharging Buck Attack for increased damage											

Egyptian Improvement Statistics

IMPROVEMENT	EGYPTIAN GOD	COST	BENEFITS
Medium Axemen	All	100 food, 100 gold	+10% to attack and hit points, +1 to line of sight
Medium Slingers	All	100 wood, 100 gold	+10% to attack and hit points, +1 to line of sight
Medium Spearmen	All	100 food, 100 gold	+10% to attack and hit points, +1 to line of sight
Heavy Axemen	All	300 food, 200 gold	+10% to attack, +15% to hit points, +1 to line of sight
Heavy Slingers	All	300 wood, 200 gold	+10% to attack and hit points, +1 to line of sight
Heavy Spearmen	All	300 food, 200 gold	+10% to attack, +15% to hit points, +1 to line of sight
Heavy Chariot Archers	All	150 wood, 150 gold	+10% to attack and hit points, +1 to line of sight
Heavy Camelry	All	150 food, 150 gold	+20% to attack, +15% to hit points, +1 to line of sight
Heavy War Elephants	All	200 food, 150 gold	+10% to attack and hit points, +1 to line of sight
Champion Axemen	All	400 food, 300 gold	+10% to attack, +20% to hit points, +1 to line of sight
Champion Slingers	All	400 wood, 300 gold	+10% to attack and hit points, +1 to line of sight
Champion Spearmen	All	400 food, 300 gold	+10% to attack; +20% to hit points, +1 to line of sight
Champion Chariot Archers	All	400 wood, 200 gold	+10% to attack and hit points, +1 to line of sight
Champion Camelry	All	400 food, 200 gold	+10% to attack; +20% to hit points, +1 to line of sight
Champion War Elephants	All	500 food, 400 gold	+10% to attack and hit points, +1 to line of sight
Levy Barracks Soldiers	All	600 food	-20% to Barracks soldiers train speed
Levy Migdol Soldiers	All	600 food	-20% to Migdol Stronghold soldiers train speed
Conscript Barracks Soldiers	All	800 food	-20% to Migdol Stronghold soldiers train speed
Conscript Migdol Soldiers	All	800 food	-20% to Migdol Stronghold soldiers train speed
Conscript Sailors	All	500 wood	-20% to ship train speed
Draft Horses	All	300 food, 200 gold	+20% to siege weapon speed
Engineers	All	300 food, 500 gold	+10% bonus damage vs. walls to siege weapons, +2 to range of Petroboli and Catapult, +50% crush damage to siege towers and Portable Rams, +25% pierce and +25% crush to ranged siege weapons.
Masons	All	200 food, 300 wood	+20% to building hit points, +5% to building crush armor
Architects	All	400 food, 500 wood	+20% to building hit points, +5% to building crush armor
Archer Ship Cladding	All	200 wood, 200 gold	+10% to archer ship pierce damage, +4 to archer ship range, +20% to archer ship hit points
Reinforced Ram	All	300 wood, 200 gold	+10% to hammer ship hit points and hack damage
Naval Oxybeles	All	500 wood, 200 gold	+9 to siege ship range, +12 to siege ship line of sight, +10% to siege ship hit points, +2 to bonus damage vs. buildings
Skin of the Rhino	Ra	50 food, 5 favor	+30% to laborer hack and pierce armor; +20% to laborer hack attack
Flood of the Nile	Isis	200 gold, 9 favor	+0.75 food per second
Feral	Set	100 gold, 10 favor	+50% to converted animal hack attack; +10% to converted animal hit points; +10% to converted animal hack and pierce armor

continued

IMPROVEMENT	EGYPTIAN GOD	COST	BENEFITS
Feet of the Jackal	Anubis	250 gold, 15 favor	+50 to Anubite hit points; +6 to Anubite jump range; +20% to Anubite hack attack
Serpent Spear	Anubis	250 food, 12 favor	+15% to Spearman hack attack
Necropolis	Anubis	250 gold, 10 favor	+10% to favor rate
Criosphinx	Bast	250 wood, 15 favor	+50 to Sphinx hit points; +20% to hack attack; +50% to crush attack
Hieracosphinx	Bast	400 food, 20 favor	+20% to Sphinx speed; +20% to hack attack; +50% to crush attack
Sacred Cats	Bast	110 gold, 10 favor	+20% to farming rate
Adze of Wepawet	Bast	100 gold, 10 favor	+10% to wood-gathering rate, villagers knock down trees in one hit
Shaduf	Ptah	200 wood, 10 favor	Reduces farm cost by 33%; Increases farm build speed by 200%
Scalloped Axe	Ptah	100 food, 10 favor	+10% to Axeman hack attack
Electrum Bullets	Ptah	150 gold, 10 favor	+15% to Slinger pierce attack
Leather Frame Shield	Ptah	200 wood, 20 favor	+20% to Spearman pierce armor
Crocodopolis	Hathor	400 wood, 30 favor	+4 to Petsuchos range and line of sight
Medjay	Hathor	250 food, 25 favor	+30 lifespan to Mercenary and Mercenary Cavalry
Sun-dried Mud Brick	Hathor	300 wood, 20 favor	+20% to building hit points; reduces cost of buildings by 15%
Spirit of Ma'at	Nephthys	200 gold, 25 favor	Reduces Priest cost by 20%; increases Pharaoh and Priest healing rate by 200%
Funeral Rites	Nephthys	200 gold, 16 favor	+4 to Pharaoh and Priest bonus damage vs. myth units
City of the Dead	Nephthys	300 wood, 20 favor	+30% to Pharaoh hit points; +20% to Pharaoh pierce attack
Bone Bow	Sekhmet	250 wood, 10 favor	+4 to Chariot Archer range
Slings of the Sun	Sekhmet	200 gold, 20 favor	+30% to Slinger bonus damage vs. infantry and Throwing Axeman
Stones of Red Linen	Sekhmet	300 wood, 25 favor	+20% to Catapult and War Barge crush damage
Rams of the West Wind	Sekhmet	400 gold, 20 favor	+20% to Siege Tower hit points and crush damage
Axe of Vengeance	Horus	300 wood, 25 favor	+3 to Axeman bonus damage vs. buildings
Greatest of Fifty	Horus	300 food, 20 favor	+20% to Spearman pierce armor; +1 to Spearman bonus damage vs. archers
Spear on the Horizon	Horus	200 gold, 25 favor	+10% to Spearman hack attack; +30% to Spearman hit points
Atef Crown	Osiris	300 gold, 30 favor	+40% to Mummy hack attack; +20% to Mummy hit points; +200% to Minion lifespan
Desert Wind	Osiris	400 gold, 40 favor	+20% to Camelry speed, hit points, and hack attack
New Kingdom	Osiris	200 gold, 25 favor	Provides second Pharaoh
Funeral Barge	Osiris	500 wood, 30 favor	+2 to Kebenit bonus damage vs. archer ships
Book of Thoth	Thoth	400 wood, 30 favor	+10% to laborer gather rate
Tusks of Apedemak	Thoth	300 gold, 30 favor	+20% to War Elephant hit points; +10% to War Elephant hack attack
Valley of the Kings	Thoth	600 gold, 50 favor	Migdol Stronghold units train 66% faster

Norse Unit Statistics

UNIT	COST	HIT POINTS	ATTACK DAMAGE	BONUS DAMAGE	HACK ARMOR	PIERCE ARMOR	CRUSH ARMOR	RANGE	LINE OF SIGHT	MAX SPEED
Ulfsark	50 food, 30 gold	80	9 hack	3 to Obelisks	30%	5%	99%	N/A	16	4.8
SPECIAL ATTACK: Counters cavalry										
Throwing Axeman	50 wood, 40 gold	65	5 hack	2.25 to infantry	35%	10%	99%	9	16	4.0
SPECIAL ATTACK: Counters infantry										
Raiding Cavalry	40 food, 50 gold	105	8 hack	1.25 to archers; 1.75 to Throwing Axemen	10%	25%	99%	N/A	8	6.0
SPECIAL ATTACK: Counters archers										
Hersir	80 food, 40 gold	130	8 hack	6 to myth units	20%	15%	99%	20	16	4.2
SPECIAL ATTACK: Counters myth units										
Huskarl	75 wood, 40 gold	115	8 hack	2 to archers	15%	50%	99%	N/A	16	5.0
SPECIAL ATTACK: Counters archers										
Jarl	50 food, 80 gold	180	9 hack	4 to myth units	20%	35%	99%	N/A	16	4.8
SPECIAL ATTACK: Counters myth units										
Portable Ram	125 wood, 125 gold	250	40 crush	N/A	5%	99%	90%	2	14	3.6
SPECIAL ATTACK: Counters buildings										
Ballista	150 wood, 150 gold	85	9 pierce, 4 crush	3 to ships	20%	80%	80%	4 min, 30 max	40	2.4
SPECIAL ATTACK: Counters infantry and ships										
Longboat	100 wood, 50 gold	290	6 pierce	3 to transport ships	30%	20%	10%	12	24	6.0
SPECIAL ATTACK: Counters hammer ships										
Drakkar	100 wood, 50 gold	240	20 hack	N/A	30%	20%	75%	N/A	16	7.0
SPECIAL ATTACK: Counters siege ships										
Dragon Ship	100 wood, 100 gold	480	6 crush	.5 to buildings	10%	50%	10%	12 for ranged, 3 for ram	24	4.8
SPECIAL ATTACK: Counters archer ships and buildings										

Norse Mythological Unit Statistics

UNIT	GOD	COST	HIT POINTS	ATTACK DAMAGE	BONUS DAMAGE	HACK ARMOR	PIERCE ARMOR	CRUSH ARMOR	RANGE	LINE OF SIGHT	MAX SPEED
Raven	Odin	N/A	50	N/A	N/A	20%	50%	99%	N/A	16	4.0
SPECIAL ATTACK: Respawning flying scout; Odin only											
Troll	Forseti	150 wood, 15 favor	200	12 pierce	3 to myth units	50%	5%	80%	14	20	3.6
SPECIAL ATTACK: Bonus damage vs. myth units											
Valkyrie	Freyja	200 food, 20 favor	360	12 hack	3 to myth units	55%	70%	80%	10 max for healing	20	6.0
SPECIAL ATTACK: Bonus damage vs. myth units; can heal allied units											
Einherjar	Heimdall	150 gold, 20 favor	250	15 hack, 10 crush	3 to myth units	70%	60%	80%	10 for attack boost	16	3.2
SPECIAL ATTACK: Bonus damage vs. myth units; uses horn to boost nearby units by 50%											
Battle Boar	Bragi	250 gold, 30 favor	720	20 hack, 20 crush; 10 hack bonus for buck attack	2 to myth units	60%	60%	80%	N/A	16	5.3
SPECIAL ATTACK: Bonus damage vs. myth units; recharging Buck Attack for added damage											
Kraken	Njord	300 food, 25 favor	900	30 hack, 20 crush; 40 hack for throw attack	N/A	50%	70%	80%	N/A	22	6.0
SPECIAL ATTACK: Recharging Throw Attack against ships or shoreline human units											
Mountain Giant	Njord, Hel	300 food, 30 favor	1200	20 hack, 25 crush; 30 hack for gore; 120 crush for bash against buildings	2 to myth units	45%	30%	80%	N/A	16	3.2
SPECIAL ATTACK: Bonus damage vs. myth units; added damage with recharging Gore (units only) and Bash (buildings only) attacks											
Frost Giant	Skadi, Hel	200 gold, 25 favor	600	18 hack, 12 crush	3 to myth units	55%	70%	80%	4 for freeze breath	16	3.8
SPECIAL ATTACK: Bonus damage vs. myth units; recharging Freeze Attack can freeze human unit											
Fire Giant	Baldr, Hel	300 gold, 35 favor	600	25 hack, 20 crush; bonus of 10 hack, 20 crush for recharged attack	N/A	60%	80%	80%	14	18	3.2
SPECIAL ATTACK: Recharging attack, with more projectiles and increased damage											
Fenris Wolf Brood	Tyr	150 gold, 15 favor	360	15 hack	3 to myth units	40%	50%	80%	25 to boost	16	4.0
SPECIAL ATTACK: Bonus damage vs. myth units; 20% attack boost when extra Fenris within range											
Jormund Brood	Tyr	200 food, 15 favor	800	40 pierce	N/A	20%	30%	80%	20	24	6.0
SPECIAL ATTACK: N/A											

Norse Improvement Statistics

IMPROVEMENT	NORSE GOD	COST	BENEFITS
Medium Infantry	All	150 food, 150 gold	+10% to attack and hit points, +1 to line of sight
Medium Cavalry	All	200 food, 100 gold	+10% to attack and hit points, +1 to line of sight
Heavy Infantry	All	300 food, 300 gold	+10% to attack, +15% to hit points, +1 to line of sight
Heavy Cavalry	All	400 food, 200 gold	+10% to attack, +15% to hit points, +1 to line of sight
Champion Infantry	All	500 food, 400 gold	+10% to attack, +20% to hit points, +1 to line of sight
Champion Cavalry	All	700 food, 200 gold	+10% to attack, +20% to hit points, +1 to line of sight
Levy Longhouse Soldiers	All	600 food	-20% to Longhouse soldiers train speed
Levy Hill Fort Soldiers	All	600 food	-20% to Longhouse soldiers train speed
Conscript Longhouse Soldiers	All	800 food	-20% to Longhouse soldiers train speed
Conscript Hill Fort Soldiers	All	800 food	-20% to Longhouse soldiers train speed
Conscript Sailors	All	500 wood	-20% to Longhouse soldiers train speed
Draft Horses	All	300 food, 200 gold	+20% to siege weapon speed
Engineers	All	300 food, 500 gold	+10% bonus damage vs. walls to siege weapons, +2 to range of Petroboli and Catapult, +50% crush damage to siege towers and Portable Rams, +25% pierce and +25% crush to ranged siege weapons.
Masons	All	200 food, 300 wood	+20% to building hit points, +5% to building crush armor
Architects	All	400 food, 500 wood	+20% to building hit points, +5% to building crush armor
Archer Ship Cladding	All	200 wood, 200 gold	+10% to archer ship pierce damage, +4 to archer ship range, +20% to archer ship hit points
Reinforced Ram	All	300 wood, 200 gold	+10% to hammer ship hit points and hack damage
Naval Oxybeles	All	500 wood, 200 gold	+9 to siege ship range, +12 to siege ship line of sight, +10% to siege ship hit points, +2 to bonus damage vs. buildings
Lone Wanderer	Odin	175 wood, 5 favor	+10% to Ulfsark speed
Pig Sticker	Thor	70 gold, 1 favor	+5 to gatherer pierce attack; +10% to hunting rate
Eyes in the Forest	Loki	50 gold, 2 favor	+3 to infantry line of sight
Hamarrtroll	Forseti	200 wood, 10 favor	+50 to Troll hit points; +2 to Troll range; +20% to Troll pierce attack
Hall of Thanes	Forseti	300 wood, 10 favor	+10% to Hersir hit points; +10% to Hersir speed
Mithril Breastplate	Forseti	100 gold, 10 favor	+10% to Ulfsark hack armor
Aurora Borealis	Freyja	200 gold, 10 favor	+50% to Valkyrie hack attack; +20% to Valkyrie crush attack; +33% to Valkyrie heal rate
Thundering Hooves	Freyja	300 food, 15 favor	+10% to Jarl and Raiding Cavalry speed; +20% to Jarl and Raiding Cavalry hit points; +10% to Valkyrie hit points; +20% to Valkyrie speed
Elhrimnir Kettle	Heimdall	250 food, 10 favor	+6 to Einherjar hack damage; +10% to Einherjar hit points
Safeguard	Heimdall	300 wood, 15 favor	+200% to Tower and wall hit points; Reduces Tower wood and gold costs by 25%

continued

IMPROVEMENT	NORSE GOD	COST	BENEFITS
Arctic Wind	Heimdall	200 wood, 10 favor	+10% to Longboat speed and hit points
Call of Valhalla	Bragi	200 wood, 20 favor	+25% to Ulfsark hit points
Swine Array	Bragi	200 wood, 20 favor	+1 to Ulfsark bonus damage vs. cavalry
Thurisaz Rune	Bragi	200 wood, 20 favor	+12% to mythological unit speed
Wrath of the Deep	Njord	200 gold, 15 favor	+200 to Kraken hit points
Long Serpent	Njord	200 gold, 25 favor	+20% to Longboat pierce attack and crush armor
Ring Giver	Njord	400 gold, 30 favor	+20% to Jarl hit points
Rime	Skadi	200 food, 20 favor	+33% to Frost Giant hit points; +20% to Frost Giant hack attack; Frost Giant "freeze breath" recharge 25% faster
Winter Harvest	Skadi	200 food, 20 favor	+20% to farming rate
Huntress' Axe	Skadi	200 gold, 20 favor	+20% to Throwing Axeman hack attack
Arctic Gale	Baldr	250 wood, 20 favor	+20% to Dragon Ship velocity; +30% to Dragon Ship hack armor
Sons of Sleipnir	Baldr	400 food, 30 favor	+2 to Raiding Cavalry bonus damage vs. archers and Throwing Axemen
Dwarven Auger	Baldr	300 gold, 35 favor	+20% to Portable Ram speed and crush attack; -50% to training time
Rampage	Hel	300 gold, 20 favor	-95% to myth unit training time
Granite Blood	Hel	600 wood, 30 favor	+100 to Fire, Mountain, Frost Giant hit points
Berserkergang	Tyr	300 wood, 45 favor	+20% to Ulfsark hit points; +10% to Ulfsark hack attack
Bravery	Tyr	400 food, 30 favor	+0.5 to Huskarl bonus damage vs. buildings

Resource Improvements

IMPROVEMENT	RESOURCE	EFFECTS
Pharaoh Empowering	All	+20% to gather rate
Ra's Pharaoh Empowering	All	+25% to gather rate
Ra's Priest Empowering	All	+25% to gather rate
Husbandry	Herding	+20% gather rate; 30% faster fattening; +15 food-carrying capacity
Hunting Dogs	Hunting	+30% hunting rate
Plow	Farming	10% faster farming
Irrigation	Farming	15% faster farming
Flood Control	Farming	15% faster farming
Purse Seine	Fishing	+50% fishing rate
Salt Amphora	Fishing	+25% fishing rate; doubles carrying capacity
Ra's Rain	Farming	+300% to current gathering rate, but +200% to all other players, even enemies.
Isis's Flood of the Nile	Food	+0.75 food per second
Bast's Sacred Cats	Farming	+20% to gather rate
Ptah's Shaduf	Farming	-33% to cost; +100% to build speed
Thoth's Book of Thoth	All	+10% to gather rate
Poseidon's Lure	Herding, hunting	God power erects stone that lures animals
Aphrodite's Divine Blood	All	20% faster villagers; +10 carrying capacity; +25% to build rate
Hephaestus's Plenty Vault	All	+10 food, wood, gold every five seconds
Worship Odin	Hunting	+10% hunting rate
Odin's Great Hunt	Herding, Hunting	Randomly doubles a number of herdables or huntables.
Thor's Pig Sticker	Hunting	Increased villager damage to animals; +10% to gather rate
Skadi's Winter Harvest	Farming	+20% to gather rate
Hand Axe	Wood	+10% to gather rate; +5 carrying capacity
Bow Saw	Wood	+10% to gather rate; +5 carrying capacity
Carpenters	Wood	+10% to gather rate; +5 carrying capacity
Bast's Adze of Wepawet	Wood	+10% to gather rate and lets villagers chop down trees in one hit
Pick Axe	Gold	+10% to gather rate; +5 carrying capacity
Shaft Mine	Gold	+10% to gather rate; +5 carrying capacity
Quarry	Gold	+10% to gather rate; +5 carrying capacity
Isis's Prosperity	Gold	+80% to gather rate
Hades' Vault of Erebus	Gold	+0.75 gold per second
Norse Dwarven miners over other gatherers	Gold	+20% to gather rate
Pharaoh empowering a Monument	Favor	+4% to favor-gain
Ra's Pharaoh empowering a Monument	Favor	+5% to favor-gain
Ra's Priest empowering a Monument	Favor	+5% to favor-gain
Anubis's Necropolis	Favor	+10% to favor-gain
Worship Zeus	Favor	Starts with 15 favor, can reach 200 favor, +25% to favor-gain
Aphrodite's Golden Apples	Favor	+15% to favor-gain
Fortify Town Center	Population	+5 population to each settlement
Worship Isis	Population	+3 population to each settlement
Sekhmet's Citadel	Population	+5 population to the Citadel

Counter Units

UNIT	CULTURE	COUNTERS	COUNTER WITH
Hoplite	Greek	Cavalry	Toxote, Hypaspist, Axeman, Chariot Archer, Throwing Axeman
Toxote	Greek	Infantry	Peltast, Hippikon, Slinger, Mercenary Cavalry, Jarl, Raiding Cavalry, Huskarl
Hypaspist	Greek	Infantry	Toxote, Chariot Archer, Throwing Axeman
Peltast	Greek	Archer	Hippikon, Mercenary Cavalry, Raiding Cavalry, Huskarl, Jarl
Hippikon	Greek	Archer	Hoplite, Prodromos, Spearman, Mercenary, Camelry, Ulfsark
Prodromos	Greek	Cavalry	Hoplite, Spearman, Mercenary, Camelry, Ulfsark
Myrmidon	Greek	Egyptian or Norse human unit	Toxote, Hypaspist, Cataphract, Axeman, Chariot Archer, Throwing Axeman
Hetairoi	Greek	Building	Hoplite, Prodromos, Spearman, Mercenary, Camelry, Ulfsark
Gastraphetes	Greek	Building	Prodromos, Mercenary, Camelry Hippikon, Raiding Cavalry, Jarl
Greek Hero	Greek	Mythological unit	Human Unit
Petrobolos	Greek	Building	Hippikon, Prodromos, Hetairoi, Camelry, Mercenary Cavalry, Raiding Cavalry, Jarl
Helepolis	Greek	Building	Hippikon, Prodromos, Hetairoi, Camelry, Mercenary Cavalry, Raiding Cavalry, Jarl
Trireme	Greek	Hammer ship	Juggernaut, War Barge, Dragon Ship
Pentekonter	Greek	Siege ship	Trireme, Kebenit, Longboat
Juggernaut	Greek	Archer ship	Pentekonter, Ramming Galley, Drakkar
Axeman	Egyptian	Infantry	Toxote, Chariot Archer, Throwing Axeman, Jarl
Slinger	Egyptian	Archer	Hippikon, Myrmidon, Mercenary Cavalry, Raiding Cavalry, Huskarl, Jarl
Spearman	Egyptian	Cavalry	Toxote, Hypaspist, Myrmidon, Axeman, Chariot Archer, Throwing Axeman
Chariot Archer	Egyptian	Infantry	Hippikon, Mercenary Cavalry, Camelry, Raiding Cavalry, Jarl, Peltast, Slinger
Camelry	Egyptian	Cavalry	Hoplite, Myrmidon, Spearman, Ulfsark
War Elephant	Egyptian	Building	Hoplite, Prodromos, Myrmidon, Spearman, Camelry, Ulfsark
Pharaoh	Egyptian	Mythological unit	Human unit, Hero
Mercenary	Egyptian	Cavalry	Toxote, Hypaspist, Myrmidon, Axeman, Chariot Archer, Throwing Axeman
Mercenary Cavalry	Egyptian	Archer	Hoplite, Prodromos, Myrmidon, Spearman, Camelry, Ulfsark
Catapult	Egyptian	Building	Hippikon, Prodromos, Hetairoi, Camelry, Mercenary Cavalry, Raiding Cavalry
Siege Tower	Egyptian	Building	Hippikon, Prodromos, Hetairoi, Camelry, Mercenary Cavalry, Raiding Cavalry
Kebenit	Egyptian	Hammer ship	Juggernaut, War Barge, Dragon Ship
Ramming Galley	Egyptian	Siege ship	Trireme, Kebenit, Longboat
War Barge	Egyptian	Archer ship	Pentekonter, Ramming Galley, Drakkar
Ulfsark	Norse	Cavalry	Toxote, Hypaspist, Myrmidon, Cataphract, Axeman, Chariot Archer, Throwing Axeman
Throwing Axeman	Norse	Infantry	Peltast, Toxote, Chariot, Slinger, Raiding Cavalry
Raiding Cavalry	Norse	Archer	Hoplite, Prodromos, Myrmidon, Spearman, Mercenary, Camelry, Ulfsark
Huskarl	Norse	Archer	Toxote, Hypaspist, Myrmidon, Cataphract, Axeman, Chariot Archer, Throwing Axeman
Jarl	Norse	Mythological unit	Hoplite, Prodromos, Myrmidon, Spearman, Mercenary, Camelry, Ulfsark
Hersir	Norse	Mythological unit	Human unit, Hero
Portable Ram	Norse	Building	Hippikon, Prodromos, Hetairoi, Camelry, Mercenary Cavalry, Jarl, Raiding Cavalry

Continued

UNIT	CULTURE	COUNTERS	COUNTER WITH
Ballista	Norse	Human unit	Hippikon, Prodromos, Hetairoi, Camelry, Mercenary Cavalry, Raiding Cavalry, Jarl
Longboat	Norse	Hammer ship	Juggernaut, War Barge, Dragon Ship
Drakkar	Norse	Siege ship	Trireme, Kebenit, Longboat
Dragon Ship	Norse	Archer ship	Pentekonter, Ramming Galley, Drakkar
Mythological Unit	All	Human unit; other mythological unit; building	Hero, Ramming Ship (if naval)

Relics

RELIC	BENEFIT
Ankh of Ra	Provides small, continuous favor income
Anvil of Hephaestus	Reduces cost of Armory improvements by 10%
Armor of Achilles	+5% to infantry hack armor
Arrows of Alfar	+20% to building pierce attack
Black Lotus	+10% to farming rate
Blanket of Empress Zoe	+5% to building crush armor
Boots of Kick Everything	+10% to Hero speed
Bow of Artemis	Reduces cost of archer and Troll by 15%; reduces cost of Centaur by 20%
Buhen Flagstone	Reduces cost of walls by 25%
Canopic Jar of Imsety	Reduces infantry training time by 15%
Catoblepas Scales	+20% to myth units' crush armor
Dwarven Calipers	Reduces siege weapon cost by 20%
Eye of Horus	+2 to Town Centers' population caps
Eye of Ornlu	+5% to hack attack of Throwing Axemen, Axemen, Hypaspists
Fetters of Fenrir	+250 pierce damage added to villagers
Girdle of Hippolyta	+5% to hit points of Toxotes, Chariot Archers, and Throwing Axemen
Golden Bridle of Pegasus	Respawning Pegasus
Golden Lions	Respawning Golden Lion at Temple
Harmonia's Necklace	+10% to villager gold-gathering rate
Harter's Folly	+2 to scout line of sight
Head of Orpheus	+8 to building line of sight
Hera's Thundercloud Shawl	+5% to human unit pierce armor
Khopesh of Horus	+1 to Hero bonus damage vs. myth units
Kithara of Apollo	+10% to villager speed
Mithril Horseshoes	+10% to cavalry speed
Monkey Head	Respawning monkeys at Temple
Nose of the Sphinx	+15% to building hit points
Odin's Spear	+5% hack attack to Hoplites, Spearmen, Ulfsarks
Oseberg Wagon	-25% to trade caravan cost; +15% to trade caravan speed
Pandora's Box	Reduces myth unit training time by 25%
Pelt of Argus	+6 to all units' line of sight
Pygmalion's Statue	+40% to villager hit points
Reed of Nekhebet	+200% to hack attacks of Sea Turtle, Leviathan, Kraken, Scylla, and Carcinos; +200% to Jormund Brood pierce attack

continued

RELIC	BENEFIT
Ring of the Nibelung	Provides small, continuous gold income
Scarab Pendant	+1 to bonus damage vs. buildings of Portable Ram, Helepolis, Siege Tower, and Scarab
Shard of Blue Crystal	+5% to villager wood- and gold-gathering rates
Ship of Fingernails	Provides a small, continuous food income
Sistrum of Bast	Reduces villager cost by 10%
Staff of Dionysus	+20 to villager food-carrying capacity
Tail of Cerberus	Reduces myth unit special attack recharge time by 25%
Toothed Arrows	+5% to archer and Ballista pierce damage
Tower of Sestus	+30% to Tower pierce attack; +10% to Tower Burning Oil attack
Trios Bow	+2 to archer and Ballista range and line of sight
Trojan Gate Hinge	+20% to wall hit points
Tusk of the Iron Boar	+10% to hit points of cavalry and Chariot Archers
Wand of Gambantein	Reduces cost of Temple improvements by 20%
Wedjat Eye	Reduces the cost of myth units in food, wood, and gold by 10%